# PRODUCTIVITY IMPROVEMENT

EDITORS:
**Vernon M. Buehler**
**Y. Krishna Shetty**

# PRODUCTIVITY IMPROVEMENT

## Case Studies of Proven Practice

**A Division of
AMERICAN MANAGEMENT
ASSOCIATIONS**

To MaRee and Shabari

**Library of Congress Cataloging in Publication Data**
Main entry under title:

Productivity improvement.

Bibliography: p.
Includes index.
1. Industrial productivity--United States--Addresses,
essays, lectures. I. Buehler, Vernon M. II. Shetty,
Y. Krishna.
HD56.P822      338'.06'0973           80-69686
ISBN 0-8144-5701-0                     AACR2

First Printing

# Preface

SCHOLARS AND POLICYMAKERS are locked in a debate over the merits of two new conceptions of economic policy: supply-side economics and reindustrialization. But there is no debate about the need for more incentives for savings, investment, capital formation, innovation, and export. The benefits of such actions were explained by productivity experts participating in Utah State University's 1979 and 1980 Partners Seminars on "Productivity Improvements." The college is pleased to collaborate with AMACOM in using the proceedings of these seminars as the basis for this book.

Our Partners who provide the life blood for these programs are our industrious faculty and students, as well as hundreds of business and community managers and loyal alumni who generously contribute their time, advice, and resources. For example, they include George S. Eccles who funds our prestigious George S. Eccles Distinguished Lecture Series, which sponsored Professor Murray L. Weidenbaum's scholarly address on excessive regulation at the 1980 seminar.

Assistance in arranging for these seminars was provided by many individuals and organizations, including Dean Richard L. Smith; the seminar co-chairman, Lynn Richardson, Vice President, First Security Bank, Ogden; the American Productivity Center in Houston; the Productivity Institute at Arizona State University; and the Center for Productivity and Quality of Working Life and the Office of Research Services, both of our College of Business. Professor John W. Kendrick of George Washington University, and a board member of the American Productivity Center, significantly influenced the design, content, and successful outcome of these seminars.

Generous assistance was received also from the seminar participants representing Corning Glass; Nucor Corporation; Kaiser

Aluminum & Chemical Corporation; Beatrice Foods; Crompton Company; Hughes Aircraft; General Foods Corporation; Continental Group, Inc.; Burger King Corporation; Chicago Title & Trust; Detroit Edison; The Tanner Companies; U.S. General Accounting Office of Chicago; and District #38 of the United Steelworkers of America in West Covina, California. Typical accomplishments of our participants include: Nucor Corporation has the world's most productive steel mills; Crompton's productivity in textiles makes it a booming exporter; Burger King's productivity techniques are the key to its exploding growth rate; and Corning's phenomenal 8 percent productivity rate makes it a competitive price leader despite soaring prices of inputs.

Student and staff assistance was provided by Carey Koplowitz, Daniel Harawa, Clark Parker, and many others. Dolly Young ably coordinated our efforts with the office of Governor Scott M. Matheson of Utah.

Vernon M. Buehler

Y. Krishna Shetty

# Foreword

IN THEIR INTRODUCTION to this volume, Vernon Buehler and Y. K. Shetty enumerate all the good things that flow from vigorous advances in productivity. These advantages include advancement for the individual, survival and profitability for the firm, expansion of domestic and foreign markets for the industry, and rising real per capita income, along with less price inflation for the nation.

The slowing of productivity growth in the United States since the mid-1960s and the absolute declines in 1979 and 1980, associated with accelerating inflation and distress in vulnerable industries and companies, underscore the timeliness of the concerns expressed at the first two Utah State productivity seminars, whose proceedings serve as the basis for this volume.

These concerns have taken on worldwide dimensions in recent years, as productivity growth has slowed dramatically in all industrialized nations since 1973 for many of the same reasons that it has lagged in the United States. But there is a significant additional reason: the process of closing the technological gap with the United States through international transfer of technology, which resulted in much higher rates of productivity growth abroad from 1960 to 1973, had been largely completed in many industries and was a less important source of higher growth in recent years. In the 1980s other industrialized nations will increasingly have to pioneer their own innovations, which may sharpen international competition. On the other hand, it creates an opportunity for American firms to develop means of transferring technology from abroad.

It is appropriate that a college of business should sponsor productivity seminars centered on the theme of enhancing company productivity. After all, that is where the action is with respect to the decisions and activities that result in more efficient production and the cost-reducing innovations that are the chief source of rising productivity in the long run. Company productivity programs are, of course, only one technique available to management in its continuing responsibilities for profitable operation. But such programs are a potentially powerful tool in that, if successful, they get people involved at all levels in promoting the goals of the enterprise. This volume provides a rich trove of tested experience with regard to the various features of productivity programs which are conducive to success.

The concluding chapter is particularly useful in providing summary guidelines—drawn from the entire book—which will be helpful in instituting and running productivity programs. But, as Buehler and Shetty point out, programs vary from one company to another, and the right approach for any one firm will depend on the particular circumstances. So, readers who seek guidance for commencing or continuing productivity improvement programs must go beyond the summary and study the individual chapters to find the special features of successful programs that fit their own particular situation.

Although innovations and other managerial initiatives directly affecting productivity take place in the firm, the broader social and economic environment within which organizations operate can be terribly important. In particular, the role of the government in creating the legal framework that sets the rules of the game, tax legislation that creates incentives and disincentives, and regulations that affect costs, can have a major influence on productivity. I attribute the slowdown in productivity growth since the 1960s to the following factors:

1. Macroeconomic policies that reduced after-tax rates of return on investment and slowed the growth of capital per worker.
2. A drop in the ratio of research and development outlays to GNP, particularly government-financed R&D.
3. A less favorable impact of interindustry shifts of labor and capital.
4. Reduced economies of scale and a rising trend of unemployment.
5. The great expansion of government regulation at all levels.
6. Deterioration in the quality of natural resources, and possibly some decline in labor efficiency as well.

Chapter 18, "Free the Fortune 500," by Murray L. Weidenbaum, ably addresses one of the issues: overregulation. But it must be kept in mind that there are other areas in which changes in government policies could have significant positive effects on productivity growth. Government, labor, and business must all work together constructively if we are to reverse the downward slide of productivity growth and enjoy once more the benefits of significant economic progress.

John W. Kendrick
*American Enterprise Institute*
*George Washington University*
*Washington, D.C.*

# Contents

## Part IV. MANAGING PRODUCTIVITY IMPROVEMENT PROGRAMS

# Part I
# INTRODUCTION AND BACKGROUND

VERNON M. BUEHLER and
Y. KRISHNA SHETTY

# 1
# Improving Productivity: An Introduction

ONE OF THE most alarming trends that has emerged in the United States in the past few years is the slackening in productivity—the efficiency with which outputs are produced or the ratio of output to input. From the end of World War II through the 1960s, U.S. productivity increased at an annual average of just over 3 percent. Productivity in the 1970s has been rising at only half the rate that it did in the booming 1960s—or at just over one percent per year. U.S. productivity is now the lowest among the major industrialized countries. This decline in productivity growth has contributed significantly to our prevailing inflation and unemployment, our declining international competitiveness, the declining value of the dollar, and lower corporate profits. Consequently, productivity has become an important national issue today.

Productivity has vital consequences for the whole nation, as well as for individual companies. The higher the productivity, the stronger the economy and the higher the standard of living. An increased rate of productivity growth will improve the standard of living of our people. A higher standard of living is responsible for achieving an improved quality of life; better education, health, and safety; a cleaner environment; and equality of opportunity. A rapid rate of productivity growth would also offset increases in labor wage rates and would thereby have an ameliorating effect on inflationary pressures. If U.S. productivity continues to lag, the country will have a hard time solving its inflationary problems. Finally, slowing down the rise in unit labor costs and rapidly increasing labor productivity would make U.S. products more competitive than they have been in international markets, and this would in turn have a favorable effect on our balance of payments. In other words, continued improvements in productivity are critical for maintaining our competitive position in the international economy.

Likewise, increasing productivity is critical for the survival and prosperity of companies. First, it would strengthen our competitive position in domestic as well as world markets. Second, improved productivity would counteract increased costs of raw materials, energy, and labor. Third, it would meet the pressure of rising costs of government regulation. Fourth, it would provide funds needed for capital investment for innovation, expansion, and modernization. Fifth, improved productivity would conserve scarce resources, such as energy and raw materials. Finally, the dream of all working people—higher pay, shorter hours, better fringe benefits, and improved quality of working life—can only be achieved with sustained improvement in productivity.

In other words, reversing the declining trend in productivity is a significant concern to each of us. At the national level, it is the best way to stop inflation, improve real income, and make this country more competitive with others. Productivity may be the single most important factor for ensuring national survival. At the company level, it is the only way to reduce costs, improve profits, and make the firm more competitive at home and abroad. And for individuals—managers as well as workers—improving their own productivity is central to their jobs and standards of living. It is the way to improved prosperity and quality of life.

Even though economists disagree about the reasons for the slowdown in productivity, there is some agreement on the following causes: inadequate capital investment; reduced outlays for research and development; increased government regulation; a higher proportion of output in the service sector, where it is harder to improve productivity; the changing composition of the labor force; an alienated workforce; and the power of labor unions. These and other explanations of why U.S. productivity growth is declining are not mutually exclusive; to some degree, declining productivity may be caused by all these factors in various combinations.

At the national level, government policies can positively influence the climate for productivity improvement. Given the national climate, it is the efficiency and innovativeness with which organizations combine capital, advanced technology, human resources, and creative management that largely determine the rate of productivity improvement in an enterprise. Hence the individual producing unit, which is the focus here, is a primary area for action in improving productivity.

The concern for productivity is slowly but surely reaching the corporate level. As a result, an increasing number of companies are instituting productivity improvement programs designed to supplement management's continuing effort to enhance productivity.

This book is based on the 1979 and 1980 seminars on productivity sponsored by the Utah State University College of Business. These seminars were organized to:

1. Provide a forum to discuss productivity, one of the critical issues facing the nation.
2. Analyze the experience of selected companies which have successfully developed and implemented productivity improvement programs.
3. Highlight selected issues relevant to national productivity, such as the impact of government regulation and the labor unions' viewpoint on the problem.

A brief summary of the chapters in this book is now presented.

Chapter 2, "Background and Overview of Productivity Improvement Programs," by John W. Kendrick, does a number of things. Professor Kendrick, an international authority on the subject, defines the concept of productivity, then identifies the sources of growth of labor productivity in the U.S. economy. He emphasizes that productivity is the key to profitability at the company level, and the concluding section of the paper moves from a *macro* (national) emphasis to a consideration of productivity improvement within a *micro* or organizational context. Discussing the experiences of a number of companies (such as Honeywell, Northrop, and Kaiser Aluminum), Kendrick suggests certain preconditions for the success of productivity improvement programs. These include an effective organization for productivity improvement, worker involvement, productivity measurement, specific productivity goals, and an effective monitoring and communications system.

Chapter 3, by David E. Leibson of Corning Glass Works, discusses the experience of developing and implementing a productivity improvement program at Corning. Anticipating an increase in inflation in the 1970s, Corning introduced a productivity improvement program which used the concept of the learning curve popularized by a Boston consulting firm. The concept says, essentially, that every time you double your volume, you should bring your manufacturing cost down by some measurable amount because of experience. The company set a goal of a 30 percent reduction in manufacturing costs every time the experience or the volume doubled. To facilitate understanding by the employees, Corning converted the learning curve into cost reduction percentages and used these percentages to set goals for each of their factories. Corning started its program in 1971, when it was experiencing a 3 percent productivity growth. Now the company has attained a 6 percent productivity increase without major disruption in employment.

In Chapter 4, Wilburn G. Manuel of Nucor Corporation discusses the experiences of his company. Nucor's productivity program focuses on two basic concepts: job security and incentive wages. Nucor is deeply committed to the job security of its employees. For many years, the company has not laid off a single hourly employee for lack of work. Along with this, Nucor's group incentive system has played an important role in the company's productivity performance. The foreman and the maintenance crew are part of the group in their incentive system. Nucor tries to define and measure clearly the operational performance of a group. This helps the employees understand the system better. In addition, the company maintains an open communications system so that employees are familiar with the company's plans and problems. The company pays bonuses promptly so that employees can directly relate the added effort to increased compensation.

As a result of this incentive program, an average hourly worker in Nucor's steel mill earned $23,000 last year. The absences and lateness are tied to the incentive system. If someone is late for more than five minutes, he or she loses the bonus for the day, and if someone is late for more than an hour, he or she loses the bonus for the week. As a result of this program, the company prides itself on being the most efficient steel company in the world.

Chapter 5, by James W. Mason, Jr., analyzes the productivity improvement program instituted by the Kaiser Aluminum & Chemical Corporation. At Kaiser the annual productivity improvement plan has been part of operating philosophy for more than a decade. The company has recognized the activity organizationally with a corporate productivity committee composed of six corporate officers and chaired by a senior vice president. The key elements of the Kaiser program include stated improvement goals, an appropriate measurement system, monthly reporting of results, and frequent reinforcement.

The experience of this company, which has a very successful productivity improvement program, suggests that to get productivity improvement a company should, first, obtain top management support, organize for it, establish goals, plan improvements, and measure performance. Second, it shouldn't forget to devote adequate resources to preventing slippage of current performance while striving to improve it. Third, it should establish an early warning system to detect any slippage that does occur.

Next, in Chapter 6, Ted Olson and Jerry Jensen discuss the Beatrice Foods Company's productivity improvement efforts, which got started about a year and a half ago. Beatrice became increasingly concerned about the effect of inflationary pressures causing rapid increases in the cost of materials and labor. Convinced that it would not be able to pass on all cost increases, the company saw a real avenue for maintaining profit margins through productivity improvement. The productivity program at Beatrice consists of three parts: (1) creating awareness of the productivity problem within the company; (2) providing the tools for doing it; and (3) providing the incentives all the way down to the employee level.

The productivity awareness program includes, among other things, top management emphasis in all major speeches, publication of a booklet on the "Beatrice Productivity Philosophy," a letter from the chairman of the board encouraging improvement as a top priority for the company, divisional meetings, and a management newsletter spotlighting efforts at productivity improvement in various divisions. The company supported the program by providing corporate staff services through its operating services department, developing training programs for profit center managers, and allocating capital for the productivity improvement program. Currently, the company is working on providing a companywide incentive program aimed at getting all the way down to the employee level. Such incentives include, among others, providing financial rewards to profit centers for productivity improvements that will convert into benefits at the employee level. In addition, the company is planning to provide a high degree of visibility and recognition to the top winners.

Chapter 7, by William G. Lord II of Crompton Company, Inc., looks at the productivity improvement effort of that company. To push productivity of its equipment as high as possible, the company keeps the machines running 24 hours a day, 350 days a year. Crompton also uses the combination of three-day, 12-hour work weeks and a bonus system to improve employee productivity. This three-day, 12-hour work schedule is combined with the bonus pay for employees who stay on the job. They are paid for 40 hours each week if they complete the required 36.

Since this program has been in effect, turnover and absenteeism have gone down considerably. For example, the company held the rate of labor turnover to 9 percent a year, an impressively low figure in an industry where the average rate is over 50 percent. Its productivity improvement efforts have been yielding the company an annual increase of 8 percent in output per labor-hour—well above the textile industry's average. Because of these programs, today the company believes that it is in a much better position to utilize its plant facilities and human resources more efficiently for the benefit of employees as well as the company.

Chapter 8 is by F. Cecil Hill of Hughes Aircraft. Emphasizing that management is ultimately responsible for productivity improvement, Hill outlines a number of principles or guidelines that Hughes Aircraft attempts to follow in its productivity improvement efforts. These guidelines cover a wide range of areas including employee recognition for performance, the concept of work modules, goal orientation, and designing meaningful work, all aimed at ongoing productivity improvement. According to Hill, the ability to work with people is the key to productivity.

In Chapter 9, Anthony W. Olkewicz of General Foods describes a process which was tested by a union–management team for improving productivity through worker participation. The author makes a good case for using this experimental framework, in which workers, foremen, and the support staff comprehensively examine the important variables in work situations and develop excellent ideas that produce startling results. These include reduction of waste, savings of energy, improved quality of working life, and significant gains in productivity.

Chapter 10, by Donald J. Donahue, Vice Chairman of Continental Group, Inc., argues that business has the resources and ability to increase productivity and at the same time to address wider social objectives. However, innovation and motivation are the keys. Donahue concludes by saying that we have all learned how to manage our material and natural resources—to make them maximally productive. Now we must apply our talent with just as much effort toward the management of our human resources for improved productivity. The major theme of this chapter is that productivity programs must be planned, organized, and monitored for results.

Chapter 11 is by William Swart of Burger King Corporation. Burger King exploded the myth that productivity is hard to measure and to improve in service industries such as fast food. In order to improve productivity, Burger King is using a number of industrial engineering and operations research techniques. For example, the company uses simulation models extensively for evaluating alternative methods of production; optimizing models to minimize costs; and statistical techniques for detecting the true effects of changes on its ability to serve its customers better. Burger King is using these and other techniques in every area of its operation. These techniques are used to improve productivity in individual restaurants, in service functions such as procurement, and in customer service drive-through windows, as well as for labor scheduling. In effect, Burger King has converted hamburger manufacturing to a science, and the result of that effort is increased productivity.

Chapter 12, by Frank Ruck, Jr., Vice President of Chicago Title and Trust Company, stresses that change in management and leadership are the critical ingredients to productivity. Ruck argues that productivity improvement requires the desire to enhance productivity, an environment of constant change, and active participation at all levels of the organization. His contention is that productivity improvement is not primarily a cost reduction program, but an approach toward working smarter rather than harder. It can come about only by changing output or input and by recognizing that productivity improvement should be a continuing and evolutionary effort.

Chapter 13, by Arnold Benes of Detroit Edison Company, shows how, in its continuing effort to improve productivity during an inflationary period, the company has brought together the two disciplines of industrial engineering and modern internal auditing. The industrial engineering services division of the internal auditing department has embarked on a companywide work-measurement program. This program involves the work sampling of all areas of the company to determine initially the utilization level of the company's workforce and then to set goals for improvement. Included in this work-measurement program (work sampling) is not only the nonprofessional but also the professional level, or white-collar employees. As a result of this program, the company's overall productivity has improved considerably, and there is every indication that this improvement will continue.

Chapter 14, by Carl C. Jacobson of The Tanner Companies, does two things. First, it discusses the background, approach, structure, and philosophy of The Tanner Companies' general productivity program. Second, it presents some of the details of how the company has successfully implemented a productivity improvement program. Its conclusion is that a productivity program is a continuing process.

Chapter 15, by Clement F. Preiwisch of the U.S. General Accounting Office, summarizes GAO's study on productivity-sharing programs as pursued by selected private companies. After discussing the background and scope of the study and the findings on benefits resulting from such plans, the author outlines factors considered in adopting productivity-sharing plans, difficulties encountered with the plans, the impact of federal policies on the plans, and issues that should be considered by companies in adopting a productivity-sharing program.

The experience of these 36 firms with productivity-sharing plans suggests that they derived a number of benefits from such plans:

Improved performance of employees
Change in employee attitudes and job interest
Increased productivity
Reduction in scrap, rework, and waste
Better use of materials, supplies, and equipment
Cost-saving suggestions
Improved processes or procedures
Better product quality

Despite the numerous benefits claimed for productivity-sharing plans, there are many pitfalls which can affect their success. When a company attempts to establish a productivity-sharing plan, it may have to overcome difficulties in trying to develop a workable bonus formula. Once the productivity-sharing plan begins functioning, other problems may develop because the plan was not properly implemented or management was not fully committed to it. Also, if the plan is not closely monitored or if financial reverses occur, the expected savings may not materialize. These findings suggest a note of caution regarding the effectiveness of these plans. However, the performance of the productivity-sharing programs studied indicates that they offer a workable method of enhancing productivity at the firm level. As such, these programs warrant serious consideration by firms as a means of stimulating productivity, enhancing a company's competitive advantage, increasing the monetary benefits to a firm's employees, and reducing inflationary procedures.

The next two chapters are by Cass Alvin of the United Steelworkers of America. Chapter 16 looks at the productivity problem from organized labor's point of view. Alvin briefly reviews some important historical experiences of the United Steelworkers of America with productivity improvements in the steel industry. Then he outlines past and present programs of productivity improvements in the industry, which in most cases are operated mutually by the union and management. He discusses union–management plans that concern themselves not only with improving productivity but also with the gains that should be shared among various elements in a system of production. In his concluding remarks, Alvin says that for a plan of productivity improvement to be successful, there must exist a climate of mutual respect and trust between management and labor.

Chapter 17, also by Cass Alvin, examines the productivity problem from the labor union's perspective. He says that whenever a productivity problem is mentioned, the culprit is immediately fingered, directly or indirectly: it is the worker. To many, productivity somehow is something that only the worker and his or her attitude can do anything about. Somehow, whether productivity is not enhanced—or is being reduced—becomes a function of the worker's attitude. Hardly ever in print are the other more important factors mentioned, such as poor management, lack of imagination in product design, unwise research and development strategies, the need for infusion of capital, fiscal and monetary policies of government, and the destructive policies of monopolies and oligopolies, which thwart the very creativity needed to expand our system of enterprise.

American labor unions, Alvin argues, are in full support of improving productivity. Our effort aimed at making the workplace more conducive to higher productivity is good and should be applauded. However, such efforts should have employee inputs and provide for a fair share in return to the employees. Furthermore, productivity improvements cannot possibly be met by a more efficient system of human engineering; it needs the best and the latest tools and machines, capital, effective research and development, and imaginative and creative public policy.

Chapter 18 is by Murray L. Weidenbaum of Washington University and the American Enterprise Institute. Weidenbaum discusses the impact of government regulation on corporate performance. He makes a good case that U.S. industry is being regulated to the point where its productivity is declining, its profitability is lagging, and its innovativeness is vanishing. Regulations are affecting every aspect of business: where to set up a business, who can be hired, how to operate the business, what to sell, to whom to sell it, and, of course, how much of the proceeds to keep. One direct cost of growing government regulation is the growing paperwork—the expensive and time-consuming process of submitting reports, making applications, filling out questionnaires, and replying to orders and directives. Ultimately, every consumer feels those effects in the form of higher prices. Similarly, it affects the productivity and the profitability of the company.

In addition, the costs of complying with these regulations reduce the capital available for the productive purpose. The total effect of government regulation is costing all of us: higher prices for consumers, lower productivity and profitability for businessmen. Rather than relying on regulation to control in detail every facet of business behavior, we should see the regulatory device as a powerful tool. Weidenbaum believes the prospects for the future of productive private enterprise in the United States surely would be enhanced by reducing government regulation. He calls on all concerned—public interest groups, academia, and the media—to work to improve public understanding of the implications of government regulation on the productive performance of private enterprise.

Chapter 19, by the editors of this book, provides a comprehensive action plan to institute a productivity program—and to make it work.

Taken together, these chapters provide a variety of experiences in developing and implementing productivity improvement programs. These experiences will greatly aid executives who are looking for yardsticks with which to measure their own companies' experience, and may inspire others who are seeking ideas to apply to their own situation.

JOHN W. KENDRICK

# 2
# Background and Overview of Productivity Improvement Programs

IT IS TRUE that government can do a great deal to improve the climate within which enterprise operates, but we can't wait for government to act to help facilitate productivity improvement. Productivity at the company level is the key to profitability. Our competitive system produces very real incentives for productivity improvements. We can go ahead and, as we have done for the last 200 years, continue to make those improvements and innovations at the company level to increase outputs of goods and services that people want in relation to the resources that are used in their production.

## WHAT IS PRODUCTIVITY?

That brings me to my first point: What is productivity? It is the relationship of *outputs* of goods and services in real physical volume to *inputs* of the basic labor and nonhuman resources used in the production process, also measured in physical units such as hours worked, machine hours, and so forth. If output is related to all the inputs (which I think is the most desirable kind of measure), output per unit of total input is basically the productivity formula: O/I.

If you include all of the inputs, this measure will get at the net saving of cost elements or inputs per unit of output achieved over time as a result of technological change and the other factors that make it possible to increase production with a given volume of resources. Since this input is a composite measure, including human and nonhuman resources, you can look at it as a weighted average of output in relation to weighted inputs. Output in relation to labor-hours alone is the usual productivity measure. (We used to call it output per man-hour, but now we have desexed the term "man-hour" and just talk about labor-hours or hours worked—it means the same thing.)

Then we have output in relation to capital inputs. These are the capital goods, plants, equipment, and inventory stocks. In this category we also include land and natural resources, as well as other broad major groupings of inputs: output per unit of materials, supplies, and other purchased goods and services—including energy. As we are able to increase output in relation to each of these, of course, we increase the efficiency of the productive process. Not only are we concerned with saving on labor per unit of output (thereby making it possible to increase production with the existing or growing labor force), but we are interested in conserving on capital goods because capital is scarce. It comes at a cost of saving and investment, just as labor comes at a cost of work and has the alternative use of leisure, which is desirable.

The alternative use of the investment and saving that goes into the making of capital goods is consumption, which is a desirable alternative. In the case of the raw materials that go into production, the alternative is conservation for future generations. So, by improving productivity we're able to conserve—a buzz word these days. In fact, I found nobody who really objects to the idea of improving productivity; it's only rational to try to produce a given output with fewer inputs, since these inputs have desirable alternative uses.

As I pointed out, we measure outputs and inputs in real terms. I won't go into technicalities, but most of the outputs and the inputs are aggregates of the components, which may be very diverse when you are looking at the whole business economy. The business gross product comprises thousands of different kinds of goods. So, in effect, you have a weighted quantity aggregate—quantities of given periods weighted by the prices of a base period—so that over time you are holding prices constant and the aggregate is moving as the quantities of output move. And similarly with inputs, you are measuring the quantities of hours weighted by base-period wage rates or average hourly compensation so that the labor input moves as hours move but not as wage rates move. Because this is a technical relationship, you want to look at the relative quantity movements not obscured by price changes, wage changes, and so forth. This kind of a ratio basically signifies technological improvement.

People who have studied economics should remember the production function: With varying quantities of labor and capital, you produce a certain quantity of output, and you can vary combinations to get at the least-cost combination, depending on the relative prices of the factors. What you are getting when productivity goes up is a shift of this production function in which you are now able to produce the same quantities with less of one or both of the factors, so that you have saved real cost and with given quantities of the factors you are able to produce more. Of course, this has been the source of rising standards of living in this country, which have gone up 2 or 3 percent a year on the average during this century. Also, at the national level, it is important as an anti-inflationary element, because to the extent that productivity rises, it helps offset the increases in wage rates and in other input prices. The rise in productivity strengthens our economy and our position in the world economy.

## PRODUCTIVITY AT THE INDUSTRY AND COMPANY LEVELS

At the industry level, the relative changes in productivity are great. We have a spectrum of rates of change. Some industries rank very high—airlines, pipelines, electric utilities, communications, and technology-based manufacturing industries, such as electric machinery and equipment. Others (some of the older industries such as shoemaking and the waterways of this country) have shown very little productivity increase. One industry for which I devised measures for the postwar period showed a drop—local transit. (That's not surprising: More and more people are using their own personal cars, and fewer are riding buses. Therefore, bus traffic has gone down and the roads are getting clogged.) Generally, this kind of spectrum is associated with relative price changes. Industries with high productivity change have low relative price changes. This stimulates sales to the extent that there is an elasticity of demand, which goes right along with what the economists say: If relative prices fall, people tend to buy more of the goods.

The relative changes in productivity have accounted for changes in the industrial structure of the economy. In general, the high-productivity industries which have been able to reduce relative price have captured more of the market. They've grown relatively, and often their employment has grown as well. In fact, I think that labor has much more to fear from the unprogressive employer who doesn't keep up technologically than from the progressive employer who is improving products and processes.

At the company level, productivity is the key to profitability. If you are competing with other companies that are paying more or less the same wage rates and the same prices for materials and energy, and that are charging more or less the same prices for their outputs, the only way your profit can be greater is by using fewer inputs per unit of outputs so that your costs per unit are less. Higher productivity is the key to company profitability. The companies with higher productivity have higher profit margins. If they increase productivity faster than their competitors do, they can enjoy an increase in profit.

If productivity goes up less rapidly, profit margins tend to decline. Therefore, our competitive system produces very real incentives for productivity improvement. Companies try to improve their technology relative to competitors either *offensively* in order to widen their margins or *defensively* with respect to competitors who have introduced better technology. They must imitate the leaders and also improve their technology in order to preserve and maintain their profit margin. So, over the centuries before we even heard of the word productivity, companies were improving productivity. They were forced to by the competitive market system.

Incidentally, even the socialist countries are thinking more of trying to use market pricing and competition as a means of spurring their managers to reduce costs through innovation. Recently, while I was lecturing in the Soviet Union, my audience kept asking me how we stimulate our plant managers to innovate. It's a real problem there because of so much red tape in getting anything done. The managers don't particularly like to change techniques and get new allocations from Gosplan. Their bonuses are based on meeting production quotas. If you experiment, you may not meet the quota in the first year or two with new methods.

## PRODUCTIVITY IN HISTORICAL PERSPECTIVE

What is depicted in Table 2-1 is part of the reason why there is increasing interest in supplementing management efforts to enhance productivity. Because, as you see from this table, if you look at the fifth line, you have output per hour per unit of labor. Two lines below that you have total factor productivity output in relation to all real inputs. And on the basis of real product per unit of labor, we were raising our productivity by 3½ percent in the first two decades after World War II. During the next seven years, it slowed to 2.1 percent a year, and, in the last five years, to 1.1 percent, a decline in the rate of increase of more than two thirds. Similarly, total factor productivity had a slowdown of two percentage points—from 2.8 percent to 0.8 percent—which means that increases in our standards of living and in our real wages per worker have slowed.

This has, of course, contributed to the acceleration of price inflation. As labor has found its real wages going up less rapidly, workers try to make up for that by higher pay increases. This contributed to the acceleration of labor costs and prices per unit of output. I think that this slowdown has had a significance beyond its statistical amount of 2 percent and has contributed to the dynamics of an inflationary spiral.

This was brought out well in "Reaching a Higher Standard of Living," a report by the New York Stock Exchange published in January 1979. It showed that slowing productivity does have a multiplier effect on inflation. In Table 2-1 (which is based largely on the work of Edward F. Denison), the chief sources of increase in productivity are listed below the total productivity line. *Advances in technological knowledge* as applied to the production processes was contributing about half of the productivity increase in 1948–1966. In 1973–1978, it was contributing all of it, which in a sense is encouraging. But advances in knowledge did slow down by more than a third. Research and development expenditures dropped from more than 3 percent in the mid-1960s to 2.2 percent of GNP last year. The growth in technological knowledge has undoubtedly slowed and this is our best estimate of how much it has slowed. It

Table 2-1. Sources of growth in real gross product, U.S. domestic economy.

| | Average annual percentage rates of change | | | |
|---|---|---|---|---|
| | 1948–1966 | 1966–1973 | 1973–1978 [p] | 1980–1990 (Projected) |
| Real gross product | 3.9 | 3.5 | 2.4 | 3.4 |
| Factor Input—total | 1.1 | 1.9 | 1.6 | 1.8 |
| Labor | 0.4 | 1.4 | 1.3 | 1.3 |
| Capital | 2.8 | 3.3 | 2.3 | 3.2 |
| Real product per unit of labor | 3.5 | 2.1 | 1.1 | 2.1 |
| Capital/labor substitution | 0.7 | 0.5 | 0.3 | 0.5 |
| Total factor productivity | 2.8 | 1.6 | 0.8 | 1.6 |

Sources of total factor productivity growth (percentage point contribution):

| | | | | |
|---|---|---|---|---|
| Advances in knowledge | 1.4 | 1.10 | 0.8 | 0.9 |
| R&D stock | 0.85 | 0.75 | 0.6 | 0.6 |
| Informal | 0.30 | 0.25 | 0.2 | 0.2 |
| Rate of diffusion | 0.25 | 0.10 | — | 0.1 |
| Changes in labor quality | 0.6 | 0.4 | 0.7 | 1.0 |
| Education and training | 0.6 | 0.7 | 0.8 | 0.8 |
| Health | 0.1 | 0.1 | 0.1 | 0.1 |
| Age/sex composition | −0.1 | −0.4 | −0.2 | 0.1 |
| Changes in quality of land | — | −0.1 | −0.2 | −0.3 |
| Resource reallocations | 0.8 | 0.7 | 0.3 | 0.3 |
| Labor | 0.4 | 0.2 | 0.1 | 0.1 |
| Capital | 0.4 | 0.5 | 0.2 | 0.2 |
| Volume changes | 0.4 | 0.2 | −0.1 | 0.4 |
| Economies of scale | 0.4 | 0.3 | 0.2 | 0.3 |
| Intensity of demand | — | −0.1 | −0.3 | 0.1 |
| Net government impact | — | −0.1 | −0.3 | −0.2 |
| Services to business | −.1 | −.1 | 0.1 | — |
| Regulations | −0.1 | −0.2 | −0.4 | −0.2 |
| Actual/potential efficiency and n.e.c. | −0.4 | −0.6 | −0.6 | −0.5 |

p = preliminary.
n.e.c. = not elsewhere classified.
Source: John W. Kendrick, based in part on estimates by Edward F. Denison, *Accounting for United States Economic Growth, 1948–1969* (Brookings, 1974), and statement in "Special Study on Economic Change," Hearings before the Joint Economic Committee of Congress, June 1978.

was caused by both a drop in government funding of R&D and a leveling out of privately financed R&D.

*Changes in labor quality*, another source of productivity growth, include not only more eduation per worker (which has gone up very nicely), but it also reflects the age and sex composition. In the middle period the increasing bulge of youth tended to dilute the experience levels and was more negative. It is still somewhat negative now but will become positive, because youth is a condition that cures itself with time, and young workers are going to get more experienced and attain higher wage levels as they mature.

*Quality of land* is another factor. At last, diminishing returns from land is catching up with us as we have to go beyond the continental shelf for oil and as the quality of mineral ores declines. This is a minor negative factor because of the relatively small importance of extractive industry in the total GNP. It is less than 5 percent actually; otherwise, it would be more important. *Resource reallocations* were a bigger factor when people were shifting from farms to industry, and from marginal self-employment to employed status where they made more. Much of this reallocation is over now, and this contributed to the slowdown.

*Volume changes* should also be considered. First, economies of scale mean opportunities for greater specialization of personnel, material, equipment, and plants, and the spreading of overhead items over more units. With the slowing of growth, this economies-of-scale factor became less. In 1973–1978, you have another minus due to less intensity of demand, as the ratio of actual to potential GNP was not back up to full employment levels yet. *Net government impact* is shown in Edward Denison's estimates of the effects on productivity of environmental regulations, OSHA, and so on, which have increased the cost of business and thus the inputs, but have not increased the outputs measured. (Improvements in water and air quality don't get into the GNP so this has contributed to the slowdown.)

The last line of Table 2-1 is particularly important, because this is the factor that company programs and joint labor-management committees try to address. This is the ratio of *actual to potential labor efficiency*. In terms of work measurement, all of us have related actual output to standard output, which is one element in the productivity picture. We have certain standards under a given technology, and actual output increases relative to a standard of 100 percent.

This is the industrial engineering work measurement: The standards change if technology improves. You may start out lower than you began, but with better equipment you can work up to a higher level. With another technological change, you will be up to still higher levels. Often labor is not producing as much as is feasible, for one reason or another, and you may end up well below the 100 percent. Some industrial engineers estimate that when pay is not related to performance, people in general are operating at perhaps only 75 percent of potential efficiency. This is a challenge to management, of course, to try to improve the degree of labor efficiency. Over the long run, it is the improvement of technologies that get into productivity change.

Better labor efficiency contributes under any given technology, but there is a limit to how much you can do, even with the best motivation of the labor force. But still, there is a good deal that can be gained. It is this reservoir of untapped potential that many of the company programs are directed at (with labor cooperation), because this is where incentive, motivation, and the work ethic come in and where you can supplement normal management efforts to decrease costs and increase productivity. (Incidentally, one way to look at productivity is just as the other side of the coin of cost reduction: When you raise productivity, you are decreasing costs per unit.) You can account for the negative efficiency figures by saying that productivity was measured largely in terms of hours paid for, but that as a result of agreements over the years since World War II, hours paid for have gone up faster than hours worked. About 0.2 of the factor is because hours actually worked have risen less than hours paid. There's nothing wrong with that if it is agreed that we have more paid holidays, vacations, sick leave, and so forth. There is some tendency also for productive hours at work to decline—that is, the percentage of unproductive hours due to break time, personal business time, and so forth, some of which are part of contractual commitments. This unproductive time at work has tended to increase somewhat, also. Table 2-1 gives some background on the efforts now to improve productivity at the company level.

Basically, productivity improvement and cost reduction are normal functions of management. It is axiomatic that the unique function of management is innovation: doing things better; trying to figure out better ways to produce better products at a lower cost, and also to manage an enterprise or an organization efficiently with a given technology—that is, to operate at maximum efficiency relative to potential, and to increase levels of efficiency. But by systematically tapping the reservoir of knowledge, creativity, and productivity inherent in the workforce, management can enhance productivity.

## PRODUCTIVITY EFFORTS AND GOVERNMENT REGULATION

The first efforts to set up labor-management committees go back to World War II when Donald Nelson, the head of the War Production Board, called for the formation of joint labor-management productivity committees throughout American industry. Before the end of the war, more than 7 million workers were under such organizations. In general, it was felt that these committees were effective in enhancing productivity with meetings in various organizational units, offices, or plants, and with workers contributing or receiving ideas and being motivated to improve productivity and to recognize its importance to the war effort. And, indeed, during World War II, productivity did rise quite dramatically.

Since then there have been other developments that have promoted labor-management efforts and company programs in nonunionized as well as unionized companies. One of these has been in the area of international competition. In 1971, the United Steelworkers of America, in its contract with the steel companies, agreed to set up productivity committees in all the plants in the industry. That clause was renewed in 1974 and 1977 because of the competition from Germany and Japan, where productivity was rising faster and prices were falling relative to U.S. prices.

Another cause for the formation of these committees and programs has been government regulation. First of all, in regulated industries, such as the telephone industry and electric and gas utilities, the public utility commissions often want evidence that the companies are improving efficiency before they grant rate increases to cover increased costs; they don't want just a cost-plus pass-through to the customer.

I have testified for the Bell Companies (particularly with respect to Western Electric productivity, since I helped set up the productivity measurement program in Western Electric) as to the success of their efforts in improving productivity. In a National Productivity Center pamphlet called "Improving Company Productivity—A Description of Selected Company Programs," one of the five or six companies included was Detroit Edison. It so happens that before it would grant rate increases, the Michigan State Public Service Commission required measurement of productivity and evidence that Detroit Edison was improving its productivity.

In 1971, we got into much more regulation, partly because of the productivity slowdown and the acceleration of inflation. In August of that year, President Nixon called for a 90-day wage–price freeze, followed by Phase II of the anti-inflation program, in which controls were instituted. Jackson Grayson, the man chosen to head that effort, later formed the American Productivity Center in Houston, because he was convinced that the best way to combat inflation was through increasing productivity—not price controls.

Under Phase II, companies had to justify their applications for price increases by showing that their cost per unit had risen. However, with regard to the labor costs per unit, they had to show how much of the wage increase could be counteracted by gains in output per hour. Most companies didn't know how to measure their productivity. Jackson Grayson substituted, at my recommendation, the industry rates of change, because this gave companies an incentive to beat the industry rate and thus be able to widen profit margins if they could.

Actually, in 1972 and 1973, under the price-control program, productivity increased quite rapidly, because there was a built-in incentive to increase productivity. Similarly, when utilities' rates are set and their wages are rising, they have an incentive to improve productivity to offset that cost increase and preserve their profit margins or at least minimize the erosion of profit margin while they are waiting for the commissions to increase their rates to help cover their increased costs.

## JOINT LABOR–MANAGEMENT PRODUCTIVITY EFFORTS

The main areas which have been addressed by joint labor-management committees in the industries where they operate and by the productivity improvement programs are generally those where labor has a particular input, because in the end management has to make the big decisions on how much to invest in new plant and equipment and how much to spend for R&D. But these committees can address areas where labor has a particular significance, and some of these areas include the more efficient use of materials and reducing defects.

Beech Aircraft, for example, had a zero-defects program. This meant trying to improve reworking, improve quality, improve recovery and salvage of materials—which is particularly important in a period where material prices are rising rapidly—and likewise to conserve energy which is another major cost factor today. Even such things as agreeing to reduce the temperature in the winter by two degrees or to increase the temperature in the summer by two degrees saves energy.

The committees try to suggest ways to improve on maintenance and on the repair and use of equipment, to reduce machine set-up time and downtime, and to improve work design. This is particularly important, since nobody knows his job better than the worker. He often can suggest very important ways either to simplify the job and get greater productivity, or to enrich it.

If the job is too boring, you want enrichment rather than simplification. But the whole area of job design is one in which cooperative efforts can be very fruitful. Some of the simple personnel matters are important, such as absenteeism, tardiness, amount of overtime, the amount of unproductive time, and so on. It is important to increase safety, reduce accidents, improve health and morale, and prevent alcoholism and drug abuse. Although some unions don't like the industrial engineering approach, in some companies, with the cooperation of labor, it has been able to expand work measurement and productivity measurement. Labor can help in the planning of training programs, in the design of tools or of products, and in layouts and organization of work. These committees can help reduce grievances and improve communications in order to catch developing problems and nip them in the bud through better communication. One important problem in the office is to reduce paperwork. Business is always complaining about all the paperwork the government requires, and yet within companies, there is a lot of paperwork which can often be cut down, thus reducing costs.

But productivity improvement programs are not for every company. First of all, you have to have a top management that is willing to experiment, that is not autocratic (or is at least willing to involve workers at all levels to a greater extent in production problems), that believes in the importance of human resources, that is serious about trying to improve performance, and that is able to get the support of front-line supervisors and foremen. Also, if there is a union, you need the union's cooperation, particularly in those industries that have problems, like apparel, shoe, or steel, or other industries facing foreign competition.

Unions recognize that the health of companies in their industry is very important to their job security and their improvements in real wages. I think that basically unions recognize the importance of increased productivity and are willing to cooperate if there is a good enough atmosphere in the company. And if it's a nonunion company, you would of course need a good enough relationship with labor and enough mutual trust to permit a fair try at a program of this sort.

## SEVEN KEY ELEMENTS OF SUCCESSFUL PRODUCTIVITY PROGRAMS

In summary, here are seven key elements of any successful productivity program. First of all, there has to be an effective organization for productivity improvement with top-management support, and someone must be responsible to top management for the program. Honeywell called him the productivity administrator. There were also productivity coordinators in the various divisions, plants, and departments, who chaired the group meetings with workers in these various organizational units. There was a steering committee of productivity coordinators at Honeywell. There are various ways the productivity improvement program can be organized: It can be carried on through existing line management, although even there, there has to be somebody responsible. There should be training of the supervisors and foremen and of the productivity coordinators, if you have a special organization, in how to go about tapping the ideas of workers through meetings or suggestions.

Second, the program should involve workers at all levels with groups in each self-contained unit within the company, whether office or plant. The committees are basically advisory to management. This isn't participative management with labor participating in the final decisions; the committees make recommendations, but management maintains ultimate decision-making authority. As far as the joint labor-management committees are concerned, here again their work should not and does not infringe on provisions of the labor contract, but it is supplemental to the contract. And not only are workers involved, but their contribution should be recognized through awards and rewards. This is a somewhat controversial area involving how monetary incentive should be worked in. Everyone is aware of the Scanlon Plans which provide bonuses. As their measures show reduced costs per unit, or increased profit, a bonus is periodically paid to workers. In other cases, individual workers are paid bonuses for particular cost-saving suggestions. In general, it is felt that some kind of monetary incentive helps in addition to recognition. Some people argue that since a major element in the wage increases is productivity improvement anyway, labor is being paid for the productivity improvement in a generalized sense. I think that in many programs, it is felt that something additional is certainly motivating to a greater extent than not having a special incentive.

Third, the productivity improvement program should be linked with measurement. This means measurement not only of company productivity in terms of output per hour or per unit of input, but of other supplemental measures that are helpful: work measurement, measurement of personnel matters, absenteeism, and so on. All of these measures help in the program in that they make it possible to set goals to monitor and evaluate results. Productivity measurement in companies got a big boost back in the late 1940s and early 1950s when the Bureau of Labor Statistics had a program of plant-level measurement and a good many companies continued these measurement efforts. Then, with price controls and price standards, many more companies have come in. But accurate measurements depend on meaningful definitions of productivity.

Fourth, there should be adequate information resources available to the program—materials relating to productivity improvement techniques and the worthwhile suggestions that are made within the company, as well as resources from outside such as the publications of the National Productivity Center or the American Productivity Center. Resources also include the 28 private productivity centers. (There are about two dozen states that have productivity centers and private quality-of-work centers.) Material about all these outside resources should be available in the company.

Fifth is the development of plans, goals, and objectives with respect to improving productivity through reducing waste and accidents, or through whatever objectives may be set jointly by labor and management.

Sixth is the need for effective communication, both "up" and "down." This is an effort to get an input from workers, and should be "up" even more often than down. But it is also a way of transferring technology from one department to another where it is applicable. Where one department has hit on some good scheme through the productivity committees, you can transfer these ideas throughout the company. Usually there is a productivity newsletter which also contains material of use in the various units.

And finally, there should be a periodic review, evaluation, and analysis of the program, its results and benefits, and the obstacles encountered (such as fear of job insecurity), and so on. In conclusion, the question to be posed is how to keep these programs living and vital after the start-up period. The United Steelworkers program has been going since 1971. Here it is 10 years later. Can interest be maintained and continued at a vital and creative level? Presumably many of the good ideas come in the first year or two, but with less frequent meetings, I would think that the kind of organization that I've discussed could continue to yield good results, although perhaps at a lower level, thus making a continuing contribution to greater profitability.

# Part II
# PRODUCTIVITY IMPROVEMENT: A Description of Selected Company Experiences

## A. MANUFACTURING COMPANIES

**DAVID E. LEIBSON**

# 3
# Getting on the Productivity Learning Curve— Corning Glass Works

IF THERE IS to be any meaningful progress in productivity in this country, government and business must discontinue their adversary behavior and work together to remove the contraints and disincentives which inhibit the marketplace. During the past decade, our economic system has lost a lot of vitality and power. The many constraints on the economic system have reduced it to a state of catatonic shock. For example, the number of federal and state regulations placed on industry in the last decade has tripled. There are three times the number of regulations in 1979 as there were in place in *all history* through 1970.

## PRODUCTIVITY IN THE UNITED STATES: AN OVERVIEW

Productivity is a national concern to government, labor, and industry. This concern has been increasing over the past ten years because it affects our standard of living. The lack of productivity increases inflation and unemployment and clearly depresses profitability. There was a sharp drop in productivity starting in 1970 and continuing throughout the decade. During 1979 there was a further decline, accompanied for the first time in history by a drop in our standard of living.

One of the major factors affecting our economic system is the cost of labor, or what we call the unit labor cost. *Unit labor cost* is the difference between the gains we make in productivity and the awards that we give to ourselves and others in wages, salaries, and benefits. That gap has been growing (see Figure 3-1).

As it grows, we pay out more money, and if we don't manufacture more goods, then we bid up the price of goods. This causes inflation. There is a strong relation between inflation and unit labor cost. Whether this relationship is cause or effect could be argued, but the close correlation between the two is apparent.

Manufacturing productivity has also decreased in its rate of gain. For example, from 1967–1972 manufacturing productivity for the nation was rising at a rate of 3 percent per year. By contrast, from 1972–1979, it was rising at a rate of only 1.6 percent per year (see Figure 3-2).

There is a great difference in productivity in various industries (see Figure 3-3). The hosiery industry, for instance, has a productivity gain of 10 percent per year through the use of new equipment imported from Germany for the production of panty hose. Great strides have also been made in electronics and in telecommunications. The malt beverage industry, too, has made substantial gains. I visited the Anheuser-Busch brewery at Williamsburg, and learned that automation there is so extensive they allow the operator to turn a few valves so that he feels he is part of the total

Figure 3-1. Productivity, inflation, and unit labor costs.

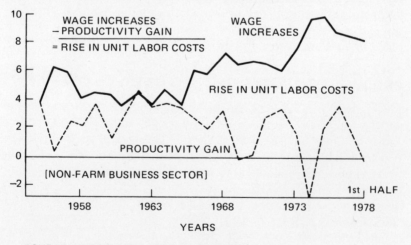

SOURCE: BUREAU OF LABOR STATISTICS

operation. Steel industry productivity has slipped. Steelmakers have been giving substantial increases in wages, salaries, and benefits, so the difference between productivity gain and higher wages causes a sharp rise in the unit labor cost.

A decline in productivity also causes a decline in purchasing power. Although wages increase, real wages are not going up as fast

Figure 3-2. Productivity index, U.S. manufacturing industries, 1967–1979.

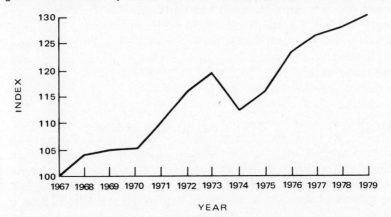

Figure 3-3. Growth in output per employee-hour in selected industries, 1971–1976.

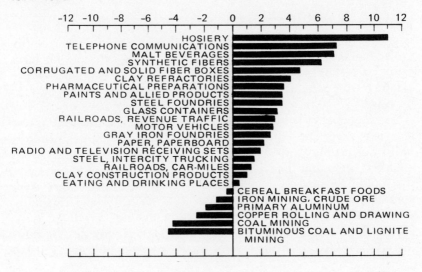

as inflation. There is also a close relationship between the use of industrial capacity and productivity, which I will discuss later. The capital-labor ratio is coupled closely with output and productivity, and it is almost self-evident that capital investment has a significant impact on productivity.

Some of the reasons for the national slowdown in productivity are insufficient capital investment, decrease in research and development, and growth of government regulations that require investments in environmental and safety improvements. There is no single reason for the decline in productivity. Declining productivity causes rising unit labor costs, which lead to higher prices, which cause declining sales volume, which reduces employment and plant utilization, which lowers productivity, which leads to more inflation—a vicious spiral.

## PRODUCTIVITY AT CORNING GLASS WORKS

Now let me discuss productivity in the company I represent. In the decade of the 1960s, Corning had rapid growth and our attention was on new products and marketing. When we came to the end of the 1960s and viewed the 1970s, we realized that we had neglected the state of our manufacturing strategy, one aspect of which dealt with cost reduction. We anticipated an increase in inflation in the 1970s and realized that cost reduction would be an important program.

In this strategy, we planned our cost reduction on a three- to five-year program. It would be funded over the duration of the project and not on a year-to-year budget. Our hurdle rate for most capital investment is a 20–25 percent return on investment, but we set the hurdle rate for the investment of cost reduction capital at 15 percent.

We set a goal to achieve a 70 percent slope in the experience or learning curve. The experience curve was developed by the aircraft industries during World War II. Later the Boston Consulting Group enlarged upon that theory, which says that as we gain experience, we should become more efficient. In manufacturing, every time volume is doubled, manufacturing costs should come down by some measurable amount. For example, with a new product whose volume is doubling rapidly, inexperience should provide a base for learning rapidly, and the experience curve should show a sharp decline. We set for ourselves a 30 percent reduction in manufacturing costs every time the experience or the volume doubled.

Corning operates 50 plants in the United States and about 30 plants in other parts of the world. The ages of these businesses differ widely. With a 70 percent slope, doubling of older businesses would take much longer than doubling of newer businesses. This makes it difficult to set goals. So we designed a more definitive, understandable, and communicative measurement tool.

We converted the learning curve into a cost reduction percentage that everyone could understand. Our cost reduction percentage represents the savings that we would make every year when expressed as a percentage of our total manufacturing costs. We converted the experience curve into percentages of manufacturing costs and used those percentages to set goals for each of our factories.

If, for instance, a plant was 15 years old and was growing at 10 percent, we would know from our charts on plant age and growth rate that the plant should have a 6 percent cost reduction program: it should show a savings of 6 percent of its total manufacturing cost per year. If the total manufacturing cost were $20 million, then we would expect the plant to develop a program for saving $1,200,000 a year. If it were an old plant with slow growth or none at all, we would expect that plant to have a cost reduction program of only about 2–3 percent. The system was equitable since we were not making new investments in older plants that were yesterday's breadwinners. We couldn't expect them to have high cost reduction goals.

Approximately 46 percent of our total manufacturig costs comprise wages, salaries, and benefits. Since these items are a large part of our manufacturing costs, we developed a productivity program to help promote cost reduction in labor, but in so doing we encountered a difficult measurement problem. It was easy to set goals, but those goals really had no meaning unless we had some way of measuring our progress.

In 1970–1972 we started developing a productivity measurement. Corning Glass Works makes 50,000 different products, has 11 basic technologies, and uses about 25 secondary manufacturing processes. There is such a tremendous variety of products and processes that we were unable to find a common unit by which to measure productivity in all plants.

## VALUE-ADDED SYSTEM

Rather than give up, we adopted the universal system used by governments for measuring productivity. It is called *value added*. The system has its deficiencies, but it was close enough to reality to give us a technique for measuring progress. It is used by the U.S. Commerce and Labor Departments and by almost every government in the world. One of its advantages is that we can compare ourselves with the outside world and assess our progress.

*Value added* is output measured by sales dollars adjusted for inventory change for transfers in and out, minus the purchases of materials and energy, and minus price increases adjusted to the base year of 1967. By devaluing sales for price increases and taking out raw materials, fuel, and energy, value added can be measured. Value added of one grouping of plants has gone from 100 to 160 and is a measure of their output. As long as there is no significant change in the product line, this is valid for measuring unit output. Corning's output growth in those plants from 1971–1979 was about 7 percent per year (see Figure 3-4).

Our measure of input was the 24 million hours worked in 1967; in 1979 we also had 24 million hours worked. As previously stated, Corning had been growing at a rate of about 7 percent per year, so

Figure 3-4. Corning Glass Works, U.S. plant sales—value-added system.

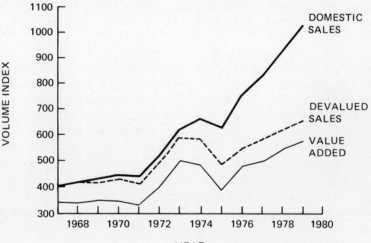

we had been realizing a productivity gain by increasing our output but using about the same number of hours worked. By applying the value-added data and hours worked, we can now compute our productivity. The value added for each hour of work in 1967 was $14, as compared with $24 in 1979.

Taking 1967 as the base year and converting both years into indexes, our productivity from 1967 through 1979 increased from 1.0 to about 1.65. Manufacturing productivity in the United States increased from 1.0 to about 1.3 in the same period (see Figures 3-5 and 3-6).

We started our program in 1971 when we were matching the 3 percent productivity growth of all U.S. industries. Because we believed 3 percent per year was totally unsatisfactory, we decided to embark on our productivity program. Now we have attained almost a 6 percent productivity gain per year, which was our goal. We believed that if we could match our plants to our growth, we could achieve a 6 percent productivity gain without major disruptions in

Figure 3-5. Hourly productivity index: Corning vs. average of U.S. manufacturing industries, 1967–1981.

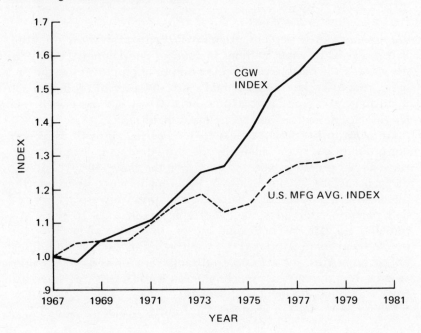

Figure 3-6. Productivity index: Corning vs. total U.S. manufacturing, 1967–1971 (base year = 1967).

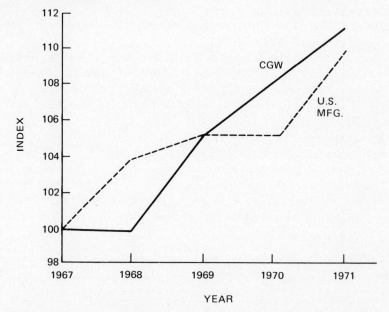

employment. A 6 percent productivity gain represents doubling output every 12 years without increasing employment. If we did not grow, we would have half the number of employees at the end of 12 years. We knew that would cause us a lot of problems and more than just employment problems. If we had no growth, we would experience serious economic difficulties.

We were able to achieve close to the 6 percent growth. However, our problem has been balancing this growth among our plants, because they cannot be expected to grow at the same rate. We tried on many occasions to move new or different product lines into the plants where product lines were not growing. We were achieving a 6–8 percent—and, in some places, as much as a 10 percent—productivity gain. We had some success in making such shifts, but we also had some failures. For instance, when we installed different technologies, we encountered inefficiencies and complexities as a result of the mixing of technologies. By and large, we have had fairly stable employment in our plants.

Productivity doesn't apply to the hourly workforce alone. Cor-

Figure 3-7. Productivity of Corning's exempt and nonexempt employees, 1967–1979.

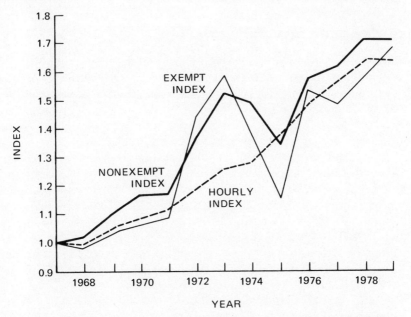

ning has three classifications of employees: the maintenance and production workers, the office staff and technicians, and the management and professional workers. We watched the productivity for all and noticed that by the end of 1979 all classifications balanced out at about 1.65, or a 6 percent per year gain in productivity (see Figure 3-7). However, there was a large deviation in the productivity curve for the exempt and nonexempt. What happened?

According to the growth curve mentioned earlier, we had a period of stable growth in 1967–1970 and held our employment for those two payrolls very constant. But we had rapid growth during 1972–1974. We tried again to keep our employment under control, so with that rapid growth we realized a large gain in productivity. Of course, the pressure grew and we had difficulty getting our work done. So we started hiring in 1974, but as we did, the economy started to decline. In 1975 the economy turned down sharply, and with those new workers, our productivity in those payrolls dropped substantially. Finally, we achieved a balance, and we are hoping that we can maintain it. In our system we don't have the flexibility in the exempt and nonexempt that we have in the hourly payrolls.

## COST REDUCTION PERFORMANCE

Returning to our discussion of cost reduction performance, we set goals for savings as a percentage of the total manufacturing costs in starting the program. By the way, this wasn't just a paper exercise; we put resources behind it. We tripled the amount of resources in terms of expense and capital dollars that we had spent in cost reduction prior to that time. Our performance rose rapidly.

It should be noted also that in our savings program we allow the plants to count their cost avoidance. That practice is extremely important since about 2–2.5 percent of the total cost reduction percentage does not reach the bottom line. We had more than a 9 percent savings in the early part of the 1970s, but it fell to around 8 percent. Now we are running at about 8 percent per year in total company savings in manufacturing cost. I have avoided saying "reduction of manufacturing cost," because cost avoidance doesn't reduce the manufacturing cost in the year when the cost was avoided. Overall, the cost reduction program on the worldwide basis amounts to about $100 million per year.

Another goal we set was to remain above what we call the dollar-for-dollar line. That's a dollar of investment for a stream of savings of one dollar. This amounts to about a 25 percent return on investment, or around $50–$60 million, and we hope to obtain a savings of around $90 million. This will result in a good return on investment. Cost reduction has provided excellent return for us.

As shown on the company's experience curve, we have not achieved our 70 percent slope, or our 30 percent reduction curve. We have come close to our goal and are still working on it.

Profitability is associated with the rate at which prices are reduced in real dollars and the savings or reduction made in manufacturing costs. If during inflationary periods prices are not raised commensurate with the sum total of inflation minus cost reduction, prices are in essence being reduced. And if prices are reduced at the same rate or faster than costs go down, the profit margin will be narrowed (see Figure 3-8).

One of the difficulties we have experienced at Corning is that we

Figure 3-8. Productivity and profitability at Corning, 1975–1979.

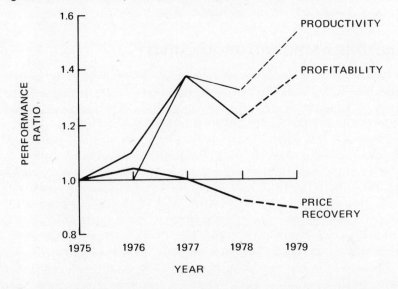

have not raised our prices to make up the gap between what we have saved and the inflation rate. We are a material- and energy-intensive industry, and it has been difficult for us to raise our prices as fast as our own costs have been rising. We have been holding about even, but we have not been putting the savings from our cost reduction program into profits. Being a manufacturing person, I like to see all that hard work go right into profit. And if we are not raising our prices to cover inflation, it won't go into profit. On the other hand, the marketing people like to see our prices come down so that we can be more competitive in the marketplace.

We have another measurement that we are now using in a number of our plants and will implement on a companywide basis this year. We call it *total factor productivity*. The measure was developed in 1955 from a thesis written at the Wharton School, University of Pennsylvania. The American Productivity Center in Houston has picked up the idea. We have found it to be a useful tool, but I don't know that it will be useful for everyone. If plants are profit centers, the measure will probably be more meaningful than if plants are cost centers. All Corning plants are profit centers and are judged on their gross margin performance. We use this system to analyze total cost and to measure our productivity. I will discuss the details of this technique later.

## FACTORS AFFECTING PRODUCTIVITY

A number of factors influence productivity profoundly in our plants. The first is growth. Growth is a great contributor to productivity gains, because with growth in the marketplace, we buy the best of equipment and the most advanced technologies. This gives us the greatest possible gains in productivity and return on investment. It justifies capital outlays on equipment, because we are bringing in new sales, new markets, and new profitability. Growth also creates an atmosphere in our plants where we can have more opportunity to do things in terms of labor crews and labor sizes in production lines. Therefore, the plant atmosphere is more conducive to productivity gains. If we are not growing, or if we are growing slowly, then we may be losing some of the benefits of productivity.

Downtime is a direct cost. If people are on the job, and if the processes go down, productivity is lost. If a machine is operating with ten heads and one head is not functioning properly, 10 percent of productivity is being lost. Whenever I go into a factory and see empty heads, I see lost opportunities. That machine had the capability of producing more, but it didn't.

Automatic controls are extremely important to the reliability of operations. Standard operating procedures are also important to industries, especially in process industries, which have many process variables that need to be controlled. The more we leave to humans, the more human error we are going to get. We should try to understand thoroughly the interrelationships between the process variables and build logic into our computer system controls. The practice will increase output and yield from processes.

Process speeds have a tremendous impact on productivity, although if the same number of people are added proportionately to a process as the speed is increased, then the productivity gain will not be achieved. But increases in speed with automation increase productivity tremendously. The output from the speed must be sold, however: If the speed is increased but the output can't be sold, there is little benefit. If the output is sold, great gains can be made in capacity, and savings can be made in capital investment.

Plant size can also have an impact on productivity. For instance, it takes so many people to open the door—a plant manager, a production superintendent, a personnel man, a maintenance crew, and so on. In Corning plants we need 25–30 people just to open the door. After that, as we gain in volume and increase the variable portion of the necessary people, we are gaining in productivity. For example, it takes one plant manager to manage a plant with $50 million in sales and one plant manager for a unit with $100 million in sales. So if the volume doubles, we double the productivity of our plant manager, our personnel man, and everyone else. In our plants we have found that the productivity of our plant staff and of indirect labor increases rapidly up to approximately $100–$150 million in sales. Beyond that, it seems to level off. We set a goal of doubling the output of indirect labor. But as volume doubles, the operations become more complex and the opportunity for confusion and mistakes increases and can reduce output.

Past experience at Corning indicates that we run into trouble with productivity as we approach 85–90 percent of our total capacity. (See Figure 3-9.) During 1979 we had a bad productivity performance. We had practically no productivity gain because we were running very close to total capacity. As we are moving up the business cycle with orders coming in, we gain rapidly in productivity. But as we begin to approach plant capacity, the marketing people and the sales people are yelling at the plant people to "get that order out." We start to make shorter runs and faster job changes. Mistakes increase, and we start to hire more people to make up for our inability to deliver goods on time. We try to make up production shortages by hiring more people. We bring in marginal operational facilities. We have a worn-out piece of machinery sitting in the corner, and because of the sales pressure, we bring in that marginal machine. Productivity starts to decline rapidly and, as we approach 100 percent of capacity, the problem intensifies. In the United States in 1979, employment increased by the same percentage as output increased. This means that there could be no gain in productivity. That happened to us at the plant level, too.

## PRODUCTIVITY MEASUREMENT

*Total factor productivity* is a measure of all the factors that go into manufacturing: labor, materials, energy, and capital. Therefore, output is a modification of the value added. The inputs are labor,

Figure 3-9. Productivity varies sharply with capacity utilization, 1972–1978.

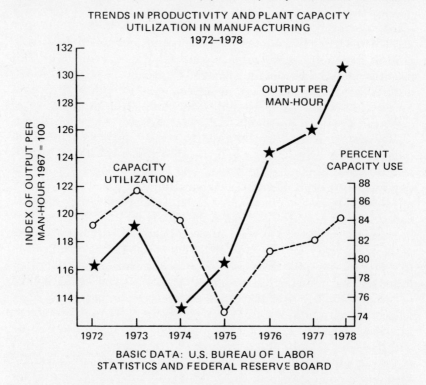

TRENDS IN PRODUCTIVITY AND PLANT CAPACITY
UTILIZATION IN MANUFACTURING
1972–1978

BASIC DATA: U.S. BUREAU OF LABOR
STATISTICS AND FEDERAL RESERVE BOARD

material, energy, and capital. They are adjusted for the price index in providing a common base. The sales volume less inventory change multiplied by the price index equals ouput. It is simpler than value added, because energy and material are not subtracted. In using capital as an input, the total investment is multiplied by the expected return at the plant level. Corning uses a 30 percent expected return on capital before taxes at the plant level. By multiplying the targeted return from operations on that capital, we get our capital input.

Data from one of our plants in which we make this measurement shows the change in labor from 1975–1978. It is difficult to obtain all the statistics needed to get this measurement. We must have all the price changes for all the materials we buy and the price changes for the material in the products we sell. We were able to get those figures only back to 1975. During 1980 we will put them in our computer for all our plants and will obtain that information more readily. In order to make sure that we tie this to our measure of total manufacturing cost, we back-out the cost of capital. The total input was $57 million, whereas our total manufacturing cost was $42 million. So our capital input from investment was $22 million, which we backed-out to tie our manufacturing cost. This can be tied indirectly to gross margin. To get input, we take sales and deduct inventory changes from transfers in and out.

We can get a measurement of the productivity of capital, labor, energy, and material, because we have an output and an input. Some plants fell badly in 1976 and again in 1978. But our gains have overcome the losses in productivity, all traceable to things that we did. For example, investments in capital dropped in 1976. We took a high depreciation so we didn't get it back that year, which resulted in lower productivity.

In summary, when looking at the whole productivity picture for a plant, including the benefit that accrued to the gross margin from the productivity program, we didn't get the full benefit because we didn't get the full price recovery. However, we certainly improved our gross margin for the plant during that period.

In conclusion, I would like to leave this one thought from Peter Drucker: "Productivity is the first test of management competence."

# WILBURN G. MANUEL

# 4
# Productivity
# Experiences
# at Nucor

NUCOR CORPORATION basically is a simple company with a limited range of products and a readily understandable corporate structure. Our sales in 1969 were less than $30 million. In 1979 they were $430 million. Our return on stockholders' equity of 38 percent is substantially higher than the average return in the steel industry, and our annual compounded growth rate of both sales and earnings for the last ten years has exceeded 24 percent. All this growth has been internally generated.

We are a manufacturing company. We produce steel, steel joists, metal decking, and cold finished steel bars. Steel joists are used in the roofs of shopping centers, warehouses, churches, schools, and hospitals. Our joists are produced under the trade name Vulcraft. We have five Vulcraft divisions employing about 1,600 people, producing joists in South Carolina, Alabama, Texas, Nebraska, and Indiana. We are the largest supplier of joists in the nation. Last year we supplied 400,000 tons of steel joists—more than 20 percent of the total market and more than twice the volume of the second largest producer. We intend to build our sixth joist plant in Utah during 1981.

Nucor entered the steel-producing business by constructing a steel mill in South Carolina in 1969. A second mill was constructed in Nebraska in 1973 and a third in Texas in 1975. The South Carolina mill was doubled in capacity in 1978 and the Nebraska mill in 1979. The Texas mill expansion was completed in August 1980.

In 1970 we produced 50,000 tons of steel. By 1982 we expect to produce 2 million tons. We have started construction of a new $60 million mill near Plymouth, Utah, which is scheduled for start-up in 1981. The mills are all basically the same design. Our new mill in Plymouth will consist of electric furnace melting of scrap, continuous casting, and automated in-line rolling and straightening facilities.

We produce angles, rounds, flats, and channels in our mills, each of which has a workforce of about 400 people. We intend to be national in scope and to concentrate on those products we can make most efficiently. One of our specific objectives, for example, is to obtain at least 20 percent of the United States market for steel angles.

For a number of years the price of our products, FOB our plants, has been equal to or less than the foreign price at dockside. We are confident we can produce steel as efficiently as any steel mill in the world. How has this occurred? Primarily by constructing plants economically and operating efficiently and with high productivity.

With regard to construction, we have low capital costs. The three original mills constructed between 1968 and 1975 had an average cost of less than $80 per ton of annual capacity. The expansion of these facilities will average close to $100 per ton of annual capacity. This compares with an industry average of $600 per ton of annual capacity by big steel during the same time period. Scaling up, therefore, does not always result in either lower capital costs or better productivity.

As a small company, we serve as our own general contractor, and design and build much of our own equipment. In our existing mills, we have designed and built our own continuous casting units, reheat furnaces, cooling beds, automated straightening operation, and, for the past several years, even our own rolling stands.

As to operating efficiently and with high productivity, we believe that we produce steel cheaper than anyone else in the world. We use less than five man-hours per ton of production, including maintenance, clerical, sales, accounting, and management personnel. On the basis of hourly production by workers alone, it is less than three man-hours per ton. Our total employment costs last year were less than $50 per ton, compared with an industry average of $120 per ton. We have attempted to reduce as much as possible inventories and handling. The total time in our mills from scrap charging to finished steel is under three hours, and metal is normally handled only twice—when it comes out of the furnace and caster, and after the straightener when it is loaded for shipment.

Yield is one of the most important factors in both energy cost and energy conservation. The average yield of steel mills in the United States from molten metal to finished product is in the range of 75 percent. Our yield from molten metal to finished product is more than 90 percent, putting total energy cost at about 12 percent of sales. Despite new sophisticated equipment and the use of the latest technology in steelmaking, we believe that our high productivity and the success of the company is attributable to our organizational structure and our company programs and policies.

Peter Drucker once said that the size of a company is not determined by its sales but by the number of management layers in its organization. He said that when a company had nine management levels, it became unmanageable and that there was no clear communication from lower-level management to the top. In the next sentence he said the U.S. Army has nine management levels.

At Nucor there are only four effective management levels: the president, the vice president and general manager of each plant, department managers, and foremen. Staff functions are minimized. We have no "assistant to" or no executive vice presidents. We also do not have company cars, company airplanes, or company boats. There are no company apartments, hunting or fishing lodges, or executive dining rooms. Everyone in the company, including the Chairman of the Board, travels economy class. Last year our sales were $430 million and our corporate offices consist only of 13 people, of which six are secretarial or clerical help.

We believe our incentive programs have played an important role in our productivity performance. There are currently many articles on job enrichment, personal fulfillment, and participation management. We believe that the best job enrichment and the best motivation is "green." Most of our workers are unskilled or semiskilled. They have real problems in maintaining a modest standard of living and they are primarily concerned with two areas: what can I earn today, and will I have a job tomorrow? (Number one, salary; number two, security.)

With respect to security, we believe a company cannot get productive people to work nine months a year or to work for a company with a history of frequent layoffs. In addition, it is necessary for workers to understand that their job security is enhanced rather than threatened by added productivity. This cannot be accomplished by discussions or explanations; the worker has to see over a number of years the actual results of the increased productivity before he becomes convinced that it is not a threat to security but is central to improving his job and standard of living.

As to salary, part of our philosophy is a real commitment to the extra production/extra pay concept. You can find any number of managers who give lip service to this principle ("You can pay a man twice as much if he produces twice as much"), but not many are willing to make the payment. As soon as anyone or any group produces at that level, managers immediately rationalize that the standards are wrong or the group has deviously changed the process or managers find some other reason to reduce the compensation. Probably the greatest single factor in the failure of productivity incentive systems is a less than total commitment by management.

At Nucor we are deeply committed to incentive systems. All our systems are designed around groups, not individuals. We try to clearly define and measure the operations a group is performing and believe that programs should be simple so they can be readily understood. We believe bonuses should be paid promptly so that an employee can directly relate the added effort and added productivity to increased compensation. More than 60 percent of our production workers' total pay is incentive pay and is paid weekly on the basis of the previous week's performance. The bonus is paid as a percentage of the classified job rate. The average hourly worker in our steel mills last year earned $23,000 and many who hold key positions earned more than $35,000.

Any incentive program depends upon the mutual respect and confidence between employees and management in order to avoid serious problems. There is an old saying that goes something like, "Tell them everything or tell them nothing." We definitely believe in telling employees everything about the company—its successes, its failures, its mistakes, its good decisions, and its bad decisions. We encourage communication from the worker about his job and about better and safer ways to do it. The most important part of our approach to safety is through a volunteer rescue squad at each plant manned by the employees. Nucor pays for their training and their equipment, and they take it from there.

In our incentive system, we do not pay a bonus when equipment is not operating. We have a maintenance crew as part of each shift. They participate in the bonus with the regular members, and they feel the urgency to repair equipment promptly.

The foreman is also part of the group and receives the same bonus. The rules for absenteeism and lateness are simple: except for the death of a close relative, if someone is late more than five minutes, he loses the bonus for the day, and if he's late for more than an hour, he loses the bonus for the week. We do not have a problem with tardiness or absenteeism.

The main lines of communication between employee and management are reasonably simple with only four levels of management. In addition, however, weekly crew meetings are held with the department managers, and semiannual dinners are held with the general managers.

The management of this company has strong feelings of responsibility and loyalty to its employees. For many years we have not laid off a single hourly worker for lack of work. In addition, we have a number of unusual employee benefit programs. One of the most unusual is our scholarship program. The company provides a scholarship of $1,200 per year for four years of college or vocational training to every child of every employee in the company. We currently have children of employees enrolled in some 115 learning institutions.

With regard to the future, we have an ambitious expansion program. During 1980 and 1981 we anticipate capital expenditures in excess of $90 million, the major portion of which will be financed in-house.

At present, our backlogs are higher than they were a year ago, and we expect sales and earnings for the first half of 1980 to be 20 percent higher than they were in 1979. We believe that Nucor has laid the foundation to maintain a five-year growth in real earnings of 12–15 percent per year.

Our new mill at Norfolk, Nebraska, started operations in July 1979. Five years in development, this mill and an expanded one at South Carolina are the only mills in the world where a continuous cast billet is rolled directly into a finishing product. We are constantly working toward new techniques and methods of increasing production.

JAMES W. MASON, JR.

# 5 Productivity Achievement at Kaiser

KAISER ALUMINUM & CHEMICAL CORPORATION (KACC) is a large, diversified manufacturing firm, and our productivity program is manufacturing-oriented. We are the 114th largest corporation in the United States on the basis of sales and the 71st largest on the basis of assets, according to the 1979 listing of the Fortune 500. We had sales in 1979 of approximately $3 billion. We employ about 26,000 people in 89 manufacturing locations around the world. We are a fully integrated aluminum producer, mining bauxite, converting bauxite to aluminum in chemical process plants, smelting aluminum, and fabricating annually 1.75 billion pounds of the metal we produce. We also produce fertilizer, a variety of industrial chemicals, and refractories. Our plants range in size from 15 to 3,500 employees, and our productivity program is used in all but the smallest plants.

## ELEMENTS OF KAISER'S PRODUCTIVITY PROGRAM

The elements of our company's productivity program are probably much the same as those for any company with a formal program. We recognize the activity organizationally with a corporate productivity program coordinator who works for me. We also have a corporate productivity committee composed of six corporate officers and chaired by a senior vice president. Our Chief Executive Officer

(CEO) is involved in a review of each plant's annual improvement program and a monthly monitoring of results.

Other key elements of our program include stated improvement goals, an appropriate measurement system, monthly reporting of results, frequent reinforcement of objectives, and programs to recognize plant performance. In our organization the annual improvement plan has been part of operating philosophy for more than a decade. Management people, down to the shop foreman level, accept the principle of annual improvement, which in itself is an important contribution to our program's success.

Our productivity improvements result from activities that can be grouped into three general categories: improvement, breakthrough, and control.

I have defined *improvement* as "using what we've got better." By this I mean those programs which get incremental improvements in manpower utilization, material recovery, maintenance spending, and the like, without large capital expenditures.

Since productivity change is the sum of improvement and regression of performance, it is as important to prevent performance erosion as it is to implement programs to improve it. Our experience indicates plants and departments usually are successful in installing their productivity improvement projects. When plants show negative trends, it is almost always because something such as quality, employee relations, or equipment conditions got out of control, and the improvement projects, although implemented, were not enough to offset the disaster.

*Breakthrough,* on the other hand, I use to describe productivity gains generated by process changes, usually requiring large amounts of money. I will devote the balance of the chapter to describing how Kaiser Aluminum & Chemical Corporation gets productivity gains through control and improvement activities. I will not discuss our breakthrough projects, since they are process-oriented and not of general interest.

*Control,* of course, begins with measurement. Our corporate productivity measurement system is a one-number measure. This index is expressed in dollars rather than in percentages, an approach we have found quite effective. At headquarters, my office publishes a monthly report, addressed to the CEO, that indicates the productivity improvement or regression of each plant in the company. The report shows by month and year-to-date how each plant is performing compared with the previous year. Elements outside the control of plant personnel, such as energy price increases and natural disasters, are excluded from the calculation.

## KAISER'S PRODUCTIVITY MEASUREMENT SYSTEM

The foundation of our productivity measurement is the standard cost system. By comparing this year's cost performance with last year's, we get the improvement or regression that we equate to productivity change. Of course, the procedure must handle standards revisions, mix changes, and that sort of thing. Our productivity index measures *the difference between what conversion cost (value added) was for the period and what it would have been at last year's performance level.*

Although we believe our measurement system is appropriate, we believe it can be improved. The concept of total factor productivity measurement came to our attention several years ago. The concept should be familiar to anyone who knows John Kendrick's work or the measurement activities of the American Productivity Center in Houston. Total factor productivity (TFP) is output divided by the sum of the various inputs, here listed as *labor, capital, material,* and *energy.* National productivity trends are usually presented as output per man-hour, which is a partial productivity factor: output divided by labor input. This factor indicates an annual improvement of productivity in the United States since World War II of 3.2 percent. When we look at the TFP indexes for key industries in the post-World War II era, we see from Figure 5-1 that the chemical industry exceeds 2 percent. The big difference in the two approaches is the addition of capital as an input in the TFP calculation.

As you can see from Figure 5-2, Kaiser's system of productivity measurement falls somewhere between the partial labor productivity factor and a total productivity factor. Kaiser's system measures labor productivity, material productivity, and energy productivity in a combined index. Our system does not include capital or "white collar" costs on the input side.

We have the capability to handle what are sometimes difficult problems in productivity measurement. Our system copes easily

Figure 5-1. Total factor productivity: Average annual change in various U.S. industries, 1947–1973.

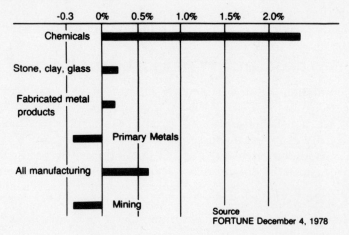

Source
FORTUNE December 4, 1978

with output mix changes, labor input mix changes, contracted labor, and purchased material price variances.

Our plans are to develop a total factor productivity index by plant and division and for the company as a whole. We will use this in addition to our current measurement (see Figure 5-3). We would like to have the impact on productivity expressed as a percentage of cost reduction capital, regulatory capital, labor (including white-collar costs), material, and energy. The algebraic sum of the parts would be our TFP.

As useful as our single measure of productivity is, it has a potential to be harmful as well as helpful. In a 1974 *Harvard Business Review* article entitled "The Decline, Fall and Renewal of Manufacturing Plants," Wickham Skinner said, "Simplistic performance evaluation is one of the four principal causes of failure of manufacturing businesses." He explained that there is a tendency in most companies to evaluate manufacturing on a single performance criterion, such as profit or cost or efficiency, at the expense of such other factors as customer service, quality, and employee relations.

We utilize a companion measurement system with our productivity measurement system to help prevent any imbalance in emphasis of key performance criteria. This system is part of an

Figure 5-2. Kaiser Aluminum & Chemical Corporation's system of productivity measurement.

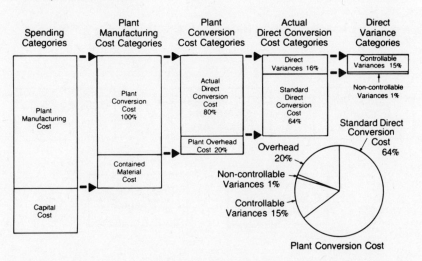

annual recognition program we call the "Best Operating Team Competition." Now in its eighth year, the program recognizes and rewards the best overall performance by plants in each of eight groups. Plants are divided into groups solely on the basis of size. Winners are selected annually from each group. Appropriate recognition ceremonies and awards are part of the program with participation of company officers and, frequently, board members.

Whereas winners are selected annually, performance is evaluated quarterly, and contending plants are publicized quarterly. The criteria on which performance is evaluated include cost performance, productivity, customer service performance, safety, profit plan performance, community and government relations, environmental control, quality performance, maintenance of assets, energy management, affirmative action and employee relations, capital spending, and inventory control.

Within the company we still use the term *productivity* to describe labor performance against standard and cost performance as the measure of overall cost performance this year versus last year.

The significance of a criterion for a particular plant is established by assigning weighing points. A total of 100 points is spread out

Figure 5-3. An equation showing Kaiser's productivity goals.

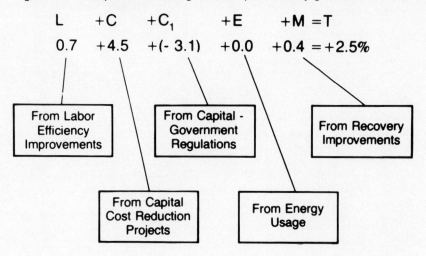

over the 14 criteria. High points are assigned to important criteria, fewer point to less significant criteria, and no points when the criterion does not apply to a plan's mission. Point assignments are made by division management and reviewed by the Best Operating Team administration committee.

A plant is graded by comparing its current performance with its historical performance and its planned performance. A suitable performance index (or in many cases a number of indexes) is selected to track each criterion. Typically a plant receives 70 percent of the points assigned to a criterion if its current performance exceeds its historical and planned levels. Higher percentages are used if the plant has two, three, or five years of successive improvement. Substantially exceeding plan or historical base may gain a few additional percentage points as well. The emphasis in grading is on continued improvement in the plant's past performance.

The example of a plant's grade in Table 5-1 shows a 76.7 percent performance. This hypothetical plant did well in customer service, capital spending, and inventory control but was not as strong in environmental control and energy management. With this grading system, plants with entirely different manufacturing missions can be ranked appropriately in the same group.

Table 5-1. Sample of grading system for plant XYZ, first quarter.

| Category | Points Assigned | Grade Percent | Score |
|---|---|---|---|
| Safety | 10 | 70 | 7.0 |
| Productivity | 10 | 85 | 8.5 |
| Cost | 15 | 80 | 12.0 |
| Environmental control | 8 | 60 | 4.8 |
| Customer service | 5 | 100 | 5.0 |
| Profit plan | — | — | — |
| Quality | 10 | 70 | 7.0 |
| Production plan | 5 | 80 | 4.0 |
| Energy management | 3 | 60 | 1.8 |
| Maintenance of assets | 8 | 75 | 6.0 |
| Employee relations | 10 | 70 | 7.0 |
| Capital spending | 3 | 100 | 3.0 |
| Inventory control | 5 | 100 | 5.0 |
| Community and government relations | 8 | 70 | 5.6 |
| Total | 100 | | 76.7 |

## USE OF CONTROL CHARTS

Personnel who evaluate performance quarterly have control charts to aid them. These charts show current performance by month on a trend graph and historical performance. The form permits showing the numbers as well as the trend. The format of the trend graphs has been developed for quick analysis. With this form of presentation, it is possible to review 20 or 30 indexes for a plant in a matter of minutes—much faster than analyzing lists of numbers. These charts are currently prepared by each plant and are submitted quarterly. They often become the foundation for the operations reviews by division management. We are currently exploring the possibility of generating these charts centrally, using computer graphics. Some examples of our computer analysis involved in four functions—raw materials, building construction, forging, and sheet and plate—are shown in Figure 5-4.

These Best Operating Team performance charts are part of a positive motivational program designed to recognize superior performance. They serve another purpose which protects and enhances our company's productivity performance. In a large, diversified

Figure 5-4. Performance analysis charts for four functions: Raw materials,

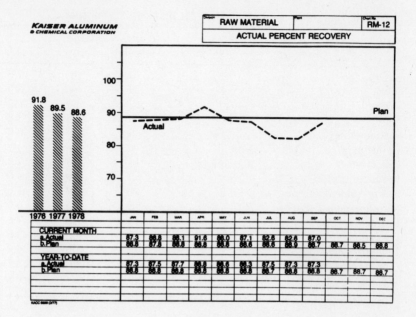

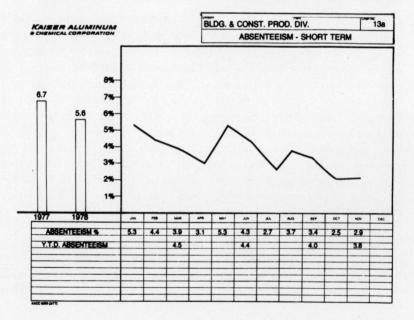

building construction, forging, and sheet and plate.

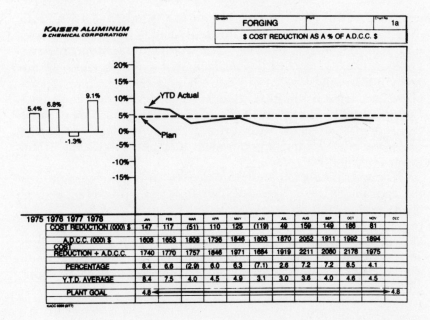

*KAISER ALUMINUM & CHEMICAL CORPORATION*

| Division | FORGING | Plant | Chart No 1a |
|---|---|---|---|
| | $ COST REDUCTION AS A % OF A.D.C.C. $ | | |

1975 1976 1977 1978

| | JAN | FEB | MAR | APR | MAY | JUN | JUL | AUG | SEP | OCT | NOV | DEC |
|---|---|---|---|---|---|---|---|---|---|---|---|---|
| COST REDUCTION (000) $ | 147 | 117 | (51) | 110 | 125 | (119) | 49 | 159 | 149 | 186 | 81 | |
| A.D.C.C. (000) $ | 1608 | 1653 | 1808 | 1736 | 1846 | 1803 | 1870 | 2052 | 1911 | 1992 | 1894 | |
| COST REDUCTION + A.D.C.C. | 1740 | 1770 | 1757 | 1846 | 1971 | 1684 | 1919 | 2211 | 2060 | 2178 | 1975 | |
| PERCENTAGE | 8.4 | 6.6 | (2.9) | 6.0 | 6.3 | (7.1) | 2.6 | 7.2 | 7.2 | 8.5 | 4.1 | |
| Y.T.D. AVERAGE | 8.4 | 7.5 | 4.0 | 4.5 | 4.9 | 3.1 | 3.0 | 3.6 | 4.0 | 4.6 | 4.5 | |
| PLANT GOAL | 4.8 | | | | | | | | | | | 4.8 |

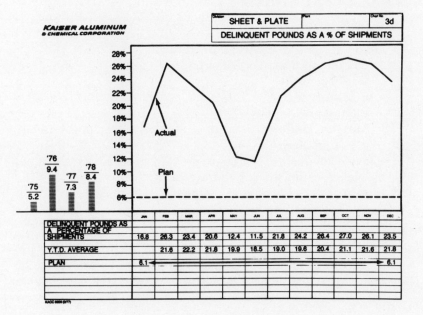

*KAISER ALUMINUM & CHEMICAL CORPORATION*

| Division | SHEET & PLATE | Plant | Chart No 3d |
|---|---|---|---|
| | DELINQUENT POUNDS AS A % OF SHIPMENTS | | |

| | JAN | FEB | MAR | APR | MAY | JUN | JUL | AUG | SEP | OCT | NOV | DEC |
|---|---|---|---|---|---|---|---|---|---|---|---|---|
| DELINQUENT POUNDS AS A PERCENTAGE OF SHIPMENTS | 16.8 | 26.3 | 23.4 | 20.6 | 12.4 | 11.5 | 21.8 | 24.2 | 26.4 | 27.0 | 26.1 | 23.5 |
| Y.T.D. AVERAGE | | 21.6 | 22.2 | 21.8 | 19.9 | 18.5 | 19.0 | 19.6 | 20.4 | 21.1 | 21.6 | 21.8 |
| PLAN | 6.1 | | | | | | | | | | | 6.1 |

company such as ours, a major problem facing top management is to detect severe performance erosion early and to intervene in a way that will encourage recovery. Knowledge of performance regression usually reaches top management slowly because of the many intervening levels. And there is a natural tendency to suppress bad news or to "fix it ourselves before someone finds out." Loyalties and long-time associations often defer personnel changes that should be executed with dispatch. An information system that provides early warning or performance decline is extremely useful in preventing disasters.

It is important not to inhibit initiative by strong central control or the appearance of such control. Our Best Operating Team control charts give us the information we need centrally without the appearance of central control. The intervention methods we use when out-of-control performance is detected are carefully selected to preserve a feeling of reasonable autonomy on the part of plant and division management. Performance charts are not used as whips and clubs.

## ESSENTIALS OF AN EFFECTIVE PRODUCTIVITY IMPROVEMENT SYSTEM

The essentials of an effective system are as follows.

1. To achieve productivity improvements:
   Obtain top management support
   Organize for it
   Establish goals
   Plan improvements
   Measure performance but avoid pitfall of "one number" overemphasis
2. Devote adequate resources to prevent slippage of current performance while striving to improve it.
3. Establish an early warning system to detect slippage.

Our productivity improvement activities are varied. We have found there is no single program such as quality circles, a suggestion system, a cost reduction program, or quality-of-work-life program, that can be applied universally to generate productivity improvements. Factors such as the age of the facility, the labor content of the manufacturing process, the value of the raw materials being processed, the amount of energy consumed by the operation, and the labor relations climate all have a bearing on the approach used in a particular plant at any given time. There are common factors in all our plants, however, concerning productivity improvement. They each must submit by the end of November an annual operating plan, which includes, among other things, the detailed projects that will generate the improvement in the coming year. They utilize the same guidelines to establish the amount of improvement to be accomplished.

The guidelines are quite simple. The acceptable range for a given plant is from 3–5 percent of its previous year's actual conversion cost *and* 25 percent of variance from standard cost. We use 5 percent for fabricating and labor-intensive plants and 3 percent for process plants that are more locked in by existing facilities with less opportunity for *improvement* productivity gains. Our process plants are usually candidates for *breakthrough* improvements.

Thomas C. MacAvoy, president of Corning Glass Works, made this comment regarding productivity improvement goals in the March 10, 1980 issue of *Fortune:* "I'll be darned if I can figure out how we are going to do it. I think, as in all technically innovative businesses, frequently you don't know what new inventions will come along, so you don't know how in heck you're going to achieve the goal." Despite a cloudy future, Corning has boosted its productivity growth up to 6 percent.

Our experience is similar to Corning's. Just where the improvements will come from when we look beyond the next 15 to 18 months is hazy, but they usually develop. Some are fortuitous; they knock on your door as new products or techniques. It's just necessary to keep an open door and an open mind to the sales people who call. I would estimate 20–30 percent of our improvements originate this way.

## OTHER AREAS OF PRODUCTIVITY IMPROVEMENT

The balance of our productivity improvement comes from a variety of activities, depending on the specifics of each plant. Although all plants have the traditional cost-reduction programs, they are also active in two or three of the following areas:

Process control improvement
Energy utilization
Elimination of restrictive work practices
Mechanized material handling
Capacity utilization
Product line streamlining
Training programs—hourly and salaried
Systems improvement—particularly production control

Another area we find has great potential for improvement in our large plants is in the utilization of maintenance manpower resources. As you can see in Figure 5-5, our typical maintenance workers perform direct work in a craft skill only about 27 percent of the time they are paid to work. We are actively pursuing the potential to improve their utilization through maintenance management programs that feature personnel development, training, and improved planning and scheduling systems. Most of the improvement potential in maintenance manpower utilization can be achieved by better management. Only a small part of the nonproductive time is

Figure 5-5. Utilization of maintenance workers in Kaiser's plants.

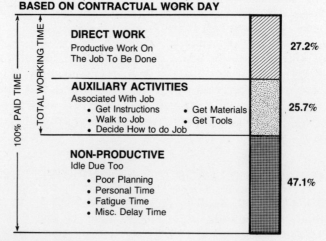

BASED ON CONTRACTUAL WORK DAY

DIRECT WORK
Productive Work On
The Job To Be Done — 27.2%

AUXILIARY ACTIVITIES
Associated With Job
• Get Instructions   • Get Materials
• Walk to Job        • Get Tools
• Decide How to do Job — 25.7%

NON-PRODUCTIVE
Idle Due Too
• Poor Planning
• Personal Time
• Fatigue Time
• Misc. Delay Time — 47.1%

Sample Size, 765 Craftsmen
Craftsmen these plants – – – – –1300
Approximate Annual Cost – – – – $39 million

attributable to restrictive work practices or general worker indifference.

In the recent past, the greatest improvements have evolved from these areas:

Plant surveys
Maintenance management
Robotics and automation
Restrictive work practices
Mechanized material handling
Inventory management

## THE ROLE OF PLANT SURVEYS

Plant surveys have been a particularly useful technique for us in identifying productivity improvement potential. We have conducted surveys in more than 30 of our plants during the past five years with extremely good results. These surveys assess manufacturing methods, evaluate the manufacturing control system, determine labor productivity level, and evaluate cost reduction activities. The surveys result in a time-phased program with cost and benefit levels established.

The survey team, which is composed of a number of people from my staff, several from the division staff, some from the plant staff, and usually a couple from "sister" plants, spends two weeks at the plant collecting data. Work sampling is used extensively as a diagnostic tool. The team takes an additional two to three weeks in data analysis and then presents a draft of the report to plant management. The final report is formally presented at the plant with key plant and division management present.

A form of data presentation we have found useful in reporting analysis methods and recommendations is what we call productivity sensitivity analysis. The key factors that affect productivity are listed in descending order in Figure 5-6, according to how much a 5 percent change would improve productivity. Our survey process then begins diagnostic work with the element at the top of the list and works down. Ultimately, we determine the improvement potential as the major factors chart, shown in Figure 5-7, becomes the center of discussion of the plant's improvement program.

Figure 5-6. Productivity sensitivity analysis (on the basis of a 5 percent change).

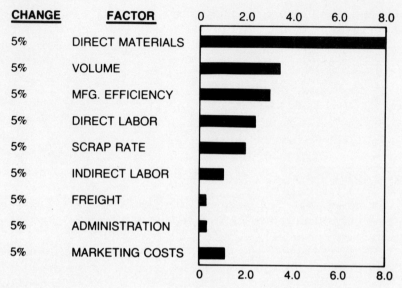

Figure 5-7. Determination of productivity improvement potential by analyzing major factors.

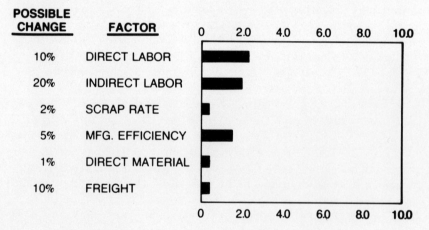

The survey technique must be applied delicately to prevent the process from being construed as a witch-hunt. We do not use the survey approach unless it is formally requested by a plant. It is doubtful that it would be successful if imposed "from above."

## CONCLUSION

This chapter has discussed what Kaiser Aluminum & Chemical Corporation is doing to improve productivity. For the future, we look to an approach that holds great potential for us in the next five years. Employee involvement programs, illustrated by the "Quality of Work Life" accomplishments of General Motors Corporation, offer tremendous opportunities. If we can tap the potential of the people who know the work best, the individuals actually performing it, the results would pale our efforts in other areas. If all employees work collectively for the improvement of the unit, there are few situations where a productivity problem would exist.

**TED OLSON and JERRY JENSEN**

# 6
# Starting
# Productivity Programs
# in a Diversified Firm—
# Beatrice Foods
# Company

OUR PRODUCTIVITY efforts at the corporate level at Beatrice really got started about a year and a half ago. The challenge, from our perspective, was to stimulate productivity improvement in probably the most diverse and decentralized corporation in this country. The question was what we could do at the corporate level that was consistent with our decentralized management philosophy. To provide some background on that perspective, we'd first like to tell you what the operating services department is and does and then give you some background on Beatrice Foods.

After introducing the company we can discuss the program as we've unfolded it over the last year and a half. The program consists of three parts to date, and we've got a pretty good idea of where we're going. We began by dealing with the issue of creating the awareness of the productivity problem within the corporation, and then providing the tools for solving it. We're currently working on providing the incentives all the way down to the employee level.

Let us begin by explaining our operating services department. We are a small internal consulting staff that provides staff support services to the operating units at their request. We have five people in the financial services area, four in the materials management field, and five on our industrial engineering staff. The primary efforts of the operating services department are devoted to providing project assistance on-site to the operating units at their request. We have a high profit center orientation. The department reports to the president and chief operating officer. Our limited staff capability made it necessary to find some ways in which we could leverage the staff and activities.

## A BRIEF LOOK AT BEATRICE FOODS

Beatrice Foods is probably the largest least-understood company in this country today. Most people don't know that Beatrice Foods is one of the largest firms in the United States. We just finished an $8.3 billion sales year. We were number 23 on the 1979 Fortune 500 list. We're the third largest Chicago-based corporation, and we have 430 operating companies or profit centers. The company is a highly diversified organization with 17 operating divisions in 28 countries. Our products are distributed in over 90 countries. Approximately 75 percent of the organization is food-related; the other 25 percent is in nonfood areas.

Our products fall into ten SIC United States industry codes. These include products in the dairy and soft-drink division, which is represented by Meadow Gold, our national brand. The company got its start in the dairy business. We're currently the largest dairy supplier in the country with brand products such as Dannon Yogurt and Swiss Miss. Our grocery products are represented by companies like LaChoy, Aunt Nellie's, Martha White, and Tropicana. Food distribution and warehousing are represented by companies such as Sexton, Inland Cold Storage of Kansas City, and a whole series of warehousing operations such as Quincy Cold Storage in Boston.

Confectionery and snack companies include Switzer, Clark, Halloway, Jolly Rancher in Denver, and Fisher Nut. Fisher is the second largest nut producer in the United States. The specialty meats division is represented by companies such as Peter Eckrich, Lowrey's Fresheries, and Kneip. Our Agri-Product companies include Vigortone and a number of rendering plants such as Regal in Lynn Center, Illinois.

Our institutional and industrial divisions include companies such as Culligan, Day-Timers, Waterloo Industries (which manufactures tool boxes), Hi-Temp World Dryer (which manufactures the hand dryers everybody hates), ACME, Dycasting, and Brillion Iron.

Our travel and recreation products include Samsonite, Buxton, and Morgan Yacht. We have a large soft-goods industry, represented by E.R. Moore in the school equipment, athletic apparel, and cap and gown markets, Swingster, which manufactures promotional jackets and caps, and Homemaker, whose products include sleeping bags and bedspreads. In the area of housing and home environment products, our companies include Stiffel Lamp and Charmglow. Our international food division is primarily in food distribution and dairy operations throughout the world.

Our company's major strength has been in promoting local brands such as Dannon to the regional level and regional brands to the national level.

Beatrice is probably the most decentralized organization in the country today. The profit centers are stand-alone businesses. All our operating decisions are made at the profit center level. The corporate office consists of only 310 people. Our profit center managers have total autonomy in making their own operating decisions.

Beatrice Foods consists of many small companies. Our average company size is under $20 million in sales, with most companies being in the $10 million–$30 million range. We have a few large companies with sales of more than $100 million, represented by companies such as Culligan, Samsonite, Sexton, Eckrich, and Tropicana.

Beatrice has enjoyed a unique growth record—we are the only company today on the New York Stock Exchange that can talk about 28 consecutive years of increases in sales, earnings, and earnings per share. Few companies have successfully weathered as many economic downturns as we have. The company is currently doubling in size every five years, which is a significant rate.

## HOW THE PRODUCTIVITY PROGRAM STARTED

Our motivation for getting the productivity program started at the corporate level was that we wanted to stimulate productivity improvement on a broader basis than was occurring. Obviously, we were concerned about the national productivity problem. Figure 6-1 shows that some countries—in particular, Canada, France, Germany, and Japan—could surpass the United States in productivity growth rate within the next ten years. But basically, our motivation for starting on the corporate productivity efforts was an

Figure 6-1. Projections of domestic output per employee-hour, United States and four other industrial nations, selected years.*

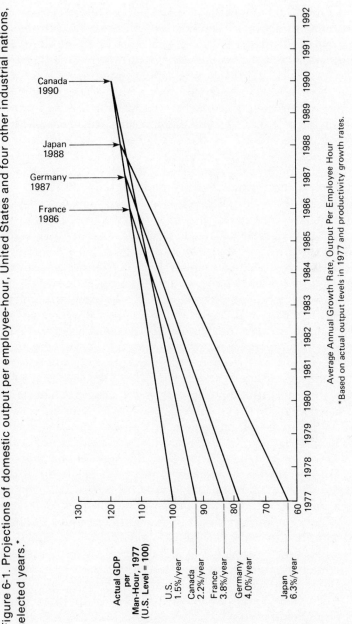

Average Annual Growth Rate, Output Per Employee Hour

*Based on actual output levels in 1977 and productivity growth rates.

internal one. Our Chairman and Executive Officer became increasingly concerned about the effect of inflationary pressures and the resulting rapid increase in costs in materials and labor. He was seeing signs that we would not be able to pass-through all cost increases, especially if the government imposed voluntary or mandatory controls. Therefore, the only real avenue for maintaining margins was through productivity improvement. We began this program about a year ago, and the first issue we addressed was how to bring an awareness of the productivity problem down to the profit center level on a broad basis.

In March 1979, we made the first attack on the awareness problem at our second annual management conference. This is a conference where the 430 profit center managers, plus division, group, and corporate executives, meet for two days to talk about where they have been, but mainly where they are going. Although it had not been planned, all the major speakers on the program, except Henry Kissinger, stressed productivity in their talks, pointing to it as a major issue and challenge for the coming years. We did not exert influence on a single speech on the program. One of our executives spoke specifically on the issue of productivity and described how an individual profit center manager could affect his operation. He spoke from the perspective of what he had done himself. In order to reinforce the message, we published a little eight-page pamphlet entitled "The Beatrice Productivity Philosophy" (reprinted at the end of the chapter). This pamphlet was handed to all the managers and provided some very simple ideas on maintaining awareness of the problem. They carried it back to their companies as an aid to stimulate discussion on productivity. This brochure was hastily produced but has been highly effective and now is in its third printing. It has been distributed throughout the company and also outside the company. Many people, including contractors, call for it and ask how to implement a productivity program such as the one outlined in our pamphlet. To put it briefly, there are four steps involved:

1. Establish productivity goals and objectives.
2. Develop productivity measures.
3. Encourage participation of all employees in the productivity improvement effort.
4. Consider productivity training programs.

Within a couple of weeks after the management conference, our Chairman of the Board sent a letter to all division and group managers indicating that he considered productivity a major challenge and a major issue for the coming year. He encouraged the division managers to maintain the theme of productivity throughout their divisional meetings and their various activities. Indeed, a number of divisions did follow through and spent a great deal of effort throughout the year talking about productivity. Our confectionery division inaugurated its first annual productivity award. One plant had achieved a very dramatic 60 percent improvement in productivity during the preceding year. That is an astounding figure. Although the plant was not in the greatest shape to begin with, it wasn't a losing company. The key to this particular success was the very simple technique of analyzing people's skills and their jobs and matching the right people with the right jobs. That may sound simplistic, but it was the heart of this program and it yielded a dramatic result.

The corporation also published a monthly newsletter to its managers, and in every issue there was a highlight of a productivity program at individual companies. One example was our Royal Crown bottler in Los Angeles, which had achieved an increase of 3,500 cases per shift to 10,000 cases per shift by a rather small adjustment and some minor capital modifications to its bottling line. It is this type of emphasis on the simple, very attainable things that can be done that is stimulating the program.

Beyond that, we also felt that there was a need to provide some other tools on how to approach the productivity problem and exchange ideas. We also wanted to provide backup from the corporate level. Therefore, we placed a high degree of emphasis on providing our staff services functions and on working on projects aimed at improving productivity. The lion's share of the capital expenditures during the past year has emphasized the results expected from productivity improvement and cost reduction activities.

## PRODUCTIVITY SEMINARS: HOW THEY WORK

We also organized a quarterly training seminar for about 25 to 30 managers from the profit centers to provide some discussion and some tools for productivity improvement. I think it might be interesting just to briefly look at the seminar agenda, because it encompasses a rather wide range of the productivity issues. The sessions emphasize interchange by providing extensive time for discussion among the participants. These managers are generally top performers and come to the table with a lot of ideas. They arrive with the attitude that they've done a lot but that more can be done.

The agenda begins with an address by either our Chairman or our President to this group of 30 people to reinforce top-management support of this activity. They emphasize that the corporation is truly behind the program and believes in it. The address includes a brief discussion of the national problem and relates that to why productivity is important to Beatrice Foods.

We spend the remaining eight hours of the first day dealing with the management issues that affect productivity. We cover such areas as how to better motivate our employees, how to better manage *ourselves* through proper time management, and how to tone up our communications skills, which are very important in setting up productivity improvement programs at the plant. We cover team building, since that is one of the best approaches to get at the problem. A high degree of emphasis is also placed on improving our supervisory effectiveness. Finally, we put it all together with an action plan. We are anticipating modifying this seminar so that with our next-generation programs, we will have the individuals work on specific action plans that they will carry back to their companies for implementation.

We use numerous materials to support the program over the two days, including Alan Lakein's book on time management and two books on productivity: Joel Ross's general management study on productivity, and Clair Vough's book on how IBM views a total productivity program in its Selectric plant at Lexington, Kentucky. The latter two are relatively brief and very readable books, and we receive good feedback on them. [Editor's Note: The full titles of all three books are provided in the Bibliography.] Finally, we furnish a small pamphlet on the "Truths of Productivity," which helps bring the message home to the employees on the floor.

In addition, we have a speaker from a small company outside of Beatrice who is very much committed to productivity improvement. He has approached it primarily through his family-owned company, using quality-of-work-life approaches. He really didn't know he was using a quality-of-work-life approach until someone told him. He said, "I was just trying to get better productivity, and trying to get it through my employees." He comes from a $10 million company and speaks very effectively to those of our managers who come from a similar environment of family-owned companies.

The second day we talk about some specific industrial-engineering tools that may be useful in improving manufacturing productivity. These are familiar approaches, including materials handling, space utilization, and control techniques such as standards and short-interval scheduling. We also discuss the roles of the purchasing department and distribution department and their effect on productivity. Beatrice has the largest private truck carrier fleet in the United States because of all the individual companies. While the small Dannon Yogurt trucks, Sexton trucks, and Meadow Gold Milk vans are all part of this fleet, there is a large number of over-the-road vehicles, which can be used to put together a rather effective distribution system. We also place a high degree of emphasis on value analysis, which is a general technique that most companies can apply. We bring in several examples from diverse backgrounds.

I should emphasize that there is a very close tie-in between day one and day two. Throughout the discussions during day two, we continually emphasize how the management techniques that were discussed the day before are used in better presenting, implementing, and organizing the types of tools that are presented on day two. We're not approaching it from a standpoint of our industrial-engineering profession. I know some of my peers are upset, but we're really looking at it from the perspective of trying to make every person in the plant his own mini-industrial engineer in designing methods of improvement. These are the people who know the best way to improve the jobs. How you tap that resource to get them working on these techniques is emphasized this second day.

Actual case examples are covered for all the techniques. Various company representatives come in person or send prepared text and slide presentations. Charmglow talks about nine improvements in corrugated packaging that snowballed into a number of improvements throughout the plant. Dry Print Foils management presents how it uses short-interval scheduling to achieve its productivity results. A Fisher Nut representative talks about that company's packaging materials substitution, and Liken Home Furnishing shows how it uses standards. Morgan Yacht discusses its organized value analysis program, which has a very broad perspective. Richardson Mint management talks about the results of its methods improvement program.

## CURRENT AND FUTURE DIRECTIONS

Our major thrust the past year was to sharpen our message to the profit centers. Our emphasis was on getting something started and then letting the profit centers develop their own productivity program. With a corporate staff of five industrial engineers dealing with 430 companies, it wasn't possible for us to work with every company individually.

This year, to follow up on the awareness issues that we addressed last year, we wanted to answer the question, "What's in it for me?" We have put together a corporationwide incentive program that is aimed at getting all the way down to the employee level at the profit centers. The blanket theme for the Beatrice productivity programs is "uncommon people, uncommon goals." It was announced at our March management meeting this year. The program is designed to provide some financial rewards to the profit centers for productivity improvements. Those rewards will be converted to benefits at the employee levels. It's a noncash incentive program. The program will be administered through the 17 divisions and developed on a divisional basis. The financing for the program is going to be split three ways, with the corporation, divisions, and profit centers each carrying one-third. Our plant-level theme is "working smarter—together."

We expect that approximately 50 percent of the participating plants will be eligible for some group financial rewards on a quarterly basis. The program is tiered, and the outstanding achiever or best profit center in the division has an opportunity to win as much as $10,000 per year, or $2,500 quarterly. This is a contribution toward some kind of an employee benefit. The next highest achievers can win as much as $5,000, and those who surpass the threshold goal for the division can win as much as $2,000 annually, or $500 quarterly. We've even introduced a consolation prize for a certain threshold level of improvement.

The rewards are in many forms of employee benefits. They are tailored to the profit center level and could be in the form of concerts, picnics, parties, sporting events, free lunches, free coffee, and the like. In addition, we plan to provide a high degree of visibility and recognition to the top winners in *Beatrice World*. The top winners in the division will be recognized at next year's annual management meeting. Recognition is probably as important as the non-cash awards.

Each profit center and division will provide coordinators to administer its program. The profit centers will be provided with all the promotional materials and a full guidebook on implementation. The total commitment in this program with full participation can run up to about $1 million. So the corporation is putting some money behind its productivity efforts.

Looking ahead, where do we go from here? We envision that it will take us about two years to bring the incentive program to a full-participation level across the board. The program also provides a vehicle for increased exchange of information among our profit centers on productivity improvement. We will continue to focus on extension of training aids that can be used at the profit center level. We plan to develop some in-house training programs that can literally be mailed out. These will be in the form of videotape or slide presentations.

Beyond that, we view the program as evolutionary, and we're still collecting ideas. We suspect that it will have many more generations of improvement because we have a very strong corporate commitment to the issue of productivity improvement.

## APPENDIX: THE BEATRICE PRODUCTIVITY PHILOSOPHY

At Beatrice, our people are the strength of our productivity effort. They help us use our resources more efficiently and effectively. This means working smarter with our tools, our capital, and our human resources.

The most important factor in improving productivity is the positive attitude of the management team. This attitude is important for developing ways to reduce costs, compete effectively, and ease the pressures of inflation.

Within these pages are some methods and directions for making productivity work for our businesses, our employees, and our future.

James L. Dutt
*Chairman and*
*Chief Executive Officer*

*What is productivity?*

Productivity is doing more with the resources we have. It is measured as the simple ratio:

$$\frac{\text{OUTPUT}}{\text{INPUT}}$$

OUTPUT   refers to goods and services produced and may be expressed in dollars, pounds, or other currencies.

INPUT   refers to labor, material, capital, and so on.

*How do changes in productivity affect us?*

Productivity growth is a key element in determining improvements in our living standards. It contributes to economic expansion, provides healthy growth in jobs, and restrains inflation. Improving productivity within our businesses means finding better ways to do more with the resources we have. With rising energy, labor, and materials costs, we must strive to improve all levels of company operations in order to maintain our performance in profits and growth.

*What is productivity improvement?*

Productivity improvement isn't just working harder, it's working smarter. It means devising a method to get the best return on our investment in people, raw materials, facilities, equipment, and other resources. Some of the ways to improve productivity are:

Creating a more productive work environment.
Developing new products and technology.
Managing our production resources more effectively.
Utilizing machinery and equipment more efficiently.
Improving our work methods.
Motivating and training our people.

In short, we produce more when we have better tools and production techniques and are better organized and managed.

*How do I develop productivity "awareness" in my company?*

To be effective, every segment of the company should understand its responsibility for improving productivity. This understanding is communicated through various methods. Among these are the following:

1. Establish productivity goals and objectives.
2. Develop productivity measures.

3. Encourage participation of all employees in the productivity improvement effort.
4. Consider productivity training programs.

Let's break each of these steps down a little further:

*1. To encourage productivity improvement, we need to establish productivity goals and objectives*

To be successful, a serious productivity improvement effort must include productivity goals. Try some goals, even if you're not sure they are right; make corrections later.

The following is a simple five-step technique for productivity goal setting:

Decide how to monitor productivity.
Determine your productivity level.
Set attainable goals.
Establish action plans for improvement.
Implement productivity improvements.

Once you have decided on the output-to-input ratios that best fit your work, set improvement targets for the next week, month, or year.

*2. To determine our progress, it is important to monitor productivity*

To be meaningful, the productivity measure used should relate to the organizational unit. The following measures might be considered:

*Employee productivity*—Measured as output per employee or per man-hour, such as
Value added per payroll dollar.
Units per man-hour.
*Equipment productivity*—Measured as output per machine-hour, such as
Pounds per machine-hour.
Units per machine-hour.
*Assets productivity*—Measured as output per asset dollar, such as
Sales per asset dollar.
Units per asset dollar.
*Energy productivity*—Measured as product output per energy input, such as
Units of product per cubic feet (gas).
Units of product per gallons (oil).
Units of product per kilowatt hours (electricity).

*3. The greatest improvement will be achieved if all employees participate in the productivity effort*

The emphasis on productivity as a company goal comes from the top. But the best ideas for improving operations often come from the bottom. The involvement of people at all levels will ensure successful productivity efforts.

The following techniques, communicated properly, can provide a participative atmosphere for productivity improvement:

Encourage employee suggestions.
Encourage employee participation in cost reduction.
Consider methods of employee recognition, such as
    Employee productivity awards.
    Cost reduction contests.
Consider employee motivation techniques, such as
    Employee suggestion awards.
    Cost reduction contests.
Monitor employee productivity.

*4. Productivity training programs can aid in developing effective approaches to productivity improvement*

Many techniques are available to managers and supervisors for achieving improved productivity, such as:

Work simplification.
Short-interval scheduling.
Employee motivation methods.
Improving supervisory effectiveness.
Value analysis.
Automation.
Methods analysis.

There are numerous sources of information and professional assistance available on many of the above formal systems. Companies may contact Ted Olson, Director of Operating Services, for information and referrals.

In addition, training programs that will help acquaint the manager and supervisor with the application of these techniques are available from a variety of sources.

Further information on such training programs is available from Pat McCuan, Director of Management Training at the Corporate Office.

WILLIAM G. LORD II

# 7
# Becoming a Textile Exporter Through Productivity— Crompton Company

MORE THAN 150 years ago, Queen Victoria was on her yacht *Britannia* off the entrance to the harbor of Cowes on the Isle of Wight. She was watching the end of a very unusual yacht race—the entire Royal Thames Yacht Squadron was racing against one American boat, the schooner *America*. When the first sail appeared on the horizon, the captain of the *Britannia* focused his glass while the Queen asked, "Who's winning?" "It's *America*, Your Majesty." "Who's second?" The captain put his glass to his eye again, scanned the horizon, took it down and said, "There is no second, Your Majesty."

I quote that story to illustrate the point that in many situations you're either first or you don't count at all. Yet the fact is that America is losing its number one position as the greatest productive industrial power in the world—and we better believe in this case there is no second!

To reverse this process we must seriously address the issue of productivity and unit costs in the American textile industry and their effect on our position in the world. Then I would like to discuss my own company—because that is the only area I can document—and present a sort of case study on productivity improvement.

## INCREASED PRODUCTIVITY IN THE AMERICAN TEXTILE INDUSTRY

Helped to a large extent, I believe, by the absence of the inhibiting influence of organized labor, the textile industry in this country has been able to increase its productivity over the last 20 years at an annual rate of more than 4 percent. For the last five years this rate was more than 4½ percent, and last year productivity was up almost exactly 5 percent. These figures are based on the average pounds produced per man-hours worked throughout the whole textile industry.

One study based on 1978 data attempted to arrive at the unit cost of a yard of fabric and a pound of yarn in various textile industries around the world. Using the American cost as an index of 100, the Italian cost was 211; the West German, 194; the French, 185; the Spanish, 147; and the Greek, 130. Complete figures from Far Eastern countries are not readily available, but from my own observations I would say the only country in the Far East that had a chance of matching U.S. productivity in the textile industry is Japan. In many of the other countries lack of productivity is more than made up for by low wage rates, but even here the unit-cost gap is closing rapidly. I have not seen figures from Mainland China. No one I know of has been able to get close enough to the situation to do a study, and because Chinese goods are politically priced, price alone is no indication of cost.

The domestic market for our products has been increasing for the last several years at the rate of only 1 to 2 percent per year. Imported fabrics and garments have made major inroads and are allowed to increase under the Multi Fiber Arrangement at the rate of about 6 percent per annum. We have been called "protectionists," but it is easy to see from these figures that we lose a share of the market every year. Our position has been that we should not allow our apparel industry to be replaced to any significant extent by imports. We have asked for fair trade, if not free trade.

Because of our record on productivity and, of course, helped by the declining value of the dollar, we find ourselves faced with the happy opportunity of becoming the leading producing country of textiles in the world. We already hold a strong competitive edge over European countries, and we are closing the gap rapidly in the Far East. Many of our European competitors are now taking a serious look at the United States as a place for them to begin producing. They recognize that our competitive position with Europe is being enhanced every year.

My company opened the first Hong Kong office of any American textile company just two years ago. We have found that in the traditional market for Japanese fabrics—the entire Pacific Basin—we are competitive for perhaps 15 to 25 percent of the business. It tends to be a higher-quality end of the business, and our competitiveness seems to be increasing year by year. Of course, in this area, the exchange rate between the yen and the dollar is extremely important.

For the first time, then, since World War II we have the opportunity to become an exporting industry, and a great deal of this can be attributed to our increasing productivity. I am proud of the textile industry, although I readily admit that we do not seem to have a very good press.

## AN IMAGINARY JOURNEY

And now I would like to take you on an imaginary journey to demonstrate some of the techniques used in our industry to increase productivity. As I mentioned before, I will restrict myself to my company, because only with my own company can I document the figures. Crompton is a relatively small textile company that produces only corduroys and velveteens. We did $158 million in sales last year, made $9.8 million net, and returned 6.2 percent on sales and 18.4 percent on average stockholder equity. The last two figures are at or very near the top of our industry.

During the past five years, when the industry registered 4.5 percent productivity gains, we have gained about 8 percent. I must point out, however, that one of the reasons we have done better than the rest of the industry is that five years ago we were losing money. During a turnaround it is natural to expect performance gains in excess of the industry in general.

In the textile industry we pay people, not to run machinery, but to start machinery. On our imaginary journey you are going to become a weaver in one of the Crompton plants about three to four years ago. The looms to which you are assigned were stopping on an average of about 5 times an hour. Your job has been measured, and we figure you could start about 100 looms an hour. Your assignment then was obviously 20 looms. That was all you could be expected to keep running, and it was well below the industry average. At this time, however, with that low assignment you were not able to run the looms very well. All allowable incentive payments were meaningless, because you were not able to produce enough to get paid an incentive. You were being paid merely a base wage, which for the sake of a simple illustration we will peg at $5 an hour. Working a 40-hour week, you were paid $200 for each week's work. Ours is a multiprocess manufacturing operation, and some 18 to 20 of the processes involved take place before we get to the loom. To improve the running of your looms, we worked on these other processes and finally ended up delivering a better and stronger yarn to your looms. Over a period of 18 months the stop rate had gone down from 5 an hour to about 1⅔ an hour. Since you are still able to start 100 looms at an average pace, you can now run 60 looms.

Part of our technique is to assign machinery to each individual's capabilities. People who are above average can start more than 100 looms in an hour and we give them bigger assignments. Their pay goes up proportionately to the additional machines they can run, and further incentives are put in for quality and product performance.

In the textile industry the markdown from first-quality price averages about one-third, and thus we must instill in you the idea that making first-quality fabric is terribly important. With decreased loom stoppage and better-quality performance you are now running what we call a 1.18 index—in other words, you get 118 percent of base pay. Using the same $5 base rate, you are now making $5.90 an hour, or $236 for that same 40-hour week.

Because each of the looms you are running is turning out more fabric and turning out better quality, we have reduced our unit cost for three reasons:

1. We no longer have to discount so large a part of our production.

2. Looms are stopping less and thus creating more fabric.

3. This additional production is run through the same fixed cost in other processes such as dyeing and finishing, which reduces unit cost there too. We figured under these circumstances we ended up with about 10 percent reduction in unit cost. You end up with 18 percent increase in your pay. It is good for the company, and it is good for you. This is the basic approach we use to increase productivity throughout the industry.

## INCREASED UTILIZATION OF PRODUCTIVE CAPACITY

But something else is happening in the world. Our labor force is not as anxious to work the normal five days a week plus an extra day when business is good. This is reflected in industrywide absenteeism averaging perhaps 5 to 6 percent and an annual turnover rate in excess of 50 percent. Textile work is hard work, and the plants must be run round the clock. With three eight-hour shifts, this means two-thirds of our workers are working in what most of us think are normal hours. They work from 4 P.M. to midnight or from midnight to 8 A.M. The maximum schedule we can get under these circumstances is working every other Saturday, or 132 hours a week.

We at Crompton therefore decided to develop a system which would allow us to utilize our machinery to the fullest without creating a difficult work schedule for production workers. Seven-day round-the-clock running is becoming more common in our industry, but generally this is done with people swinging from shift to shift—a situation which I believe creates a sort of permanent jet lag.

We decided the real problem was getting people to *come* to work—once they were in, they were unlikely to leave the job. We therefore developed a system where we work two 12-hour shifts each day six days a week. Each worker works three days a week under this system, and 12 hours a day, either from 7 A.M. to 7 P.M. or from 7 P.M. to 7 A.M. For perfect attendance he or she gets a 4-hour bonus—40 hours pay for 36 hours worked. Now only half our people rather than two-thirds are working at what we would consider normal hours, and even they have to work only three days a week.

Under these circumstances, your pay as a weaver again is exactly the same as it was before, except now the plant runs 310 days a year—that is, 52 weeks at six days a week, with only Christmas and Christmas Eve extra time off. But you as an individual are working only half that time, or 155 days a year. Under the old system you worked five days a week for 50 weeks a year with 2 weeks vacation. For the same amount of money you had to work 250 days a year instead of 155, and the plant ran only 250 days a year instead of 310.

We then decided to run Sundays. Although state law requires only time and a half wage payment, we pay double time. Our schedule is worked out so you work only three Sundays out of eight, but the plant runs six Sundays out of eight. In weeks when you work Sunday you receive 64 hours pay for a 48-hour week. By swinging your shift not from day to night but from one end of the week to the other, we manage to give you seven days in a row off every eight weeks, or six to seven weeks a year. That amounts to a substantial vacation.

If you work this system out on paper, you discover you work an average of $40\frac{1}{2}$ hours a week but get paid for a 49-hour week. Assuming you maintain 118 percent of base pay and assuming the same $5 base rate, your weekly pay has now gone up to $289 a week.

So during the last few years, assuming a frozen base wage rate of $5 an hour, your pay has increased from $200 to $289 a week. Your hours worked have remained nearly constant, changing from 40 hours to $40\frac{1}{2}$ hours on average, but you must now come to work only 175 times a years instead of 250. Again, our production goes up, and again, the unit cost goes down.

One must of course consider the effect of a 12-hour work day—but here is one of the big surprises. With minicomputers on all the machines, we find the last four hours are generally the most productive. These computers have terminals throughout the plant, and each person in the plant can punch his own number into the computer any time he wants and get a readout of his productivity rate for the day up to the moment he hits the computer. If the job runs well, his incentive-pay rate is up. We find that workers are eager to finish the day on a strong note.

## INCREASED PRODUCTIVITY THROUGH THE USE OF NEW MARKETING TECHNIQUES

I would like to touch on another problem in our company. It has to do with marketing of our goods. Every once in a while God seems to reach up and turn a big valve off, saying, "Hey, no more corduroy down there." Things just seem to stop dead.

This is a cyclicality problem—our products tend to become more fashionable or less fashionable from year to year. If you think about corduroy from the consumer's viewpoint, you will also realize we have a seasonality problem. While we must produce our fabrics on a year-round basis, corduroy and velveteen are worn only in the fall and winter months. Running full schedules year-round meant building up unacceptable peak and valley schedules. The only way to solve these two problems—cyclicality and seasonality—was by creative marketing.

To me, the most exciting thing of all is that we have increased productivity in our company through the use of new marketing techniques. We decided that instead of making 220 million people in the United States our market, we would expand the usage to as many of the 4 billion people in the world as had the money to buy quality fabric and garments. When we ship goods to the southern hemisphere, the seasonality is reversed, since their winter is our summer. When we ship goods to Europe, the lead time tends to allow us to make shipments earlier. When we ship goods to the Far East for return in garment form to either the United States or Europe, the lead time necessary for manufacturing into garments and transportation nearly half way around the world almost exactly corresponds to the six months that our goods are out of season in this country.

Furthermore, we offer tiered pricing—one tier for the off-season, one tier for the midseason, and one tier for the height of the season. Since the off-season in the United States corresponds to the time the Far Eastern manufacturers must buy fabric, we are able to offer very attractive prices that meet Japanese competition. These same low prices create incentives for our customers here in the United States to buy goods early and to begin their garment manufacturing earlier than they normally would like.

This has let us keep our inventories at acceptable levels and at the same time allowed us to run full schedules in off-season. Once again, the additional production this creates and the fact that we need not retrain extra workers for peak season months reduce considerably our unit costs and increase considerably the quality of our product. You, as a weaver, are assured of steady work.

## CONCLUSION

So, at Crompton—and I think we are quite typical of the industry—we have managed to increase productivity at a satisfactory rate by various approaches. There is a common thread running through them all, however, and that is recognizing each worker as an individual and trying as best we can to engineer our schedule and method of operation to this individual's needs.

F. CECIL HILL

# 8
# Motivating Workers
# for Increased
# Productivity—
# Hughes Aircraft

OUR PHILOSOPHY at Hughes has been, and is becoming more so, that the responsibility for productivity lies squarely on the back of management. The common denominator for success is a potential for improvement and an ability to work with people. We are busy right now trying to overcome some of what we've done in the past as managers. We're trying to put the emphasis back on our management people. We normally think of return on investment (ROI) in relation to *capital equipment* and facilities. During the past few years we have spent double our earnings in capital outlays. However, we are now looking at ROI from the *return-on-individuals* point of view. We feel our biggest potential currently lies in our employees. Now that we have the capital equipment we can truly go to work with "people."

I'd like to discuss briefly the principles that we're trying to espouse within the company in our management programs. We know that if we use these principles in assigning work, developing new jobs, and dealing with our people, we will have a productive organization, regardless of the specific techniques and programs we use. Credit for our results ultimately goes back to management and its acceptance of responsibility for assuring that we have motivated and productive people.

1. Let's consider ROI as being return not only on investment in capital but also on individuals. We are talking about the necessity to

structure our operations to encourage employees, regard
their job, to use their talents, ability, and knowledge. This is
tled the principle of utility. We have found that if we follow a
principles that we are going to discuss, we have a much more
ductive organization.

### PRINCIPLE OF UTILITY
Effort and interest levels depend on the amount
of our capabilities we use in accomplishing the job.

Structure all operations to encourage employees (regardless of their
job) to use their talents, abilities, and knowledge. It goes without
saying that people possess varying capabilities, but we must also
assume that they do want to use them.

2. We also use the principle of work control.

### PRINCIPLE OF WORK CONTROL
The amount of control an individual has over the job directly
affects the level of commitment to accomplishing the job.

Allow employees to have the maximum possible amount of discretion and decision-making leeway concerning how the job is to be
accomplished.

Both of the principles discussed so far tell us that we have to *ask
the people* on the job how they are doing and how they think the job
should be done. We must get feedback from them. Our analysis
indicates that we often tend to *demotivate* our employees. They
normally come to us with a fairly high level of intrinsic motivation,
but we often try to whip that intrinsic motivation out of our new
employees as rapidly as possible. We unconsciously want to get
them down to our level.

A while back, I read a scholarly article on how to train fleas.
Believe it or not, in Europe they still have some flea circuses. If you
allow your flea performers one hop, they may all disappear, because
fleas are capable of jumping to great heights. They train fleas by
placing a clear glass over them, and fleas do not like to bump their
heads. The trainer progressively lowers the glass until the fleas
jump to a level that is acceptable, and thereafter the fleas jump only
to that level. I think that's what we often do in business, schools,
and other organizations: we tend to hold down people's motivation
by our own negative attitudes, thoughts, and whatever traits we
happen to possess.

A typical organization tells a design group to design a product, and the group often designs it in a vacuum. The group then gives it to a production organization, which attempts to put together a product which the designer has conceived. Then, at the end of the line (when, as is often the case, the product doesn't work), the quality people try to figure out just how to make the product work. They don't even go to the design people; they go back to the fabrication supervisor, who says, "It meets specs. It is exactly what the prints call out." But, because of the separation of our functions within most organizations today, we tend to limit and even eliminate the intergroup communications that are so necessary.

3. The principle of communication is, ostensibly, fairly simple.

PRINCIPLE OF COMMUNICATION
Involvement and effort levels result from the
amount of information communicated to individuals.

We simply say, "Communicate with employees." Unfortunately, we find that inadequate communication is the norm in typical organizations in the United States. Most of us as managers feel that we are superior communicators. "That's why we got where we are—because we are good communicators. That's just basic to management." But, upon closer analysis, we find we are not effective communicators. Many people in organizations really don't know where they are, where they're going, what's happening in the future, or how their portion of the job affects the overall picture. Our company has been conducting a study for several years on the subject of productivity. It is almost a classic in industry, as far as studies on productivity go, and it emphasizes the importance of getting back to fundamental, simple principles, such as we are discussing. These principles, although they sound simplistic, are not, and they are also not simple to implement.

4. Recognize and acknowledge the effectiveness of all employees who work for you.

PRINCIPLE OF RECOGNITION
The output of an individual is directly affected
by the amount of recognition received.

Recognition is a major factor in everything we do. We may not want to admit it to ourselves, but the fact is that we want recognition for our efforts and accomplishments. This is true of all of us, and it is true of every person working for us. However, we must carefully avoid the tendency to give "token" recognition. So many times in management we say, "You did a great job, Charlie." Week after week we tell Charlie the same thing. Before long he realizes that this is insincere and reacts negatively. We have to sincerely show employees, by whatever means we have, that what they have done is important. And you would be amazed at some of the things that occur when we recognize our people. Recently, I talked to a young Ph.D. who assumed management of a department in which 50 percent of the employees had Ph.D.'s, 30 percent had master's degrees, and the balance had bachelor's degrees. This was a technically oriented department in which the morale was terrible. In a two-hour interview with each employee, the new manager turned the morale in that department around: he spent two hours simply asking employees what they were capable of doing and what they wanted to accomplish. Through recognition and acknowledgment of those people and their goals, he changed their attitude.

We might mention that money, of course, is an important form of recognition. This is one reason for dropping the idea of giving *everybody* a 5 percent increase this year and just giving true merit raises to the deserving performers. Discretionary use of money as recognition is extremely important in motivating people to be productive.

5. The next principle requires that we assign work in logical modules that have a reasonable starting point and a reasonable stopping point.

### PRINCIPLE OF WORK MODULES
Work is more effectively accomplished if it consists of a
"whole" job with logical beginning and ending points.

If this principle is followed, it allows people to perform what they consider a complete job. We have found this to be extremely important. If we do not have functionally complete jobs, or if we leave people with a task that lacks logical starting and stopping points, they end up being frustrated. Some of you, I'm sure, are familiar with the Zeigarnik effect—the frustration that people have when they are interrupted before they complete a job. Many times we program this frustration right into the job. We're not just talking about production line operations; we're talking about services, administrative functions, finance areas, and all of the many functions in the typical organization. Any task should be logical, and it should result in a definable product.

6. Now we go to the principle of regular customers, or the principle of product flow.

### PRINCIPLE OF REGULAR CUSTOMERS
Work is more effectively accomplished when workers know who the recipient of the work is and what the recipient expects.

Organize operations to assure that, regardless of work type, the output of each job goes to a regular recipient or "customer." If we regularly deal with the same people, before long they will give us feedback on what's wrong with the product or service. It's amazing how much we have accomplished by giving people regular "customers" or recipients for their work. We find that there is a great deal of communication and "cross-fertilization." Adherence to this principle has enhanced our work flows greatly.

7. Each job should be structured so that it provides every worker with immediate, direct information on how well he or she is accomplishing the work.

### PRINCIPLE OF FEEDBACK
Effective performance depends on immediate knowledge of how effective or acceptable the work is in relation to specifications or requirements.

Organization structures today often force such fragmented performance that there is inadequate or unsuitably delayed feedback. An employee assembles a part of a widget, which goes to the next person, who adds another module to it. This occurs down the line, to the point that the original worker seldom knows whether or not he has been effective. And, because of the way we build our businesses today, we often assume low-quality products. It's extremely important that people know whether or not they are producing something that is acceptable—and they should know immediately. This is accomplished by setting up a job that is clearly defined and logical, with some method of verifying adherence to prescribed standards.

Tom Fullmer and I talked about a situation in Japan recently, where an American quality manager visited a Toyota plant. He asked the Toyota manager, "How many employees work here?" The answer was 4,300. He then asked, "How many inspectors do you have here?" The answer was 4,300. Every person knew whether or not the product he or she was producing met the standards. This, again, tended to eliminate the Zeigarnik effect and the negative thoughts that people have.

8. Management must provide clear-cut goals.

PRINCIPLE OF GOAL EFFECTIVENESS
Accomplishment and productivity levels
depend on the goals employees perceive.

Each job should be designed and assigned to include clearly understood goals that provide structure and direction for all work activities. Effectiveness, accomplishment, and productivity levels depend on the perceived goals. We, as managers, must set up goals. We need to set up broad as well as immediate and specific goals. If we give our people goals to achieve, they will almost invariably achieve them, especially if the people are actively involved in developing those goals. Management people must provide leadership by developing and communicating goals.

9. Give employees meaningful work. This requires work that is "meaningful" in our *employees'* minds.

PRINCIPLE OF MEANINGFUL WORK
Motivation levels depend on the perceived
"significance" or "meaningfulness" of a job.

Any job that has a low perceived value will never motivate employees. People consistently report that meaningful jobs are the greatest source of motivation.

There are some jobs that are truly meaningless; you probably should eliminate those or combine them with another job. Consider yourself, how many jobs have you worked at that were really meaningless in your own mind? Before long, we develop an attitude that says, "No matter what I do, it's going to be meaningless work." It may take a little analysis and work to come up with a job that is truly meaningful. Employees indicate that there is nothing more frustrating than going home every night with the thought, "No matter how many widgets I've turned out, it still doesn't mean anything." Often the work is very meaningful in terms of the product itself, but we never communicate this fact to our people. We need to let them know what the product does, where it fits into the overall picture, and so on.

10. Assure that management, supervision, and operations are geared to emphasize success, raise employees' self-esteem, and enhance their image of their own capability.

### PRINCIPLE OF ESTEEM
Employee attitudes and intrinsic motivation to perform depend on employees' perception of their own value and capability.

This requirement applies at every level in the organization. Supervisory contact that emphasizes *only* the problems will perpetuate those problems. For instance, the "management by exception" principle can foster low self-esteem because a person or area may be contacted only when there is an exception or problem. This tends to reinforce shortcomings rather than strengths. On the other hand, experience indicates that contact and activities which are heavily weighted to emphasize success—and the potential for success—will improve the achievement of results.

Poorly assigned work given to people or areas not mentally or physically equipped to handle it assures failure, which reduces esteem, which leads to increased failure—ad infinitum. Even poorly prepared, outdated, or inaccurate work instructions can contribute to a vicious cycle which progressively causes inaccuracy, poor quality, and reduced motivation and productivity. Employees trying to follow a poor instruction will experience frustration and low achievement. This causes them subconsciously to place some of the blame on themselves, which leads to an image of a less competent self, which leads to a less productive person, and so on. Ridicule is devastating to every employee and should never be used. In other words, every action or result which tends to raise an employee's self-image is beneficial because an enhanced self-image causes that person to be more productive.

11. Assure that all management and supervisory people are trained to encourage and support those reporting to them.

### PRINCIPLE OF SUPPORT
Motivation and productivity are increased whenever we
know that management and supervision will assist and support us
and our actions because we are important to them.

Observation and studies verify that normal humans never outgrow
their need to be loved and to know that others are available to
assist, support, and defend them, if necessary.

Whenever our people know with some certainty that those who
represent "the organization" are there to help them grow and to
achieve, their attitude becomes more positive toward the achievement of organizational goals. Whenever they understand that they
are perceived as human beings and are important to supervision,
they automatically strive more readily toward achievement of organizational goals. Their security is enhanced, and this carries over
into motivation and productivity. Conversely, perceptions that they
are merely "a number," "a machine," or some other nonentity de-
motivates them significantly.

It is important that employees perceive supervision as a "resource" and a source of help on specific problems and assistance in
goal achievement.

12. Management at every level must take time to teach those
reporting to them exactly what is to be accomplished. The process
is as important as the material taught.

### PRINCIPLE OF TEACHING
Employees at all levels improve performance when properly
taught by their immediate supervisor.

Experience indicates that managers who see themselves as
teachers generally have more motivated and productive organizations. Again, this applies to everyone from the CEO down to the
first-level supervisor.

The process of teaching clarifies to the supervising person exactly
what he or she wants, and the process of conveying this to the
subordinate crystallizes those needs in the mind of both the teacher
and the student.

Managers should never "fear" teaching subordinates, but they
often do. They are afraid they will "offend" the very "expert" hired
to do the job. If the teaching is done in a noncondescending and

positive way, it will accomplish several things. It communicates that the boss is interested enough to help the employee understand the goal and how it is to be achieved. It sets the stage for future two-way communications and reduces the fear that subordinates often have of bothering the boss, who always seems busy.

It is also very common for the superior to have had more experience, and he normally has a broader view of the enterprise. His additional knowledge usually enables him to perceive more rapidly an effective method for achieving the goal. Simply communicating this at least gives the respondent an excellent starting place.

The process of teaching fosters the idea that the boss is really interested in the employee and in his or her accomplishments.

What I'd like to do now is give you a brief recap of a program that uses the principles we have developed. We recently sent an employee to Japan to examine Japanese practices, and he verified what other people have said: "Japanese people are taking ideas that originated in the United States and whipping us with them economically." We have implemented a Hughes Quality Circle Program based on the Japanese Quality Circle approach. It is not a "quality control" program. We are using the word "quality" in the generic sense—that is, we assume that no matter what our job, service, or product, it can be improved. I know I can improve my output, and I'm sure you can improve yours.

Responsibility for our program rests with small volunteer groups of four to ten people, who meet once a week. Now, keep in mind this is just one program that we have used successfully, and it does use the twelve principles just mentioned. We emphasize that people volunteer to participate in the programs—and this includes management people in a given area. The Circle is led by the supervisor of the area. So, we don't interfere with the normal chain of command. Someone from outside the group trains the group and assists in the process of achieving the Circle's goals. We meet on company time, and the company pays for the Circle, which meets for one-half hour to one hour per week. (We emphasize the term *voluntary*. We've had about 600 people volunteer in the last two years since we started the pilot program.)

Training is a very important part of the program. The facilitator—the person from outside the group—is a key element in the success of the Quality Circle. He/she trains the group, and the group leader, in certain analytical techniques, such as Pareto analysis and cause-and-effect analysis. Each group is trained only to the level required to overcome its problem. We have a few groups that have been trained to handle some very sophisticated statistical analysis techniques, simply because they relate to the problems they are attempting to solve. The facilitators we have at Hughes spend part of their time working as facilitators. They must be people-oriented and able to communicate, understand group processes, and encourage participation.

The Circles meet, as I said, for one-half to one hour a week. They identify problems, conduct research into the problems, and devise methods for overcoming the problems. One Quality Circle just recently came up with a list of 22 problems at its second meeting, and in the next few weeks was able to save more than $100,000 in production costs in that area. This was a group of people on a production line. The interesting thing about that particular case was that the supervisor of the area—the assistant manager of the entire department—said, "Well, I think this would be fun to try. We really don't have any problems, but I think this might help us avoid some in the future."

The Quality Circles may also request help from another area or another department. We've had excellent results when our production areas call engineering and design personnel to give them a hand. Those of you who are familiar with what's happening in Japan know that one of the three major elements in Japan's productivity philosophy is the absence of the "we–they" syndrome between the design/engineering and manufacturing departments. They avoid that dichotomy that is so prevalent in the United States.

We at Hughes are emphasizing the use of Quality Circles initially in manufacturing areas, because we get a higher return there, and we get it immediately. But we're now spreading it into some other areas. We've even had one Quality Circle that consisted of nothing but high-level managers. Quality Circles take a manager or supervisor and make him or her the "official" leader of a group, thereby giving genuine on-the-job training. At Hughes Aircraft, our managers and supervisors are our highest-paid "expeditors." They rarely have time to manage. They always have time, though, to chase down tools and materials, make phone calls, sign papers, and so on. This program is one way we encourage them to communicate with their people and to manage.

Quality Circles work because they are people-oriented. They're based on sound behavioral theory; they are structured; they give everyone a format that is simple to follow. And they acknowledge that people are interested in doing something about their work. I might mention also that some of the most prolific producers in our Quality Circles have been our union stewards. They have been a very strong part of this process, because apparently they are aware of many problems.

Quality Circles have been successful in every area. I think the common denominator for success is simply the potential for improvement in an area, and our ability to work with our people and recognize their ability.

Quality Circles allow us to recognize employees as individuals and to listen to their input. Although we have considered ourselves very progressive for quite a few years, we have never truly listened to people who worked for us. We now acknowledge that they have special abilities, skills, and ideas that concern our own job, and we let them feed these to us through the Quality Circles. I don't care how negatively employees feel about an organization; if they can do something about the problems that beset them every day, they will be interested.

We might also point out that Circle members do not discuss problems in somebody else's area of responsibility. They discuss problems that relate to their own work.

One of the major points of the Quality Circles is that line management still has the responsibility for accomplishments and for making the final decisions. Quality Circles recommend solutions; supervisors and management still have the responsibility for implementing them. In any organization, management support from the top down is extremely important. Our program has been a "soft sell," and we haven't pushed it on anybody. If an organization says, "I don't like it," "I don't want it," or "I don't have time to fool with it," we forget it. We go to someone who wants to try the concept, and now it's selling itself.

Most problems are resolved in the Circle itself. However, if a problem cannot be resolved, we go to the responsible manager. We sit down and talk to him at a scheduled meeting. We explain the problem and make recommendations. The manager has the option of saying "go ahead" or recommending an alternative. We haven't found a manager who wasn't satisfied with the recommended solutions.

These presentations to managers are important. It's probably not nearly as important to communicate the problems and recommendations to the managers as it is to recognize the group members. Management recognition is a key item in this whole program, and it's worked amazingly well. You'd be surprised at the effort people put into these presentations, and the positive reinforcement they receive from the recognition received from the manager.

Another thing that we have avoided is the development of any new tracking programs for the Quality Circle. We already have several programs in the company that keep track of performance improvement ideas and cost improvement ideas. We simply use them to document and track Quality Circle results. In fact, we don't insist on attacking only problems whose solution will result in verifiable money savings. For instance, how do you cost out morale? Or how do you cost out the fact that employees, even after the Circle is concluded, continue to talk to their supervisor and avoid many problems that they would have otherwise encountered?

We have also found that we have greatly improved quality in our own products. Many of you will relate to the chart in Figure 8-1. The defects on a particular electronics board had been running at .6 per unit, for two years. The quality control people got together and said, "We ought to do something about this." They obtained some new equipment, revised operations, and were able to cut defects down to .3 per unit. That level was maintained for more than a year. We started Quality Circles in January 1976 and cut defects by another 66 percent to .1 per unit, and it continues to operate at that level.

The following are some of the things Quality Circle participants say they like about the program:

Discussing and solving problems as a team.
Freedom to express themselves.
Influencing decisions about their work.
Getting engineers, supervisors, and others interested
    in their problems and working with them toward solutions.
Reduction of conflicts in the work environment.

Figure 8-1. Industrial Products Division—quality control chart.

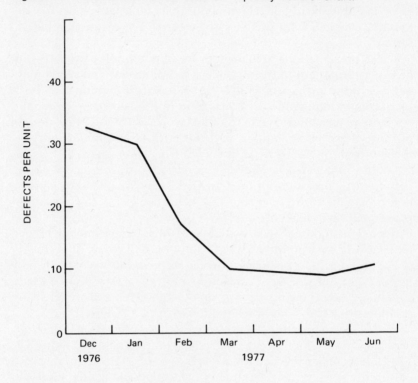

Telling management about their successful projects.
Recognition by management.

The last item in the participants' responses, recognition by management, probably should have been at the top. We also found that employees were spending their own personal time attacking problems, even outside work. They would go to the library, conduct research, and prepare excellent material.

Here are some of the comments that foremen and supervisors made about the program:

"Many problems have been identified and solved by the workers themselves."

"Engineers have been responsive to circle problems when
called in for help."
"Several problems which have been around for years have
been solved."
"The Circle meeting gives me an opportunity to listen to my
people without interruption."
"The program gives me on-the-job training in improving
communications with my employees."

Again, this program sounds almost too simple, but it works, although the effort hasn't been completely problem-free.

In conclusion, I would like to say that management is responsible for productivity improvement. It is the element that makes or breaks efforts to improve productivity and motivation.

ANTHONY W. OLKEWICZ

# 9
# Productivity Experiment at Maxwell House– Hoboken

TO IMPROVE productivity, all departments must be willing to talk about the issues and problems in a constructive way. I would like to describe some joint union-management work on productivity that was done at our Maxwell House Hoboken plant some two years ago. I will cover the process used in an experiment for improving productivity through worker participation at the Hoboken plant.

## BACKGROUND

General Foods has many manufacturing plants across the country that vary from new to old. We have a vital interest in keeping these units economically productive as long as possible. Tremendous capital investments and talents and learning experiences exist in these organizations. During the life of these investments we have experienced much change concerning the workers, the environment, and the economy. Many of these plants are no longer as efficient as they were in the past. Combine that with the costs of energy, utilities, and taxes and you wonder whether you can keep these operations going. Most of our manufacturing occurs in these older plants, so our interests are to bring these plants up to speed as quickly as possible.

The problem was not just one of the workers; it also involved unions and management. Our practices and work processes were really preventing us from getting effective use of the energies, talents, skills, and abilities of the people. That applies not only to the workers, but also to the foremen. The foremen face some real problems. Over a period of time they gradually have begun to lose their identity with management, and they don't feel that they are a part of the workforce either. They are very much threatened and concerned about their security. So our concern was for the total effort. It is not something directed at any one group, but requires everybody working together.

The Hoboken plant had about 1,500 employees at the time of our study. It has been considerably reduced in numbers since then, but now has stabilized. That plant has been a part of the whole coffee business which has experienced violent price movements and other problems. The plant has been in place since 1939, so it's an old plant. It is overbuilt in terms of the amount of equipment and processes put in one place, and it has all the problems of a plant sitting in the middle of a residential area. That was the testing ground for our experiment.

## PURPOSE OF THE EXPERIMENT

The objective of our experiment was to provide an experience for the union and the management people. We wanted to test some ideas for improving productivity and the quality of working life for the people. This particular presentation covered about 80 people in one department. It was truly an experiment, since we said that all bets were off—on *either* side—if we felt uncomfortable with it. So we had control over the outcome of our efforts.

The purpose was to test a process that the union and management could use in learning how to improve the work and the results that come from it. This involved examining the human relationships—including the feelings that people had about themselves—in that particular unit. The perspective for this was to have a learning experience concerning plant operations. We found that the union, management, and the workers all felt good about it. The results began to make a lot of sense for the stability of that particular unit.

## STEPS IN THE EXPERIMENT

The steps of the process we went through in implementing the experiment included:

Forming a committee with members from all departments connected with the process
Having the group set objectives
Determining the procedures to be used
Plotting the mission of the operation
Reviewing the state of the business
Gathering the necessary data
Analyzing the data
Reporting the findings
Proposing changes in the operation

The first step was to form a committee of people who could contribute skills in knowing how the work gets done, could represent other people in the unit, and could provide knowledge about how the work gets performed. The committe consisted of stewards, a union coordinator, a couple of maintenance stewards, and three production stewards. We have a person from quality control, three shift foremen, the general foreman, the maintenance foreman, and the department head. I served as the internal consultant for the unit, and we also had consultants from the corporate level.

Our committee set some objectives for the group. The objectives were:

1. To improve the quality of working life through joint exploration of ways for reorganizing work and through improved communication.
2. To improve the assurance of product quality.
3. To improve job security through fair pay and worker recognition. (Reducing product costs helps achieve this objective by improving product competitiveness and job security.)

The group talked about these objectives before they started their investigation. In terms of improving the quality of working life, we would use some basic tests to see whether we felt that things were improved at the end of our study. We agreed to this before the investigation began.

When you assemble that group of people, you've got people who have been negotiating in grievance (win-lose) situations. You need some agreement on how they should work together. The group was organized under these concepts:

Introduction and clarification of member roles
Joint participation rather than negotiation

Discussion of objectives
Role clarification

We introduced and clarified the member roles for the union, management, and support group. We agreed on the need for joint participation rather than a negotiating posture. We discussed the objectives for the work group. We agreed on role clarification, which says, for example, that as a union person you have a responsibility to present the union view on any solutions so that when we go out to the membership, it makes sense to them. The maintenance person must make sure that the maintenance issues are properly covered, since we may specify some changes on how to maintain equipment. Similarly, the foremen must make sure that the proposals make sense and that other foremen aren't going to look at you and say, "What the heck are you up to? What are you doing—giving the place away?" Role clarification was necessary so that everyone knew what they were supposed to do.

We talked about the department's purpose and its mission—it's a technical one. We questioned why the plant is there, why we are concerned about it, and what we are supposed to do about it. Its mission is to transform or change in-specification blend of roasted whole bean into in-specification bulk powder at the maximum possible rate with minimum waste. Thus, this statement says what we're working on and what outcomes we'll be seeking.

We then looked at the state of the business. The main considerations included

Measure of performance
Plant organization
Union contract
Technical system
Economic considerations

We talked about how we're going to measure ourselves so we can know if things get better. We wanted to look at how many pounds of in-specification product per day we should produce (the yield). We examined the electrical usage and ways to improve that. We explored water usage and refrigeration, which is very costly. We looked at the plant organization and the contract. We recognized that we could not make contract changes because that exceeded the authority of this particular group. We looked at the existing procedures and practices and talked about the problems they created and the protections they provided.

We talked about the fact that we compete with the product produced at our own plant in Houston, Texas. It is the same product and it could be shipped across the country and put on our dock at a cost lower than we can manufacture it here. That's very real. Houston is another Maxwell House plant and if the coffee market goes down, you know where we will produce coffee in order to stay in business—and you know what that will mean for Hoboken. We talked about the high cost of utilities in the area. We discussed competition and what was happening in the marketplace. Marketing people and other resources helped provide a common base of understanding about what we were doing.

We performed the laborious process of looking at every piece of equipment in that particular production unit. This took several weeks, and sometimes we wondered whether it was worthwhile. But the idea was to find out the relationship of the technology to the people and to the factors which are part of the process. That is, how does one piece of equipment affect another piece and thereby affect people in the operation? What kind of information is needed to better control that process? What kinds of information would they need in order to make improvements? We provided some formats for this analysis, showing the inputs, outputs, specification, and the relevance of quantity and quality. This data never really gets down to most workers—or, in many cases, even to the foremen. It generally goes all the way up to the engineering department, the production scheduling department, and top management. It's never used within the processes for people to learn and to improve their jobs. This data is plotted to show how one area affects another and is broken down in terms of teams and groups.

We looked at the kinds of things that go wrong in the operation and identified those that are caused by operations outside the department, by the technical process, and by human error. For example, somebody makes a mistake because of lack of information or because maintenance hasn't done its job. Those discussions really air the issues that have been bothering that unit and others for years. It gets people talking about you and me and about what we can do to improve productivity and what has prevented us from doing it in the past. This is a very important step. I don't think it's possible to pursue the analysis unless you've made it legitimate to talk about the issues and problems in a constructive way.

We did interviewing to find out what people thought about their jobs and what kinds of things were happening in the place. We found that a very large number of people work at low-level jobs, but they have a tremendous effect on the quality and productivity of the unit. They get paid the least and are valued in a way that doesn't reflect their true impact on the operation. That analysis helped us identify the kinds of inputs they can have as well as the inputs that they were prevented from having.

Having talked about changing jobs and other weaknesses, we turned to job analysis. We found that the current pay structure was too restrictive, and we decided that, as we made job changes as a result of some experimenting, we would use our existing evaluation system. We couldn't see ourselves inventing a new pay system and experimenting with uncertain outcomes; we needed some stability in being able to say, "We're familiar with this way of doing it, and we'll continue to do it that way."

We combined all the data that we had about the people and the technical system and explored ways of improving the work. We looked at the key places where things go wrong, where the problem occurs and is observed—who controls it and the kinds of things they do to solve it. For example, machine X breaks down, and I call the foreman; the foreman calls the maintenance foreman; the maintenance foreman calls the mechanic; the mechanic looks at it. We considered all those things and talked about ways of shortening the process. What can we do to bring maintenance closer to production? What can we do to provide timely, quality information to the operator? What kinds of decisions could the operator make other than those he's presently making?

Our findings from these deliberations were:

1. Information deficiencies exist particularly in terms of real-time information. (You can't use data that is a week old or even two days old.)
2. Many frustrations are inherent in the operation, and solutions are not readily available. These problems are *not* the fault of the workers or foremen.
3. The best opportunity for improvement is through internal motivation of people.

We then decided to implement the experiment. We agreed that the union, management, workers, and foremen would evaluate results and determine what the future would be for this kind of a process.

That briefly describes the process. I think it is important that we have this structure for the workers, union, foremen, and management to use in this analysis. What we all have in common is the work itself and how we work together. So if we can focus on the work and provide a structure that gets away from the old adversary relationships, we then have a chance of looking at things differently and of obtaining useful inputs and outcomes from the process.

## USING THE PROCESS

We then set up problem-solving meetings. The idea is that this is a committee at the department level for involving workers and the foremen. These problem-solving meetings provided them with a great deal of data and the feelings that we had about the way things were going. We said, "Hey, if you want to make changes, it's OK. Make the changes as you see fit, if it will result in improved operations in your opinion. Work with the foremen in coming up with those solutions, and we will support that. If those changes make sense, we'll reevaluate jobs and make sure that people are amply rewarded. We'll go back, in fact, to the point where the change was made and recapture it so that people will get rewarded."

In those problem-solving groups, we brought in research and engineering people to talk about the issues and problems. There was a fear throughout that when we sat down with those workers, they were going to talk about the parking lot, the cafeteria, and the old issues that we always spend a lot of time discussing in grievance meetings. Well, the fact is, by providing this kind of format, and helping them focus in on the issues, they directed their efforts and energies right on the issues. There was no waste of time, and no talk about old issues. We didn't say they couldn't do it; the format was open. And sometimes the old issues did come up, and we did deal with them, but basically they talked about the work, the results, and ways to improve them. They came up with some excellent ideas which they tried and confirmed in their own mind. They destroyed some myths about that particular technical process and the control of it, and produced results that were startling. It actually resulted in significant improvements in productivity, significant reductions in the use of energy in that high-energy area, and significant reductions in product waste. When you're talking about a $6- and $7-a-pound product that gets washed away, you're talking about very, very important dollars. It resulted in people working together in a new way, including maintenance, engineering, the workers, and others.

The results started almost immediately: Within a couple of weeks we started to see trend lines go up. We shared that information with them; we developed new information systems for them so that they could get feedback on the work. We put an accountant to work with them to analyze and change information so that it would make sense to people. It works. Coming out of that, they find ways to improve the work and to participate in the decision making at lower levels. They end up doing a lot of problem solving that they hadn't had an opportunity to do before. Also, union and management then had a base of learning and experience from which we could say, "What do we do next?" And the workers say, "This makes a lot of sense. Why didn't you let us do that before?" I don't know why we were afraid to let that happen.

DONALD J. DONAHUE

# 10
# Reversing the Decline in U.S. Productivity Growth

FINDING SOLUTIONS to the recent decline in U.S. productivity will not be an easy task. The causes are complex, explanatory theories abound, and some possible solutions to this problem may in turn exacerbate other problems or threaten the attainment of other national social goals. However, the implications of *not* finding solutions are so frightening that all of us must direct our attention to that task.

One of the things that scares me most is the thought, on the part of at least some of the public, that declining standards of living are not such a bad thing—that low growth or no growth is necessary if we are to survive as a society. Let me make it clear that I do not agree. In a free market society, the reduction in standards will not be uniform. You and I will not be the ones to suffer most; rather, it is the poor, the uneducated, the minorities, and the faceless millions who'll do the hurting.

One possible consequence is much greater government control of the economy. The alternative could be social chaos and eventual repression. If there is one common thread to our society, it is that everyone has a shot at the good life. My parents worked hard to improve themselves during their lives and, more important, to offer their children a better opportunity than they had . . . and you and I have done the same for our children. To close off productivity growth will, in my view, so undermine the American spirit that it will create divisions in our society which might lead to the loss of our freedom. Until we repeal the laws of human nature, it will be true that unless the pie keeps growing, those who "have" will fight to protect their share, and those who see themselves condemned to remain "have nots" will not be willing to sit back quietly and accept their lot.

For most of the last 40 years, our economy has had sufficient growth overall that we could all participate in rising expectations. It is only recently that a decline in national productivity has begun to put pressures on our society that inhibit our ability to fulfill these expectations. In a time of low economic growth, inflation creates pressures by increasing the public's demands while inhibiting the ability of the economic machine to adjust. More limited opportunities for advancement and lower standards of living have given rise to reverse-discrimination suits and taxpayers' revolts. It is a contradiction to believe that we can maintain a reasonable standard of living and provide for the rebuilding of our environment while at the same time requiring less personal effort. A clean environment calls for *more* productivity, not less—unless we are prepard to accept a sharply lower standard of living and all that that portends.

Now that I have painted such a dark picture, let us see if we can find a few rays of hope.

First of all, some of the factors that have contributed to recent declines in U.S. productivity are nonrecurring, so at least part of the problem will be alleviated just by the passage of time. Recent demographic trends, which have vastly increased the proportion of unskilled and inexperienced workers, will soon be reversed as a result of lower birth rates and extended working years.

Second, a high percentage of the costly expenditures for controlling pollution in existing plants is behind us, and the continuing costs of maintaining the environment have probably stabilized.

Third, the decline of the dollar has somewhat slowed the shift of our economy from a high-production, goods-oriented society to a low-production, service-oriented one.

A final reason for encouragement comes in the beginnings of recognition on the part of our government that something has to be done to encourage capital investment, to increase expenditures for research and development, and to find ways to achieve social goals without excessive costs. Despite this change in attitude, however, we cannot realistically expect government to move quickly to change its policies. For better or worse, our system of government is based on a principle of checks and balances. This protects individual liberty, but largely at the expense (in peacetime) of blocking direct activist solutions to problems which affect segments of the population differently. Getting Congress to move will require that all of us make our opinions known as to which solutions are most appropriate.

For example, it is necessary to adjust levels of corporate and personal taxation from time to time to accommodate the noneconomic increases in the progressive tax system caused by inflation. The easy way to do this is to cut taxes and put more money into the hands of the public, which would thereby stimulate further inflation. I would suggest that a better alternative is to cut both corporate and individual taxes by encouraging capital investment—in the case of corporations by either increasing the investment tax credit or shortening the depreciation lives of equipment. For individuals, I suggest permitting supplemental retirement benefits funded out of tax credits (and perhaps matched by additional personal contributions), provided these are deposited in a certified investment account, much as Keogh Plans and IRAs are today. These investment accounts, managed by private-sector banks, insurance companies, and investment managers, would be invested solely in stocks and bonds of domestic industry. In one step, we would withdraw spending from the inflation cycle, create an enormous fund of new capital, reduce the pressure to increase workers' pensions, and give our people a stake in society.

Continued pressure to reduce the economic loss created by unwise and often unproductive regulation is another mother lode to mine. In addition, generally accepted accounting principles which take into account the unreality of current high profit percentages could help correct unrealistic public perceptions.

Business should also be working on the local level, with educators, to correct deficiencies in schooling that produce graduates with inadequate basic skills. We should also encourage more vocational training, and be prepared to develop programs to make those young people already out of school useful, productive citizens.

We must also direct our attention toward improving productivity in the increasingly large public sector, both by encouraging administrative reform and by offering workable private alternatives to some municipal services.

Let us turn now to what business can do itself to halt the decline in productivity. The two areas which I think offer the greatest promise are innovation and motivation. In the postwar, postdepression era, the exchange between labor and capital moved sharply in the direction of spending for capital, which led to a new surge in productivity as machines were used to do what men formerly did. Measurement and control of production and of quality became increasingly automated. And we witnessed tremendous productivity gains from "scale up"—that is, the use of large volumes of size and horsepower to do the job. For example, we now haul ore in 300-ton trucks versus 20-ton trucks in the 1940s. There is probably some gain in productivity remaining from scaling up, and there are still opportunities through automation—particularly in the areas of maintenance of standards and using robots for purely repetitive or dangerous manufacturing functions. We can also improve the design of operations like shipping and receiving.

However, we are beginning to reach the point of diminishing returns in the substitution of capital for labor. The ability to deliver power to a machine is now often greater than the ability of the materials to stand the power. The costs of new equipment often require round-the-clock operation, yet many products do not lend themselves to this kind of continuous operation. Increases in interest costs and wage rates, inflation, and the faster pace of technological obsolescence of machines, combined with new schemes that guarantee income even when workers are not employed, all point to the reality that future increases in productivity are going to come more from people than from machines.

That leads us to prescription number two—motivation. There is no doubt that many of the old incentives have been dulled at a time when unemployment benefits are generous, welfare and Medicaid are available, and a high percentage of workers comes from two-income families. The old money carrot and the old layoff stick do not carry the same meaning that they did not too many years ago. Even more importantly, values have changed. The old ethic that a man out of work was ashamed to tell his friends or was a pariah if his wife worked while he sat home, has ended. Overtime—once fought for—is now avoided. The young particularly feel that much work is unsatisfying, dehumanizing, and a waste of their lives.

In an earlier age, the need for food and shelter was such that workers were prepared to subordinate other fundamental needs—like self-respect and the respect and regard of others—to them.

Today's employees are no longer willing to do this. You don't work only for pay; you work for *pride*—you work because you want the respect and admiration of your fellows. Not only do our employees have the same needs, but they have a reasonable right to expect those needs to be satisfied.

In short, we've got to find new ways to motivate workers for the simple reason that the old ways are no longer working. The traditional hierarchical boss-employee relationship, in which I tell you what to do and you do it, is no longer workable. Since employees' reactions to the traditional relationship are not likely to change, it is up to management to do the changing.

Finding ways to enhance worker self-respect benefits not only the individual, but the company as well. Workers who are proud of themselves because they are proud of the job they are doing and have gained the respect of their fellows because they have earned it are likely to be more productive employees.

This is an area where there are no ideal solutions—each company will have to develop programs to fit its particular situation. I can, however, suggest a couple of concrete applications of this philosophy. Greater use of flexitime is a scheme that will allow all workers more control over their schedules. We should also make more use of part-time employees and should be looking for ways to take advantage of the skills of older workers while lightening their physical load.

Business has the resources and ability to increase productivity and at the same time to address wide social goals. Innovation and motivation are the keys.

What it all comes down to in the end is management. We have all learned how to manage our material and natural resources—to make them maximally productive. Now we must apply our talent with just as much effort toward the management of our human resources. Our employees are one of our most valuable resources—and, as I have noted, the one to which we must look for the greater part of any future increases in productivity.

**B. NONMANUFACTURING COMPANIES**

WILLIAM W. SWART

# 11
# The Burger King Corporation Productivity Program

WHAT THE Burger King logo does for bringing customers into the store and producing revenues, our productivity programs do for decreasing our costs. We have grown substantially over the years in both size and image that is reflected in the changing facade of our units. All the changes in architectural properties that our stores have taken on over the years are made with one concept in mind: increasing productivity.

Let's contrast Burger King with other Fortune 500 corporations such as Allegheny Ludlum Industries, with sales of $1.55 billion per year, or Grumman Aircraft, with 1979 sales of $1.49 billion. You might ask, what does this have to do with Burger King? Well, directly it doesn't, except that as a system, our sales are substantially higher. We sell more dollars worth of hamburgers, sandwiches, and french fries than either of those companies do in steel or aircraft. Specifically, we sell roughly 600 million "Whopper" sandwiches in one year and a like quantity of associated products such as french fries and drinks. So, in that sense, we are a large corporation. We are the second largest restaurant corporation in the world, second only to McDonald's.

Although we are bigger than Grumman or Allegheny Ludlum in unit sales, we have more in common with them than one might think. You may think of us as a service industry or a restaurant industry. However, in terms of productivity, Burger King is really a manufacturing industry. Our philosophy allies us more closely to a General Motors assembly plant than to the typical restaurant.

## SPECIAL CHARACTERISTICS
## OF THE BURGER KING CORPORATION

As a corporation, Burger King has some interesting characteristics. Our production facilities consist of what in effect constitutes a number of assembly lines. In terms of the size of our individual facilities, we are not large. What makes us large is that we have approximately 2,800 plants across the Unites States plus a few more in other countries of the world. We employ about 130,000 people. It is not unusual for our plants to manufacture more than 1,000 hamburgers an hour. This typically happens right after having sold only 50 in the previous hour—and may drop off to 50 in the subsequent hour. Furthermore, you cannot store the product for tomorrow, because the shelf life of the product is only 10 minutes. Consequently, you cannot take advantage of lulls in your demand to replenish your inventories. We must be able to produce whatever is demanded when it is demanded.

Burger King must deliver large volumes in short periods of time. We originally organized our stores to take advantage of mass production efficiencies by organizing for assembly-line operations. Our product flow starts with raw material inventories and progresses through in-process storage and through various production processes. The production line involves the manufacturing process of grilling buns and broiling meat; preassembly into "undressed" sandwiches as output from the broiler; product transformation in the microwave oven; some more assembly to dress the sandwich; packaging; and, finally, end-product inventory.

We originally designed our stores to be efficient with this production process in mind, but we have made some changes since then. We introduced a new product line, the specialty sandwich. When you introduce new products or an entirely new product line, the efficiencies that you originally enjoyed tend to become liabilities instead of assets. In order to accommodate these new products, we had to modify, augment, and redesign our original production facilities. This created many problems that had to be solved in order to maintain our productivity.

Not only did we introduce a new product line but we scored a classical marketing coup when we introduced our "Have It Your Way" concept. This concept means, for example, that if you do not like onions, you can walk into one of our stores and ask for your product without onions. What does that do to productivity? All of a sudden you go from a mass-production, assembly-line operation to almost a customizing, job-shop operation. So by introducing the specialty sandwiches and various marketing campaigns, such as "Have It Your Way," we created severe production problems.

A review of the performance of Burger King Corporation for the past several years shows that the demand for our products has increased dramatically. This growth is in part the result of the increased well-being of the American consumer. We are able to predict what people will spend on food away from home. This is closely correlated to their disposable income, which has gone up dramatically. The fast-food segment is the fastest growing part of the restaurant industry.

When we look at the future, even with the ongoing recession and the continuing energy problems, we find that we are going to continue growing. In 1976, Burger King system sales were approximately $750 million; in 1980, we expect to top $2 billion. By 1983, we expect to continue that growth by increasing average sales per restaurant from $750,000 to $1 million. We expect to increase the number of restaurants from 2,800 to 3,700 in those three years. Also, we expect to have 250 restaurants abroad. So the future can be envisioned as one of constant growth.

What will that constant growth coupled with our increasingly complex manufacturing environment do to us? We clearly cannot service a constantly increasing number of customers with our present methods and facilities. The first step in our plan to meet the future is to increase our productivity in everything that we do today and then to plan our capacity expansion in the most productive manner possible. This joint attention to current and future productivity will be the key to our future success.

## PRODUCTIVITY PLANNING AT BURGER KING

The foundations of our productivity planning and improvement activities are the integration of the industrial engineering and operations research functions. The time study, methods improvement, facility layout, work sampling, and human engineering aspects of the industrial engineering function are the grass roots of the productivity effort. The modeling and systems analysis aspects of the operations research function provide the overall framework used to coordinate, direct, and evaluate the industrial engineering efforts from a total systems point of view.

The crucial role of models in our efforts can perhaps best be understood when you consider that our productive capacity is deployed over 2,800 restaurants. Consequently, it is impossible to focus individual attention on every manufacturing facility. We must bring our manufacturing facilities to a central location for analysis, as opposed to taking our expertise to each of our individual facilities. For this reason, we use simulation models to evaluate alternatives that will increase our productivity. We employ optimization models to minimize our cost. We use statistical models to detect the true effects of changes in procedures, equipment, layout, or manning on our ability to service customers better. When we look at the use of these types of models, we are concerned essentially with two levels of productivity analysis:

1. Increasing the productivity in our individual stores.
2. Increasing the productivity of the service functions that provide materials and other services to the stores.

In the area of increasing the productivity of our overall service functions to the stores, we have, for example, developed models in our procurement function that optimize our meat-buying process. In one week we use approximately 3 million pounds of hamburger. By focusing on how that particular purchasing function is performed, we were able to save approximately one cent per pound. By this one application of what we call productivity analysis, we have been able to save the corporation more than $1 million a year.

Not only are we focusing on the individual product-buying optimization; we are also increasing our productivity through improving our distribution. We have our own distribution fleet, called Distron. We now have the ability to improve our productivity by optimizing our costs for transportation from our distribution centers to our individual warehouses. That activity adds another $200,000 per year savings.

When we think of the implementation of increasing productivity at the store level, we think of increasing what we refer to as people productivity. As is generally acknowledged, there is a tremendous amount to be gained by soliciting input from people who are actually performing the work. We have developed an organized process in order to obtain franchisee or store input about suggestions to increase productivity. Furthermore, through the use of our models it has been possible to test and evaluate productivity improvement suggestions. Two areas in which we have been particularly successful are labor productivity and drive-through operations.

In the area of labor productivity, it is important to realize that we are at a point where labor threatens to become the largest cost element in our balance sheet. With the new labor laws, our wages have risen from just a couple dollars an hour a few years back to well over $3.25 an hour now, and wages continue to rise. We cannot pass on that labor cost to our customers and still maintain our leadership in this industry. Consequently, we are performing a substantial amount of work in improving our labor standards.

Industrial engineering efforts are continually employed in studying methods and procedures for integrating the store layout and equipment characteristics with the most productive positioning and staffing strategy at every conceivable sales level. These results must also assure that our product quality and service standards are met. The way we go about that is through a systematic analysis of all types of stores. We have approximately ten different layouts in our 2,800 stores. In the past, these stores were staffed without a lot of attention to labor cost because labor was relatively cheap. Now, that has changed. We are examining and analyzing the integrated operation of each store through our store simulation models. This process starts out by simulating the least staffing possible and then systematically subjecting the simulated store to an increased sales level. At some point, we are then able to observe where the bottlenecks that impede productivity occur. We explore the alternatives of adding additional people at the various positions in our manufacturing facility or using different equipment. On the basis of the results of our models, we determine where the next person or equipment change should be added. By exploring each alternative, we can observe how the store operates by additional staffing or equipment improvement.

We are also able to observe the effects of these changes on our cashiers and other parts in the sales area. We can also observe the effects on our production system and our customers, including how long it will take to obtain orders. This is the single most important determinant of our performance in the competitive marketplace. What we have accomplished so far indicates a savings of well over 1 percent of sales a year in labor productivity through systematic analysis and fine tuning of labor utilization. It has also resulted in improved customer service and product quality.

In another aspect of improving our labor productivity, models have been used to develop a more effective crew scheduling system. This is an area of particular difficulty, since our demand can fluctuate as much as 1,000 percent within a half-hour. This demand fluctuation also has an impact on the amount of labor required in each of those half-hours. Unfortunately, it is not possible to hire someone to come in just for the half-hour you might need him. Most states have laws that require an employee to work for at least a certain number of hours. Our models allow us to improve labor productivity by matching actual people to our labor requirements during the day so as to minimize the amount of excess labor in the store.

The productivity of our drive-through operations has been considerably enhanced with the aid of franchisee input together with corporate personnel. An early examination of Burger King's drive-through speed of service versus that of Wendy's and McDonald's revealed that all three corporations provided comparable speed of service. On the basis of this information, Burger King defined the drive-through area as one where a competitive advantage could be attained over our major competitors if the speed in which customers could be served could be increased without imperiling food quality.

Extensive method and procedure studies culminated in a list of changes in the way the drive-through operated. Although none of the changes was revolutionary, the joint effect of all changes resulted in a 30 percent reduction of the time it took to service a customer. At the drive-through, this improvement in service capacity is tantamount to an increase in drive-through sales capacity. Since this was achieved without additional resources being required, it constituted a substantial net gain in productivity.

## AIMING FOR FUTURE PRODUCTIVITY GROWTH

After optimizing productivity within our store, the next step in our productivity program focuses on future growth. Specifically, we concern ourselves with optimizing our capacity expansion over time to meet our growing needs. This is accomplished through a program we call Productivity Planning for Profit, which, like the rest of our productivity program, is based on the results of our industrial engineering and operations research efforts.

Our findings have been placed in a kit that is easily understandable at the store level. The computer models have provided the foundations for improving the sales projections and for developing and evaluating productivity improvements at various stages of growth. The results have been embodied in easy-to-use kits that are obtainable by our franchisees. We provide training sessions in each of our ten regions for our district managers. These district managers, after being trained, play the role of productivity consultants.

The first phase of the productivity consultant-franchisee interface is a productivity audit for the store during which diagnostic tools are made available and used to assess the productivity level of the store. As one example of the diagnostic tools, corporate service standards for stores suggest that, on the average, a customer should receive an order within three minutes from the time of entry. Furthermore, with our particular production capabilities, we should be able to service a car in 30 seconds or less after the car reaches our drive-through window. If any of these is not achieved at a particular store, then there is an indication that the store has productivity problems.

Our productivity planning-for-profit kit enables a store manager or franchisee to diagnose why he may not be meeting company standards. It helps pinpoint the problem to a specific area of the store (such as the counter) or any of the production stations (such as the fry station, drink station, and so on).

Once we have analyzed the store's current productivity and have provided suggestions for meeting standards, then we focus on the future. The productivity consultant works with the individual store operator to plan sales on a year-to-year basis. We project sales increases attributable to inflation and real growth. The resulting information is applied to an *improvement decision path*. This indicates to the store operator at what sales level he is likely to reach certain bottlenecks. It also indicates what investments will be needed to increase productivity. For example, we have found that when a particular type of store reaches approximately $700,000 a year in sales, the productivity can be significantly enhanced by introduction of kitchen read-out devices that are tied to the cash register. In most of our stores, orders are transmitted to the kitchen by a microphone. Once a store reaches a level of about $700,000 a year, there is so much confusion in the kitchen because of microphone message transmission during busy periods that productivity actually declines. We have developed a series of printers/CRT devices that can be tied to the cash register, which will communicate the order to the production facilities in the kitchen.

Thus, through the application of the improvement decision path, it can be determined what has to be done at various sales levels in order to maintain the productivity of the store and prevent long waiting lines from occurring. For each suggested action, we provide an explanation of why the productivity improvement is needed, what the benefit will be in terms of the additional sales that can be realized, how long it will take that particular improvement to pay back its cost, and where these particular improvements can be purchased.

Given the special relationship that exists between a franchisor and franchisee, it is preferable that our franchisees voluntarily adopt any programs that are developed. So we work hard to sell our productivity programs to them. They must be convinced that the sequence of productivity improvements and investments that result from the joint effort between the productivity consultant and the franchisee will yield an overall contribution to the store's operating profit.

Once we have performed this type of bottleneck analysis for one particular year, we incorporate the investment into our overall profit analysis. We indicate how this particular productivity improvement will have an impact upon the net store operating profit for that particular year. We do this for the entire sequence of five years. On the basis of that, we develop what we refer to as a store operation plan, which is reviewed on a yearly basis.

Using these concepts, we expect that through productivity we can become the industry leader. We expect to increase both our top-line and bottom-line dollars. Finally, we expect to be in a growth posture which will assure us of attaining that goal.

FRANK J. RUCK, JR.

# 12 Management Techniques for Productivity Improvement— Lincoln National

THE CRUX of the management/leadership function is to create ever more effective organizations. Because enhancing productivity is a core dimension to this function, basic management/leadership theory ought to be approached via the microeconomic notion of productivity—that is, a ratio of output to input. Everyone is productive—thus, they produce some output with their input. The crux of the management dilemma is how to enhance their productivity and become ever more effective.

How does an organization enhance productivity? By changing the numerator (output) or the denominator (input), or both, so as to favorably affect the result. In other words, *change* is the essential ingredient. Since organizations are always composed of people, to enhance productivity, people must change their output or input or both. To do this effectively requires behavior change (individual and group behavior).

If these brief comments correctly state the objectives and environment, then the role of management/leadership must be that of catalyst or facilitator of "change to improve." To be totally effective, it must be a constant evolutionary process, always enhancing productivity, effectiveness, and efficiency.

How management/leadership enlists the critical human resource part of the ratio is the essence of the management/leadership theory base. Despite what behavioral scientists have been articulating for several decades, actual management/leadership practices are frequently counterproductive in that they reduce or slow the rate of productivity. In this sense, it is no exaggeration to say that management/leadership can be the critical impediment to productivity, a dilemma that many management people refuse to recognize.

These key ideas are the basis of the productivity philosophy developed by the Standing Committee on Productivity (SCOP) of Lincoln National Corporation (LNC), the parent holding company for Lincoln National Life Insurance Company, Chicago Title and Trust Company and other subsidiaries. This philosophy is as follows:

Productivity is essentially an economic relationship of output to input. It is a very complex subject, but some clear conclusions emerge. First, increasing productivity requires an environment of continuing change and demands active participation at all levels. Second, productivity improvement is *not* primarily a cost reduction program; it is an approach toward working smarter, not harder. This can only come about by changing output or input, or both. It should be an ongoing and evolutionary effort.

Productivity is a prime responsibility of the management process. The greatest potential for improvement exists with employees who face the day-to-day operating problems. They can recognize opportunities for change more effectively if they have the motivation to do so. To achieve the environment conducive to this process is the first big step toward enhancing productivity.

Change of management/leadership theory base is the first step toward enhancing productivity. To achieve big advances in effectiveness requires lots of commitment—not just at the top (because it is already there), but at all levels. Cooperation is relatively easy to manage, but collaboration and commitment must come from within each participant.

This kind of significant change cannot be dictated. Management leadership must be given the opportunity to "buy in" to the new, truly "participative" approach. This is difficult and time-consuming, but it is essential, and the payoff is immense.

These ideas for productivity improvement have been implemented by Lincoln National Life Insurance Company, as explained in the company's booklet, "Quality Commitment at Lincoln: A Way of Life." Its conclusions are summarized below. In the foreword to the booklet, Ian Rolland, President and CEO of Lincoln National Corporation and Lincoln National Life Insurance Company, describes Quality Commitment as an approach to productivity in this manner:

The first time we discussed our approach to improving productivity at Lincoln National Life—and introduced a new style of management we call Quality Commitment—was early in 1978. We said at that time that the Lincoln is a high-quality operation in every respect and that we needed to maintain that position. We further said that we needed to set the pace for our competition, not follow it, and we needed to be innovative—not reactive. I felt at the time that Quality Commitment would be our most important management effort for the next five years. Now, as we consider our experience to date, I am even more convinced of its importance. We have put in motion a process based on the belief that all work can be done better by the continuing application of creative thinking, problem solving, and energetic job performance. This is what we believe "productivity" really means.

Quality Commitment is not a cost-control device. It's a continuing way of thinking. And in this organization, it is the basis for our way of life.

The booklet describes the fundamental aspects of Lincoln's Quality Commitment program under these headings: "The Theory Behind Commitment," "Organizing For Quality Commitment," and "Two Case Histories." These are summarized below.

## THE THEORY BEHIND QUALITY COMMITMENT

Quality Commitment has been built on three basic theoretical principles: work effectiveness, total involvement, and performance appraisal. Before using case histories to show how Lincoln National Life integrated these three elements, let us take a brief look at each one.

### *Work Effectiveness*
Work effectiveness is a proven method for analyzing and designing jobs so as to structure them for better productivity through im-

provement in work climate. Many of the principles of work effectiveness are familiar through the theories of Abraham A. Maslow, Frederick Herzberg, and other authorities. Under work effectiveness, a good job has certain characteristics or "core dimensions":

*Skill variety.* The job requires the employee to use a number of talents and abilities—and ideally, to keep developing and acquiring new ones.

*Task identity.* The employee does a "whole job" from beginning to end, with an identifiable outcome.

*Task significance.* The employee can recognize that his or her work has meaning to other people, either in the company or in the world outside.

*Autonomy.* The worker has substantial discretion in decisions that affect his or her job in such matters as scheduling, work methods, and so on.

*Feedback.* The employee gets continuing, timely information about the effectiveness of his or her work. Ideally, feedback comes from benchmarks in the job itself. It may also come, however, from supervisors' comments, management reports, and other sources.

From this theoretical base, a step-by-step method was developed for analyzing jobs in terms of the "core dimensions" and for strengthening them when they are weak. This process actually changes the structure of jobs through six steps:

1. *Content analysis.* For each job, ask what its purpose is in relation to the mission of the department or group, and to the company as a whole. Then determine if every task in the job is necessary to that purpose. What is the value of every task to the jobholder and to other people? Is its value worth its cost?

2. *Task combination.* Analyze the work flow within a department or group. Are some separate tasks related in such a way that they could logically be included in an integrated job "module," which would be performed by an individual or team? Such a combination increases skill variety and challenge.

3. *Natural work units.* Instead of engaging in the random assignment of work which prevails in many offices that process large amounts of information, assign work on some logical basis—for example, geographic location of customers served or type of company.

4. *Vertical loading.* Build into the job module some of the plan-

ning and controlling function usually reserved for supervisors, as well as accountability for as many parts of a total job as can be reasonably handled.

5. *Client relationships.* Give employees continuing responsibility for a group of clients, plus the authority to make more decisions about the work. "Clients" include the company's customers and people in other departments. Client relationships build a sense of "ownership" of work, thereby encouraging better service.

6. *Feedback channels.* Client relationships are a primary source of information on job performance. Create additional sources by such means as having employees check their own work and log their own error rates. Design jobs so that the work itself feeds back an indication of success or failure.

## Total Involvement

Total involvement is an approach to employee communication in which employees suggest and evaluate procedural changes and other ways to improve quality. It consists of a communications network designed to ensure strong, continuing employee participation in the Quality Commitment effort. It is Lincoln National Life's adaptation of a social innovation developed in Japanese industry and known as a *quality circle.* A quality circle is a small group of workers and supervisors—usually five to ten members—who meet frequently and voluntarily to discuss work problems, identify causes, and develop solutions.

Total involvement emphasizes the improvement of quality and productivity through employee involvement. Barriers based on age or professional status are removed so that employees and managers of different backgrounds can collaborate in true teamwork. Members of the circles learn to use all the management tools they need—tools that have traditionally been the property of supervisors and managers. Total involvement has four basic objectives for the development of participants:

1. To get those who do the work to say how to do it better.
2. To encourage first-line supervisors to educate themselves and develop leadership.
3. To raise morale and develop employees' awareness of what quality is, and what they can do about it.
4. To unify company policies regarding quality and to provide

each department with people who can interpret and clarify those policies.

### Performance Appraisal

Performance appraisal is the use of employee evaluation for two equally important goals: 1. to foster commitment to company goals and monitor and reward progress toward them; and 2. to foster the personal growth of each employee so as to realize his or her greatest potential. Lincoln National designed its performance appraisal program to have the following characteristics:

1. Employee and supervisor should understand clearly what performance is required.
2. The employee should evaluate his or her own performance and identify growth needs.
3. Both parties should agree on clearly stated development goals that serve the objectives of the job.
4. Each side should keep the other informed of action plans, target dates, and results.
5. Managers and supervisors should reinforce desired performance by recognizing accomplishments and offering help where it is needed.

## ORGANIZING AND TRAINING FOR QUALITY IMPROVEMENT

### Organizing

The roots of Quality Commitment at Lincoln National Life go back to the Corporate Productivity Committee established by President Ian Rolland. Its mission was to examine the whole spectrum of productivity approaches and to suggest which of them might be applicable to the company.

From the beginning the committee wanted to avoid approaches to productivity which would achieve impressive short-term results at the expense of the longer-term health of the organization. They believed that true productivity improvement was best achieved by unleashing employees' creativity. Management expected any productivity improvement effort to be able to help reduce staffing costs relative to the volume of work. However, productivity improvement was not to endanger the employment security of any employee.

The committee's research identified work effectiveness and total involvement as two approaches to productivity which were in accord with employee welfare. In addition, Lincoln National Life's representatives on the committee believed that management behavior would change by these two paths, a change which must be reinforced and maintained through the performance appraisal system.

The committee devised an action plan that would integrate the three elements. Its components are shown in Figure 12-1.

*Steering committee.* This committee provides overall direction for quality commitment. As quality commitment has grown, the steering committee has been enlarged to represent all work elements. The committee meets regularly with the corporate productivity committee. It plays an important role in the evaluation of the Quality Commitment effort.

*Director, Quality Commitment.* The director is a member of the steering committee and represents it in the daily task of implemen-

Figure 12-1. Lincoln National Life quality commitment implementation plan.

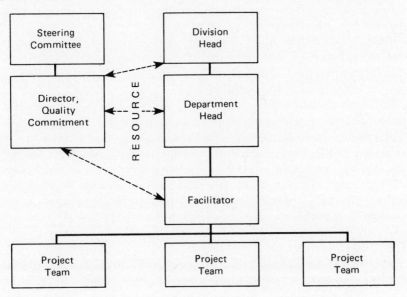

tation. The director is the sole staff support and functions essentially as a resource consultant to department and division heads as they implement their quality commitment efforts. The director also coordinates the substantial training effort required.

*Division and department heads.* It has been important for managers to understand that quality commitment does not in any way weaken their decision-making prerogatives or responsibilities, or create a separate authority structure. Division heads and department heads represent top management's strong support for quality commitment, and play a key role in its success.

*Facilitators.* Except for the one director, quality commitment is entirely a line effort. Facilitators—there are now 47 of them—are line people, chosen by department heads from among the most competent and motivated employees. Their role as facilitators is in addition to their other job responsibilities. The exact amount of time required depends on the status of the particular department's quality commitment effort.

The facilitator functions as a resource consultant within the department, maintaining communications between managers and supervisors and employees in such a way as to produce job design changes and productivity improvements. The facilitator's role is conceived as being temporary, lasting perhaps 12 to 18 months while the department's quality commitment effort gets under way and starts to show results.

All the facilitators meet regularly as a group with the program director. Thus they serve as a quality commitment network through which the practical implementing experience of one department can be made available to others.

*Total involvement project teams.* A project team is made up of 8 to 12 volunteers, with a first-line supervisor serving as team leader. The volunteers work closely with their leader and facilitator in the redesign of their jobs, meeting as often as required. After job restructuring is completed, the groups continue to meet weekly to explore further opportunities for quality improvement. Supervisors are encouraged to ask for new volunteers so that everyone has a chance to contribute personally to the effort.

### Training

The Quality Commitment effort has required substantial training in various techniques. First, higher management, from the level of department head up, received five days of quality commitment training, broken down as follows:

*General orientation* presented by the president and other officers of the company (one day).

A *work effectiveness workshop*. The highly interactive training began with the theoretical bases of work effectiveness in behavioral sciences. Participants then proceeded to test their mastery of the principles by team study of case histories from other companies. Finally they developed applications of work effectiveness for their own operations (three days).

A *follow-up session* on the performance appraisal system (one day).

The facilitators' training consisted of the work effectiveness workshop and an additional three days (developed jointly by Lincoln National Life and Walters & Associates) devoted to the techniques especially valuable to the facilitator's role: interpersonal relationships, problem solving, team building, group dynamics, and conducting meetings.

Nonsupervisory employees' training consisted of a one-day workshop in work effectiveness for prospective project team members whose department heads see a potential for effective job redesign in their areas.

## QUALITY COMMITMENT CASE HISTORIES

The following case histories describe two operations where implementation of Quality Commitment is furthest advanced. As demonstration pieces, these cases have an additional advantage: The two departments must cooperate significantly, and the cases show that Quality Commitment has substantially improved cooperation.

Because the two operations are different in kind, we have not tried to describe them in a uniform format. but we have tried to cover the following points:

What the department does
How work was organized before quality commitment
Problems under the previous organization
How jobs were redesigned
Results of the redesign

## *Word Processing Center: Case History*

The Word Processing Center is a stenographic/typing pool serving the various insurance operations. Users dictate by telephone to dictation recorders, and typists transcribe the letters on magnetic-card typewriters. They produce a rough draft and correct it as they type. The magnetic card, incorporatng the corrections, is then read by a high-speed printer, which produces a perfect copy for mailing. The center produces about 18,000 letters a month for some 200 people in 12 departments.

Lincoln National Life found that technology alone did not solve its productivity problems. In 1978, Word Processing had several serious problems. Turnaround times were as long as three to five days, and error rates were high. Employee turnover was 60 percent a year. The center's manager made a strong request for higher salaries in the hope of attracting and retaining high-quality operators and thus solving the productivity problem.

At that time, quality commitment was just getting started. When members of the steering committee heard about Word Processing's problems, they sensed that work effectiveness and total involvement might provide some solutions. The Word Processing manager was skeptical, but the three-day work effectiveness workshop convinced him that work effectiveness could help the operation. Thus, Word Processing became one of the first areas where quality commitment methods applied.

Word Processing's jobs were seriously lacking in the core job dimensions. When users called in to dictate a letter, the call went at random to any one of a bank of dictation recorders. Operators took work as it came into the department, but otherwise the assignment of work was completely random. There was no continuing client relationship and no natural unit of work. Questions and problems had to go through the supervisor as intermediary. Thus there was little chance for feedback or autonomy.

An additional problem lay in work measurement. As noted before, operators were rated by the number of lines they produced. Transcription varied in complexity and difficulty. Error rates were high, since operators were interested in quantity rather than quality. Delays were numerous because of the high rerun volume, even though figures on lines produced per day showed the department as being close to standard.

After a work effectiveness orientation, the department formed a project team consisting of one volunteer from each of four operator job grades, a trainee, and two night-shift operators. The job design strategy was to remove the random relationship with users and to service an exclusive clientele continuously. The client chosen for the pilot was Client Services and Communications (Southern Region), the largest single user of Word Processing—and one of its sharpest critics.

Ideally, under work effectiveness principles, operators should have their own group of clients whose work they would log, transcribe, correct, and run through the printer. The project team concluded that the ideal solution would be impractical: It would require too much cross-training and would present difficulties in covering for illness, vacations, and other absences. So, the team approach was a compromise. Although dictation from the client sections comes only to the team, it is assigned randomly to the team's operators. Logging work and operating the printer are rotated.

The users and the team were introduced to each other through a "get acquainted" meeting, during which tours were conducted of each area and work routines were explained. This formed a natural work unit and established client relationships. Members of the project team contact their users to resolve any questions or problems they may have with the work, and their users bring any work needing correction or revision back to the person who transcribed it. This gives them responsibility for the work through vertical loading and provides feedback by means of their client relationships. They maintain their own correction/error count, which provides feedback on the quality of their work, and take their own backlog count each morning, which tells them how much work they have and how well they are keeping up. They also schedule for vacation and personal time off within their project team.

The project team's efforts have produced several improvements in the quality and the cost of its services, as is shown here:

|  | Before | After |
|---|---|---|
| Average time per page | 14.32 min. | 12.34 min. |
| Average cost per page (@ 9¢/minute) | $1.87 | $1.38 |
| Average error rate (includes users' dictating errors) | 10.5% | 8.0% |

This last statistic reveals some significant insights into the workings of a companywide quality commitment effort. Errors occur in dictation of the letter as well as in the transcription. Very soon after the project team installed its new job design, the dictation error rate dropped, and it has stayed lower than that for the rest of the Word Processing Center. Both users and Word Processing operators say the users' better performance is a result of the more personal relationship. As one operator says:

"Before Quality Commitment, a transcriber was only a set of initials on the finished letter. Now our clients know us face to face, and they deal with us every day. They know and appreciate our problems, and they are willing to help us whenever they can."

Better communication between the project team and its users led to a significant cost avoidance through a "minor" change in procedure. Before Quality Commitment, a user would begin dictation with instructions about the carbon copies required. However, Word Processing does not produce "carbon copies" in the traditional sense, but a number of originals.

By requesting users to hold their instructions on copies until the end of dictation (the point at which instructions must be incorporated into the magnetic card), the project team saves an estimated 30 seconds per letter. That amounts to as much as the work of one person over the course of a year. Here is the calculation.

| | |
|---|---|
| Total available minutes per week, entire transcription staff | 54,140 minutes |
| $54,140 \div 11.6$ minutes, the average time per letter | 4,494.82 letters |
| $4,494.82$ letters $\times \frac{1}{2}$ minute | 2,247.41 minutes |
| $2,247.41$ minutes $\times$ 52 weeks | 116,865.32 minutes |
| $116,865.32$ minutes a year $\div$ 111,780 minutes per full-time employee | 1.04 person |

Quality Commitment has brought a new climate of employee responsibility to Word Processing. Operators talk of their reluctance to be absent, even for illness, because they do not want the feeling of "letting the team down." They feel this way especially about their days of special duty, such as logging in work and operating the printer.

If absence is unavoidable, however, team members are much more willing than before to take on the necessary extra work. As one operator said, "It used to be everyone for himself or herself, and get out as fast as you can. Now we realize we're all in it together. If I help someone today, she'll help me tomorrow. Then the team will benefit, and management will be happy with our work."

## Automatic Bank Check Payment Center: Case History

As any business expands, management often faces two unacceptable choices with regard to clerical service: Either increase staff to handle the bigger workload, or be prepared to settle for lower standards of customer service. The results of Quality Commitment in the Automatic Bank Check (ABC) Payment Center show that a more positive solution is possible.

An increasing amount of life insurance is paid for with an automatic bank check arrangement. Under this provision, the insured arranges for premiums to be paid automatically by a check drawn against his bank account and sent directly to the insurer. About 30 percent of new policies written by Lincoln National Life are now being paid for this way.

The ABC operation administers such payments. The process has two basic kinds of work:

1. *Accounting.* This includes setting up accounts for new policies on the basis of information, authorizations, and other documentation from the policyowners, from agents, and from banks; and maintaining policies once the accounts have been established, by recording premium payments and other activity.

2. *Policyholder Service* (PHS). This includes implementing changes affecting the policy, such as mode of payment, address of the insured, and name of beneficiary.

Figure 12-2 shows the structure after jobs were redesigned and the two separate functions—Accounting and PHS—were combined.

But for years, ABC operations had followed a much more complex model. Senior clerks distributed incoming mail to the Accounting section, as follows: routine account work was given to the new issue clerks; routine account change work, to the change clerks themselves; and all complex work, to senior change clerks. The work for each category was distributed among the clerks at random, according to workload demands.

If the employee handling the case found unclear information, needed advice on handling a request, or needed authorization for a decision or judgment, the case would be referred to an assistant

Figure 12-2. ABC Payment Center after Accounting and PHS were combined.

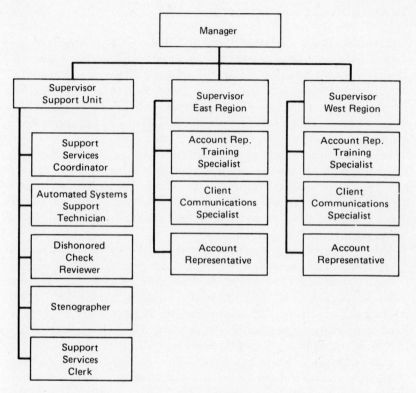

service consultant in PHS. The PHS consultant would write the necessary advisory comments and return the case to Accounting's incoming mail desk. As before, the files would be sorted for distribution to the appropriate category of clerk, and distributed at random.

In a case where a premium payment was *not* honored by the bank, it went to a dishonored-check clerk handling the appropriate category—for example, insufficient funds, account closed, or stop payment. When errors occurred in the ABC automated system as a result of an error in case handling, the file went to one of three error-correction clerks, each handling exclusively a different portion of the automated system output.

A change in technology in August 1977, which replaced a punch card system with CRT terminals, had not improved the basic organization of ABC work. Work was fragmented not only among several employees, but also between the two separate departments. When work left Accounting for PHS, the PHS consultants' backlogs often meant a delay of as much as two weeks. Meanwhile the file, which was out of its place, did not receive any information that arrived after it left Accounting. Several clerks were kept busy largely in "jacket chasing"—tracing files that were somewhere in transit.

The delays and difficulties of finding necessary information made employees feel that their two departments were adversaries, a "we–they" situation in which "they" were always to blame. Such an organization—besides its sheer inefficiency—made it hard for management to fix accountability for total customer service.

A goal of work effectiveness is to place accountability at the lowest possible level. This can often be achieved by creating "whole" jobs or combining related tasks from various positions within the same or different work units. That strategy presented some special challenges in the ABC Payment Center.

After attending work effectiveness orientation meetings and one-on-one interviews with the facilitator, each employee who had shown an interest was asked if he or she would volunteer. Out of 34 employees, there were 30 volunteers. Four teams were set up—two in Accounting and two in PHS. They met twice a week to discuss possible ways of improving work flow and quality.

After six weeks the four teams merged into two, each with representatives from both departments. The combined teams produced two independent proposals covering work flow, job content, job structure, implementation plan and time schedule, and a statement of policies and practices. Both proposals were presented to a review team of key managers, plus representatives of each of the two combined teams. The review group developed a single plan of action, which the head of the division approved with minor modifications.

*How the new plan works.* The key to the plan was the creation of a "core job" entitled account representative. Each representative is assigned ABC clients for which he or she handles all work from beginning to end. Whether the casework is routine or nonroutine, simple or complex, policy service or accounting, the representative sets it up, handles changes and terminations, and communicates with clients and agents as necessary.

The accounts are assigned geographically—work teams are

grouped by Eastern and Western geographical regions. The work team for each region also includes a client communications specialist who acts as consultant on unusual cases, reviews and analyzes communications, and initiates responses dealing with special problems.

The ABC Payment Center includes a support unit which provides the services too specialized to be incorporated into the job of account representative. For example, automated systems support technicians (formerly the error-correction clerks) review all the system's output for accuracy, acceptability, and agreement with input. They take action to correct errors, and they provide feecback on errors to the account representatives. They balance and verify bank checks before they are mailed for deposit.

The support unit also includes dishonored-check reviewers who handle all kinds of dishonored checks for their respective regions. They notify policyholders by form letter that a check has been dishonored, and either seek additional data or advise what action has been taken.

The new organization has yielded some significant work-flow improvements:

1. A stenographer sorts incoming mail by Eastern and Western Regions. Within each region, account representatives rotate the duty of distributing the mail to the person responsible for each territory. (Now, in the ongoing total involvement phase, teams are considering the advantages of having box numbers for each account representative, which would facilitate the sorting of mail.)

2. If an account representative needs information or advice on handling a case, he or she deals directly with the client (either the policyowner or the agent), or seeks the advice of the client communications specialist within the regional team.

Once the information or advice is obtained, the account representative usually completes work on the case. In a few exceptional cases, the client communications specialist completes the work. In a pilot project begun recently, the jobs of account representatives and client communications specialists are combined still further. First results are very promising.

3. Additional assimilation of functions may be possible as the limitations of the present automated systems are overcome. This will permit some tasks that are being performed by the support unit today to be handled by the account representatives in the future.

*Looking at the results.* The ABC Payment Center began operating with its new organization in mid-1978. During 1978, the number of policies handled by ABC grew from 163,000 to 178,500—an increase of over 15,000.

Under the old system, each 5,000 new policies would have required the addition of one more Accounting employee. In addition to these three employees, PHS would have required another two assistant service consultants.

In summary, the old system would have required five more employees to handle the growth in 1978. The cost in salary alone would have been approximately $50,000 a year. Under the reorganization, no employees were added.

Besides the savings, the reorganization has eliminated the old adversary relationship. As one supervisor puts it, "When there's a mistake now (and there aren't very many), it's not 'their' mistake. It's 'ours'—and we mean *all* of us."

## QUALITY COMMITMENT AND THE FUTURE

The managers and employees who have contributed to the changes described are proud of what they have done. But when you talk to them, you realize that their real excitement is for what lies ahead—what they can still do to make their operations even better for ourselves and our customers.

This commitment to the future is going to show itself in two different ways. First, those departments that have already achieved substantial improvement—like Word Processing and ABC—will be "fine tuning" their organizations in some of the ways suggested in the case histories.

Second, the departments that are in earlier stages of implementation of planning will start to show results. Inevitably, they will be helped by the practical knowledge and the spirit of the pioneering efforts.

Some expert observers have told us that Quality Commitment is remarkable in the degree to which a climate of change has been created rather quickly throughout a company. If our effort has been remarkable, it is not because we have found a quick and easy formula. But we do believe that everyone in a company can contribute to change if management provides the channels; that change has to be based on sound theory, flexibly applied; and that in a company, as in any organism, growth is not a matter of size, but of health and adaptability to a changing environment.

ARNOLD J. BENES

# 13
# Stimulating Greater Employee Commitment— Detroit Edison

DETROIT EDISON covers 7,600 square miles in southeastern Michigan. We have more than 1,700,000 customers. Our revenues are in the neighborhood of $1.8 billion, and our capitalization is approaching $6 billion. We are obviously a capital-intensive industry.

Our industry is heavily regulated. This has been the nature of the electric-power industry since it started. However, in the early years of our industry, our rates were low. We were able to install large 800-megawatt generators and pass tremendous savings resulting from technology improvement on to the customer. Suddenly, everything changed. But as recently as 1969, energy was one of those minor costs that were passed over without much attention.

I agree that there is a lot of government regulation. But I feel that just as war is the ultimate result of poor statesmanship and the lack of ability to moderate our differences and negotiate, so government regulation may be the result of weak management over the years. You may be surprised to hear that from me, but I feel that America's industrial management has not been nearly as good as we contend. I contend that the Occupational Safety and Health Act (OSHA) is not merely an invention of Congress but really the result of poor management of safety in the workplace. Strip-mining laws are not merely a creation of Congress but a result of poor management of our environment. The Federal Corrupt Practices Act did not originate in Congress, even though it enacted this law. Congress didn't cause the Equity Funding fraud, the illegal Lockheed payments, and the Firestone hidden political fund. Management is responsible for all this. Let's face reality. We have to be effective as managers and stewards of the tremendous investments and resources entrusted to us so that our investors can earn an income from their savings. Our rate-paying customers also expect us to be good stewards of the funds they pay for their utility services. Rather than hide our heads and blame the government for all our ills, we must start thinking in terms of our responsibilities as good managers.

## BRIEF HISTORY OF DETROIT EDISON'S PRODUCTIVITY PROGRAM

We started our productivity program in 1972. Our adversaries were posing questions which we did not answer effectively. We were perceived as having a cost-plus mentality. Actually, we are a pass-through-cost company. Forty-five cents out of every revenue dollar pay for fuel. We buy equipment and services from many, many suppliers and contractors. If we have a cost-plus mentality, the firms we buy from also operate on a cost-plus mentality. In fact, most of American industry operates in that same mode. I think this is a major reason for the present recession. The facts are: automobile companies are in dire straits and not making a dime because they thought auto costs could be increased and the public would continue to buy. The public is not a yo-yo anymore. Consumers are fed up with this cost-plus mentality, and I agree with them. A councilwoman in the city of Detroit called us "fat cats with automatic profits."

The public perceived us in 1972 as not being very creative. Utility managers were generally not regarded as being innovative. Some former consultants have said we were not creative and didn't rotate jobs often enough. They had an interesting concept that you should change jobs every seven to ten years. Well, I have been in this business for 40 years, and I still don't know all that I'd like to know about my job. It's somewhat like Congressmen going to Washington and trying to learn all they have to know in two years.

Today the public sees us as wasteful and unable to meet construction cost estimates. The New York State Commission recently ordered a study of the Shoreham nuclear power station of Long Island Lighting Company. A consulting firm performed a work sampling study on the construction job site. The work sampling showed only a 20 percent work utilization of the worker. The Shoreham job of Long Island Lighting Company is similar to our Fermi II plant. We performed work sampling at Fermi II and found that we are better: our work utilization is about 42–43 percent.

In our company, we've taken productivity improvement seriously. We review with all department heads their productivity improvement progress. Recently we made a presentation to about 40 managers and department heads on the present status of productivity measurement. We know our corporate performance in the utility industry. For many years we've had to furnish a report to the Federal Power Commission. It is a 1½-inch-thick report that covers everything from salaries to the number of kilowatts we have installed at each power plant. We've always been able to determine the cents per kilowatt hour, BTUs per kilowatt hour, or almost any other performance measurement.

## DESCRIPTION OF DETROIT EDISON'S PRODUCTIVITY PROGRAM

Our program at Detroit Edison is geared to work and productivity measurement of the individual and of the group. A summary of our work characteristics and measurement techniques is shown in Figure 13-1. There is no single program that fits all of our 11,000 employees. We have a large variety of disciplines and trades. So we had to select the type of traditional industrial-engineering approach, such as predetermined times or short-interval scheduling, that best applies to certain groups of workers.

From the time of the Industrial Revolution, management has tried to devise a suitable way to measure the human resource. Down through the years, many different methods have been developed to accomplish this. These include stopwatch time standards, predetermined time standards (methods of time measurement and work factor), and work sampling and short-interval scheduling. Although the objective of all of these measurement methods is to measure the human resource, the process of doing this and the results obtained are very different. Each of the methods has served different purposes for management. (Incidentally, I am opposed to the use of stopwatches. I told some of our mine contractors that if they discontinued using stopwatches, we'd improve pro-

Figure 13-1. Summary of work characteristics and measurement techniques.

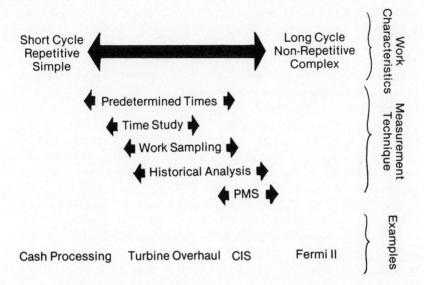

ductivity. For example, the guy who is putting up the roof bolts wants to get out of there as soon as possible. So it's really non-productive to time a worker putting up roof bolts.)

At Detroit Edison we tried several of these measurement methods with varying degrees of success and decided that our objectives for a sound human resource control program would best be served by measuring both the utilization percentage and the productivity of our employees.

To measure the utilization percentage, we designed and implemented a companywide work sampling program. This program currently covers 25 departments out of a total of 49 and includes administrative, customer service, engineering, and construction (both internal and contract construction) personnel. There are more than 1,800 people being work-sampled, many of them belonging to trade unions. And, I might add, we have had full cooperation from the unions.

Our approach to the work sampling program was unique. Rather than use the standard, conventional method of having industrial engineers or outside consulting firms conduct the actual work sampling observations, the engineers of our industrial engineering services divisions conduct observer training seminars to train selected employees from each participating department to conduct their own studies.

The benefits derived from our work sampling program have been very gratifying for us. For example, our overall productive utilization percentage from this program appears to be 62 percent, and we have every indication that it is continually improving. A continuing benefit of this program is that we have been able to identify and use methods and work simplification improvements that have had a beneficial effect on our operations. During this year, our work sampling program will be enlarged to include more departments, and an in-depth analysis of the trend indicators of our present program will be made.

After reviewing all the standard conventional methods of productivity measurement, we elected to implement a comparatively new method called "the modular system of productivity measurement analysis" to measure the productivity of our engineering and technical personnel. The system has four modules:

1. Standards design.
2. Program format definition.
3. Establishment of administrative procedures.
4. Departmental follow-up.

This method was chosen because it has been proven to be an acceptable way of measuring the productivity of senior-level engineers and other professional disciplines.

Under this system, all the elements of a position are grouped into four groups called modules. The first module is the design phase, in which all major tasks performed are identified and prioritized by frequency of occurrence as well as by complexity. A major task, for example, could be the act of thinking a design project through to a solution. The second module includes the mechanics of putting the tasks into practical or working format. The third module includes the administrative procedures necessary to implement the program. The fourth module includes the necessary engineering analysis and administrative follow-up to ensure the program's success.

The data obtained by this system form the basis for a "designated task productivity measurement methods program" to measure the productivity of the people involved. Table 13-1 illustrates the use of this method for the job of a senior design engineer. There are three major objectives of this program:

1. To identify and verify how engineers spend their time.
2. To establish engineering guidelines or standards for performing various levels of work.
3. To develop project labor costs on the basis of actual rather than estimated man-hours.

The modular system of productivity measurement analysis is a simple yet effective program with no exotic computer programming or reporting requirements. However, as with all work measurement processes, the employees who are to be measured must play a substantial part in the development and installation of the program. After all, employees demand to know what is expected of them and how they are doing in relation to those expectations.

One of our biggest problems was to train people to identify their product. It's difficult, particularly when you are dealing with white-collar workers. As a clinical psychologist, what is your product? Unfortunately, we tend to reward our professional people on the basis of the most complex aspects or the thinking part of their job. I contend that more than 80 percent of the time, professionals are expected to come up with the right answer routinely without much strain or brain work. For example, 80 percent of a surgeon's work is probably routine. If every case were a life-and-death struggle, the surgeon would exhaust himself. The same thing applies to engineers, accountants, and auditors.

We have taken a systematic approach to identifying products or the units of work. For instance, what is the product of a computer programmer? We get arguments on this, but we finally designated the product as a "line of code." We recognize that there are different levels of complexity for that product, but that's the basis for promotion and for different wage rates. We know what it costs to produce a "line of code"—we know when we should contract to buy computer programs from outside firms.

An example of another approach used to improve productivity can be found in our underground-lines area. In order to measure the productivity of our underground-lines field personnel, we use a computerized system. This system provides for payroll time report-

Table 13-1. Job description: Senior design engineer.

| Element Description | Designated Task No. | Designated Task | (Descriptive) Degree of Difficulty | Description of Standard | Standard Man-Hours |
|---|---|---|---|---|---|
| Identifies problems in engineering discipline. | 1, 2 | Thought process | Unique<br>A. New state of the art | Full project allotted time | 200 |
| | | | B. Existing method | 3/4 project allotted time | |
| Solves design problems in engineering discipline. | | | Standard (state of the art)<br>A. Moderate degree of difficulty expected | 50–60% of project time | 100 |
| | | | B. Little or no difficulty expected | 35–40% of project time | |
| Provides consulting advice to other departments concerning design projects within his discipline. | 3 | Consultation | Consulting<br>A. Specific (state-of-the-art) advice as it would pertain to the influence of the project on other disciplines | 25% of project time | |
| | | | B. General (state-of-the-art) advice | 15% of project time | |

| | | | | |
|---|---|---|---|---|
| Directs efforts of other involved personnel in carrying a design project through to completion. | 4 | Technical guidance | Technical guidance<br>A. Full guidance<br><br>B. Partial guidance | 40% of project time<br>20% of project time | 80 |
| Conducts research in new projects. Reevaluates old products or methods. | 5 | Research | Research<br>A. New state of the art<br><br>B. Existing product (large part)<br>C. Existing product (small part) | Full project time<br>3/4 project time<br>20% of project time | 200 |
| Writes technical reports. | 6 | Technical writing | Technical reports<br>A. Lengthy report<br><br>B. Short report | Actual estimates<br>Actual estimates | |
| Writes administrative reports for the department. | 7 | Administrative reports | Administrative reports<br><br>A. Lengthy report<br>B. General | Actual estimates | |

ing as well as productivity measurement. In the past two years, two changes have been made. First, the system input since July 1979 is made by payroll clerks through computer terminals to a new minicomputer. This has virtually eliminated some 300 system errors per week by making it possible for the payroll clerk to enter data directly into the system, which immediately either accepts or rejects the data. We also eliminated one day per week required by one of two employees who verified payroll and time data. With the improvement in time reporting, we are experiencing fewer payroll errors, which in turn reduces employee complaints.

Our second change was to measure operating and maintenance jobs. Currently, only new construction activity is being measured. This accounts for something less than half of all underground-lines activities. During 1979 we field-timed the operating and maintenance activities, and we are developing new job standards from this date. When those standards are completed sometime this year, we will be able to measure about 90 percent of all field operating and maintenance activities.

We have many good programs for our various departments, but we don't have time to cover them here. We have shared this information with more than 150 utilities in the country. We decided that work sampling was a recognized industrial-engineering tool for taking a quick snapshot of worker utilization at work locations. We've initiated this work sampling program on a companywide basis. I believe that we're the first utility in the industry that is attempting such a companywide program.

## THE KEY TO SUCCESS OF THE PRODUCTIVITY PROGRAM

We don't know what the rate of worker utilization should be, but the first-line supervisors should know. That's the key to our whole program. We are introducing our 1,000 first-line supervisors to the art of supervision through work sampling. To aid in this, we developed a handbook, which has been copyrighted.

When we started this productivity measurement program, we had resistance from a lot of people. I contend that for two decades we've bred managers who are waiting for somebody to devise a computer program or a black box to help them out of their problem. That black box wasn't available 20 years ago; it wasn't available 10 years ago; it isn't available today; and it's not going to be available 20 years from now. There is no such thing as program management. Let's forget it.

The key to a successful work-measurement program, in my opinion, is hard basic supervisory training for first-line supervisors. They are responsible for groups of 10 to 15 people. We need to explain to them that if they were charging Detroit Edison for products or services from their privately owned shop, they would certainly identify their good performers and know how to improve performance of the poor workers. This is the type of challenge we're giving them today. You don't need to understand the laws of probability or statistical sampling. In our work sampling handbook, for example, we provide simple instructions covering the number of observations required in work sampling and the confidence levels. You can train people to use it, and good supervisors do this anyway. We're asking them to record their observations so that later they can analyze them and determine workers' performance and relate this to expected performance.

We are committed to this program and have issued a corporate general order on it. The Industrial Engineering Division reports to me and is helping people develop the program.

I would like to summarize the results of methods currently being used at Detroit Edison. Our departments have measured human resources within their respective departments, using the measurement tools listed:

| | |
|---|---|
| Department Measurements | |
| Management by objectives | 18 |
| Strategic planning | 10 |
| Group Measurements | |
| Historic analysis | 11 |
| Work sampling | 24 |
| MBO | 18 |
| Individual Measurements | |
| Annual planning interview (API) | 16 |
| Predetermined times | 13 |
| Time study | 4 |
| Project Measurements | |
| Project management systems | 14 |

The development of work- or productivity-measurement programs must begin with the establishment of management objectives. Reaching the goals established through management objectives means improvement in productivity. Management by objectives involves the definition of responsibilities (controllable objectives) and measurement of results versus goals. Although goals must be attainable, achieving them should require some degree of stretching. These concepts are the basis for work measurement. Management objectives specify *what* is to be measured, while the work-measurement program defines *how* it is to be measured.

The effect of a productivity-measurement program on the unit cost per product (kilowatt of power or pound of steam) can be the difference between failure or success. We at Detroit Edison are using these human resources measurement methods to stabilize and/or reduce our unit cost in the face of increasing volumes and work complexities.

## TOOLS FOR MEASURING PRODUCTIVITY IN SPECIFIC DEPARTMENTS

Examples of some measurement tools used for selected departments follow.

*Accounting System and Research.* In this area we have a project management system for establishing project activities by priority and allocating hours for completion; identifying major elements for project work to enhance reporting procedures; and utilizing weekly and monthly reporting logs to monitor staff performance.

*Administrative and Technical Systems.* Here we use a computerized project management system that establishes project activities and details tasks and subtasks and time frames for completion. MBO is employed for administrative controls, and work sampling is used for comparisons with other measurements.

*Auditing.* This department uses MBO for measuring department and division performance; the Mark IV Project Management system for monitoring group performance; Annual Planning Interviews to quantify individual performance; and work sampling to identify and monitor areas for improving worker utilization.

*Electrical System.* This department employs work sampling to monitor and identify areas in which worker utilization can be improved. Department performance is measured using MBO, and a Job Management System is empoyed to evaluate requests for shutdown of substations.

*Production Organization Maintenance Division.* This division uses work sampling to monitor and improve worker utilization. The measurement program incorporates 2,281 performance standards and 309 maintenance procedures.

*Psychological Services.* This department uses a log system to monitor time spent on various work and nonwork activities.

*Real Estate and Rights of Way.* Here we use a project management system whereby activities are identified and monitored for primary or secondary activities; a cost for services is established for all activities.

*Revenue Requirements.* In this area, a project management system with two components is used. One, a monthly written report is made on project activity, status, and complexity, with reasonable target dates for completion for each project incorporated into the system. Two, a project-listing computer program is used to schedule workload and reduce downtime during assignments and prolonged waits between assignments.

## IMPROVEMENTS RESULTING FROM THE PROGRAM

The philosophy of productivity analysis relates to the effectiveness of operating units and their management in fulfilling their responsibilities. It follows that some type of program must be developed to "keep score" of effectiveness. In our case, 44 out of a total of 49 departments reported improvements in productivity. Furthermore, seven departments reported that they use productivity measurement for complement/budget controls. Examples of productivity improvements reported by various departments include the following:

- Used team approach and changed methods for processing invoices to increase productivity by 52 percent.
- Established monitoring objectives that improved keystrokes by 350 keystrokes per hour.
- Reduced overtime by 39 percent through reorganization of personnel.
- Reduced attendance problem to a controllable level through establishment of an attendance monitoring program.
- Achieved 83 percent of the yearly objectives established by the department.

- Reduced unknown work activities, through work sampling, from 18 percent to 2 percent.
- Established a Safety Coordinator Program which in the first year completely eliminated lost time because of accidents.
- Established new procedures to eliminate the presorting of mail, thus reducing manual work from 10 percent to 2 percent.
- Reduced manpower needs by 9 percent as a result of productivity measurements.
- Improved utilization of manpower from 60 percent to 70 percent.
- With the aid of effectiveness measurements, had 75 percent of recommendations implemented promptly.
- Increased sales of food by 43 percent without additional labor.
- Improved group morale and efficiency significantly since initiating a work-measurement program.
- Trended uncollectibles downward from 36 percent to 33 percent through modified policies and procedures.
- Saved $29,000 annually in postage costs through new procedures.
- Saved $59,000 annually in labor costs through productivity improvements.
- Saved $37,800 annually as a result of new procedures, methods, and materials.
- Improved work activities in primary work functions by 3 percent from 1978 to 1979.
- Increased personnel being measured from 69 percent in 1977 to 88 percent in 1979.

In sum, the program is working for us. We feel that laying off large numbers of people is not sound management. You cannot manage a company with such violent changes in your workforce. Our objective at the start was to manage our business so that people would have continuity of employment and could plan for their future. That's inculcated in all our managers at Detroit Edison. We feel that we have definitely stabilized our labor force despite the decline in the economy. And that's very important to us, because we need *all* our people.

CARL C. JACOBSON

# 14
# Making Productivity Improvement Work at The Tanner Companies

THE SUBJECT of this book, productivity, is something that we at The Tanner Companies believe in. But before we review the productivity efforts in our company, I'd like to give you a brief history of The Tanner Companies.

## BRIEF DESCRIPTION OF THE COMPANY

In 1923, with a $500 road contract and some mules, horses, wagons, and wooden scrapers, the first Tanner Brothers Company started under the leadership of Rollin C. Tanner and two brothers, Roy and Marion. Their association was short-lived, as the prosperity of the mid-1920s faded with the 1929 stock market crash.

In succeeding years, R.C. Tanner maintained his interest with various other partners in highway and bridge construction. The first highway contract in Arizona to exceed $1 million was completed by this company in 1936—with power provided by mules! In the 1940s Tanner participated in the improvement of U.S. 66 across Northern Arizona, using some of the first tractor and dozer equipment in the state.

Arizona's postwar growth demanded an ever expanding contracting service and material supply. Tanner Construction kept pace, and in 1956 Tanner Bros. Contracting Co., Inc., was organized under the leadership of R.C. Tanner's three sons, Maurice, John, and Steve. R.C. Tanner moved into a semiretirement role as consultant in 1961, contributing his knowledge and experience until his death in 1967.

The present Tanner Companies were incorporated in 1971 and consisted of a number of affiliated companies: Contracting Division, Prestressed Division, Materials Division, and Western Ash Company.

Tanner's expansion is apparent, because we currently have 1,850 employees and total annual sales of more than $110 million.

This year, The Tanner Companies are celebrating 55 years of service.

## BACKGROUND OF PRODUCTIVITY PROGRAM

Productivity has been an unspoken concern since the beginnings of the company. With the economic conditions of the 1970s, The Tanner Companies, along with many other business and industry leaders, recognized that the rate of productivity improvement within our company itself had begun to lag behind rises in the cost of doing business.

This recognition led The Tanner Companies to establish a productivity task force in the fall of 1976. This task force consisted of people from top management and at least one from each division of the company.

As the task force met frequently, the question kept coming up, "What are our goals? What do we want to achieve?" We came up with the following definition of productivity for the company:

Productivity is the way we efficiently and creatively utilize our human resources, equipment, materials, money, and information to produce, sell, and distribute products and services at the lowest possible price.

## BASIC APPROACH AND PHILOSOPHY

In order to achieve some of our goals, we asked each division to analyze its organization and pick *at least one*, but *not more than three* areas in which it was having problems with work and with workers. In order to improve any phase of the company, we had to get the involvement of the people who are doing the work. It is necessary to have ways of measuring and keeping a record of improvements. We will see later how this is done in each division.

The task force has worked together as a team from the beginning, along with Tom Fullmer, Director of the Productivity Institute at Arizona State University. The objective of the Institute is to help both private and public segments of society to improve productivity so that the quality of working life will improve and the private enterprise system will be preserved.

On a larger scale, the Institute does for its members what Tanner's task force does for its divisions: it provides research and information on productivity and acts as a focus for progress in the field. Sometimes it can offer members specific solutions to needs not always fully perceived. A good example of this is the "Data Analyzer." This is a computer program that was first brought to Tanner's attention by Tom Fullmer. He suggested to Tanner that the productivity of company management might be increased through more effective and timely use of information already residing in the firm's computer files.

One thing we all have to remember: there are always better methods and improvements in anything we do. Here are some of the ingredients of a successful productivity improvement program:

Top management must be sold on the program and be specifically supportive.

Everybody must be involved in the program.

There must be a positive attitude toward productivity from top management to first-line employees.

Inevitable discouragement must not deter the program.

Everybody must understand that survival depends on new ideas.

Success stories should be published to provide continuing encouragement.

Continuing training and education are necessary.

We will show you not only what has been done but how various measurements and techniques can result in productivity improvements. Getting back into productivity and seeing what people can do and what they can achieve is enjoyable business. Most of you realize that people will do what you expect them to do and that you have to recognize them for it. As we proceed, you will see that our program is carried out with people in mind.

## THE STRUCTURE OF THE PRODUCTIVITY IMPROVEMENT PROGRAM AT TANNER *

At Tanner, we developed an organization structure which we hoped would bring productivity closer to the people who were

* This section was prepared by Richard F. Martin.

really going to bring about productivity enhancement for us (see Figure 14-1).

We changed the name of the task force to a Corporate Productivity Committee. Then we decided we had grown up and were ready for an expert, so we selected a Producitivy Coordinator, Stephen Jones. We got further away from our task force and set up productivity committees for each division: Materials, United Metro, Prestressed Concrete, Contracting, administrative areas, Yuma area, Tucson Rock and Sand Division, and Equipment Maintenance. This way we got down to the working level. The corporate committee had officers and nonofficers selected from different parts of the company to get the program going. These divi-

Figure 14-1. Organization structure for the productivity program.

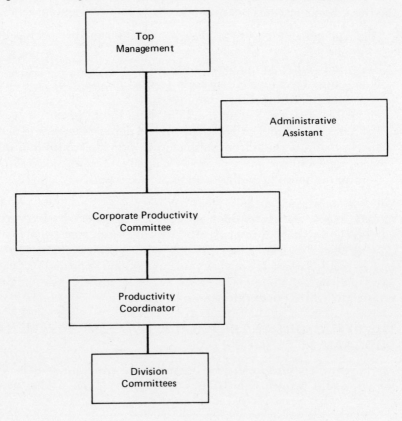

sion committees consist of representatives from management and, in some cases, union representatives among the workers, as well as office, sales, and production people. This group has been put together to try to bring productivity to the regional or department level.

In all these cases, nobody has a sole job of productivity. We wanted the program to be part of our management process. Everybody has another job in production or administration. This is to help create the awareness that productivity improvement is an additional working assignment, if you will, in each and every job. As we developed these committees, we moved into what we felt was a most important aspect of our program—education. We started holding seminars. We packaged our task force results into a small booklet. We held a seminar with our supervisory people. We have a tradition of Saturday morning seminars in The Tanner Companies. We meet at breakfast on Saturday morning, and after breakfast, we have an hour-and-a-half seminar on a particular subject. Productivity has been one of the main topics for the past two years. We use the seminar to acquaint our supervisors and unionized foremen with productivity and some of the concepts that we have begun to work with. In recent seminars we made great use of brainstorming sessions. We end each one of our seminars with a brainstorming session to bring out of each group ideas it can focus on.

Next we moved without division committees. We had seminars in which we brought divisions together. They had their own brainstorming sessions to develop some focal points for measurement during the ensuing months. These measurement points were taken back to the divisions by the division committee, and each division began the work with their people. Then we started a new series of seminars for each individual division.

Stephen Jones and I bring some framework to these seminars, but the work is done by the division chairman and his committee. One we had recently was very exciting. We finished again with a brainstorming session, and some 33 ideas ended up on the chart pad within about 15 minutes. Each of these ideas will be evaluated by the appropriate committee and worked on over the next six-month period. We also developed an Idea Catcher Program. Idea Catcher is a suggestion system with a new title. People can write their ideas on an "Idea-gram" and submit them to me. Ideas are reviewed by the people involved in that area. Of course, everybody is recognized for his or her idea, and in several cases every month, monetary recognition is also made. We use that to reinforce the concept that "ideas equal productivity."

When we kicked off the program, we also used a bumper sticker to make people aware of the fact that "ideas equal productivity." We are trying to tap our people, because they are the ones who are bringing productivity enhancement about. We use the "Idea-gram" and the Idea Catcher to advantage, all for the purpose of tapping these people and bringing their ideas to the front. *Tanner Scanner,* a newspaper for our employees, highlights productivity in every issue. As mentioned earlier, we have relied heavily on the Productivity Institute at Arizona State University to help us in our productivity program. And finally, our library of films is oriented to productivity. We have all kinds of films, but in recent months, a productivity film that is good becomes a part of our library right away. These are made available immediately for the divisions to use with their committees and with their employees.

## PRODUCTIVITY IMPROVEMENT EFFORTS AT THE CONTRACTING DIVISION *

The productivity committee in our Contracting Division has been working on a number of projects this past year. The following three will serve to illustrate the variety of these projects:

1. Right person–right machine–right job concept.
2. Crew continuity and motivation.
3. Development of equipment availability and utilization data.

1. The right man–right machine–right job concept may already be familiar to many of you. If you are acquainted with contracting operations, with ready-mix, sand, and gravel operations, or with other operations involving heavy equipment, you realize the importance of putting a skilled operator on a very expensive piece of equipment. With the prices on our equipment, which go up all the time, it's very important to keep the same skilled operator on one piece of equipment whenever possible. He gets to know it; he learns what it can and can't do. This knowledge leads to the third element of that concept, putting the right piece of equipment on the right job.

* This section was prepared by Stephen Jones.

Our contracting division strives for this three-part combination at all times. In the frequent moments of crisis, the ideal matching of the three doesn't always happen, but it is one of the division's productivity improvement goals. We install on all our equipment a small sticker that reminds the operator to check water, oil, and tires daily. This reminder is followed by a statement, "You work when this machine works." That may seem a bit harsh, but if, for example, you are familiar with a laydown machine on a paving spread, you know that if that machine goes down, nobody works.

2. Another area the Contracting Division is working on is crew continuity and employee motivation techniques. Crew continuity is simply a matter of keeping skilled people working together. They know what each other does best, they know what the equipment can do, and from there on, the learning curve takes over. If you can keep the same group of people with the same equipment doing the same kind of work, even if they are moved from one location to another, you are able to utilize your human resources and your equipment much more effectively and productively. To do this, we try to schedule all the major operations on the contracting jobs in the Phoenix metropolitan area, as well as our larger projects outside the Phoenix area, one to two weeks in advance.

Of the many motivation techniques that can be used to increase individual or group productivity, one used by one of our job superintendents is rather interesting. He selects one or two people from his crews each week. These people are given a small slip of paper and asked to write down sometime during the day a specific element of the job they feel can be improved, or to make a suggestion that will help run the job more smoothly. The slip of paper is handed back to the superintendent at the end of the day. It can be anonymous, but it's an effort to obtain the employees' ideas. It helps the employee feel his ideas are important to the superintendent. It is also a form of recognition for the employee and an example of our overall emphasis on people and on total involvement.

Another motiviation technique our superintendents are encouraged to use is setting a specific goal for each person or crew for the day. Rather than dropping off the crew and telling them only that they will be picked up at the end of the shift, the superintendent or foreman tells the crew it should try for 800 tons of material to be placed that shift, or 300 feet of curb to be formed that shift, or whatever. This is a simple leadership principle, but as in so many instances, it is the simple basic principles that are the keys to increasing productivity for the individual, the crew, and the organization as a whole.

3. Our Contracting Division has recently introduced an equipment utilization reporting system—or equipment usage report, as it is called. This is a formal effort to track how much time the equipment is available to be used and how much time it is actually used. These availability and utilization figures will be used to evaluate equipment and manager/supervisor performance and also to accumulate a long-term history of equipment performance.

To develop these figures, the system gathers the hours of downtime and idle time for a machine, as well as the hours of usage for it. Everybody in contracting or related activities knows that you keep track of your equipment costs per hour in the same way you keep track of your labor costs, so the usage figures are readily available. In addition to asking our supervisors to report usage, we ask them to report downtime and idle time and to indicate the type of downtime or idle time. From these figures we develop percentages that measure the equipment and the supervisor's use of the equipment. These figures enable not only the Phoenix office but also the individual superintendent and foreman to review their performance and the equipment and performance in their area so they can improve it the next week, the next month, or on the next job.

## PRODUCTIVITY IMPROVEMENT EFFORTS IN THE EQUIPMENT MAINTENANCE DEPARTMENT *

I suspect that the greatest problem we face today, and certainly the greatest hurdle facing us in maintenance, is how to measure our productivity. Productivity, as we have seen, can be complicated. It entails a great number of concepts, and yet I suppose it is very simple. All you have to do is do it. How do we do it? This is the question that kept plaguing us. I am reminded of one time when I was visiting Kentucky. I was impressed with the little farms I saw along the way and stopped to talk with one of the farmers. I asked him how this farm produced, or what its yield was. I will never forget the answer he gave me. He said, "Well, I raised a heap, I sold a sight, and I got a right smart left." The problem with that is, as

---

* This section was prepared by Mack R. Larson.

long as he understood the quantities that he was talking about, his measurement of productivity was excellent. I know that we have got a "heap" of equipment, and I know that we need a "right smart" work out of them, but I'm not exactly sure where I go from there. We have attempted, in some ways, to get a measurement, and started by measuring productivity from a mechanic's standpoint.

Beginning in September 1976, when we first started our productivity committee, we looked at it two different ways. First, we saw it from the standpoint of total equipment hours worked versus total maintenance hours. Then we decided we would leave out the major overhauls and the major PMs (preventive maintenance checks) and look at it from that point. When we did that, we got a ratio of 30 or 40 to 1, and we knew that that couldn't be. It just didn't look right. So this now includes all major PMs, all major engine overhauls, major component overhauls, and complete machinery buildup. With the mixer trucks, we started at 4.6 machine hours to one hour mechanic's time or service time. Then we thought that we could attain a six-point ratio and set that as our goal.

We attained that and moved to an eight-point ratio. Since then, we have remained there and haven't really progressed as much as we would have liked to. Some of this can be explained by the age of equipment. In some of our areas, the average age is about 64 months; in others, it is 85 months. With the dump trucks, we didn't make the progress we made with the mixers, although some shops did very well.

We have a total of 11 shops; however, we took our figures just from the larger shops so we would get a better feel of what we were trying to do. Even with the larger shops, much still depends on the length and location of the haul. Then the big problem that we had is how you can determine mechanic productivity when you have, on the one hand, five drivers who can drive a truck for 2,000 or 3,000 hours with no major problems and, on the other hand, five drivers who can't drive around the block without tearing it up.

In order to help us on this, we started a little committee meeting with mechanics, truck drivers, and operators. On a regular basis, we have someone from the shops, either the foreman or the superintendent, meet with the truck drivers or operators. They spend a few minutes together talking about the problems that they are having. This is starting to smooth out some of the rough spots that we were having. I guess it has been an age-old thing where the mechanics and the truck drivers locked horns. The truck driver provides security for the mechanic, and the mechanic thinks the truck driver is but a dumb yo-yo who doesn't know how to treat a piece of equipment. Both of them are wrong. Both of them are extremely important, and we are trying to get them to realize that they are there to help and work with each other, and then the trucks will work on a more regular basis.

In an effort to identify some of the specific areas in which we could improve, we created an equipment report called the EMC (Equipment Maintenance Cost) Report. We broke down our maintenance by machine component to give us an idea of where we were spending our dollars so that we could try to concentrate on those particular areas. Every piece of equipment the company owns—just over 1,450 pieces, worth about $45 million dollars—is on this system. We have a component breakdown for each piece of equipment, each group of similar pieces, and each fleet. This system told us something we would not have suspected: the item causing us the most trouble in our equipment, in general, was electrical problems. Now we wouldn't have ever thought that. We didn't realize that we were spending major dollars on electrical problems. So we decided that we would do something about that. We called a representative from a major electrical supply company. He met with me and all the shop superintendents and conducted a basic electrical preventive maintenance seminar in a matter of a few hours.

Some of the things refreshed our memory. Some of the things were new concepts. Then each shop superintendent was to have this same individual hold a similar seminar with his mechanics. So now everybody in maintenance in The Tanner Companies has attended a seminar on electrical problems. We reduced our electrical service calls from 41 per month to 14 in a matter of three weeks.

Speaking of service calls, the EMC system keeps track of service calls and identifies the problem causing the service call. We are not using this yet for our contracting equipment, but we are in our materials division truck fleet. In October 1977, we were making a total of 153 road calls on 293 units. In February 1979, we were able to reduce this to an average of 80 road calls per month simply by isolating the problem and keeping track of what the road calls really consisted of. We estimated that a road call costs us $150. In essence, we saved over $10,000 in road calls alone.

Another productivity component in maintenance resulted from a problem we were having with our service people. We just didn't feel that we were getting the equipment serviced as quickly, efficiently, and properly as we were entitled to. We talked with the service people and asked them what we could do to help them. We started by making out a list specifying which trucks and pieces of equipment were to be serviced on a given day. We found that by giving the service people a list each day, we increased their productivity by 50 percent in just a matter of a few days simply because they had a list to work from. That system has now been computerized. Every week, each serviceman gets a sheet of paper that tells him which items he serviced last week and which we want him to service this week. Another column on the sheet indicates why they are being serviced—whether the cause was overtime or overusage, for example. The third of these report sheets tells him which items are overdue for servicing. In that way he gets another reminder that these need to be done, and again, the reason for servicing the equipment indicated. Another element of this servicing report enables us to change the service interval for an individual piece of equipment or a group of machines. For example, the service period can be set for 400 hours or 83 days, whichever comes first. We have made many changes on the basis of our experience and the areas in which the equipment is working.

In another area, we devised a report on average fuel use per 100 hours. We set up a base so that, on each given job, if a truck or vehicle used more fuel than we had established, we knew there was something wrong with it that we had to check out. Maybe it was mechanical, maybe it was waste, but something was wrong. This fuel report includes an exception report that shows which machines use more than a certain amount of fuel. This has helped us a great deal in getting control of the use of our fuel.

Incidentally, we made a study on the idling of our equipment. Just idling all our equipment during the lunch break (30 minutes) was costing us $35,000 per year. Needless to say, we corrected most of that; we quit idling our equipment. We decided that starters and batteries were cheaper than fuel. Almost everything now is electrical start, not the old pony motor, so it's very easy to shut it down and then restart it when we go back to work.

I hope that I have given you a glimpse of some of the areas we have attempted to cover in preventive maintenance. We know that we have a long way to go. We know that we have made some progress in this field. We know that we have areas we need to concentrate on that will help us become more effective and more efficient in the utilization of our equipment, the utilization of our human resources, and for the overall productivity of The Tanner Companies.

## THE PRODUCTIVITY IMPROVEMENT PROGRAM AT THE PRESTRESSED CONCRETE DIVISION *

We have discussed the background, approach, structure, and philosophy of The Tanner Companies' general productivity program. Now we would like to share with you some of the specific applications and operations of the productivity program at our prestressed concrete plants. The Prestressed Concrete Division designs, fabricates, delivers, and installs structural and architectural prestressed and precast concrete products. Our division has approximately 200 employees at three plants.

### Structure of the Program

We have not employed or assigned specific personnel to be solely responsible for productivity. A division productivity committee has been formed, and an Assistant Plant Manager acts as chairman. This committee formulates a plan of action, sets goals, discusses techniques, and follows up on the progress of small task groups. A task group may consist of foremen at the various castings beds, the Quality Control Manager, the Chief Draftsman, and others. We ask these groups to discuss areas in which they think they can improve productivity and to confine their efforts to areas under their control. Every employee must be involved. Productivity improvement is not accomplished by decree, only by constant desire and action by everyone. The plan and the goals and reasons for productivity improvement are explained to everybody. We suggest to each task group to *begin* with only one or two relatively small goals that are easy to reach until the group gets into the habit of thinking and acting on productivity. An example of this would be to improve the effectiveness of one piece of equipment by considering the type, size, and number of vibrators we use for a specific product.

* This section was prepared by Ted J. Gutt.

One of the easiest ways to get started is to have a task group brainstorm on a job, process, or service item that is *dull* and *monotonous* and that nobody likes to do. You will receive a lot of cooperation and involvement on how to improve this type of work because everybody can relate to it and feel that it is a goal he can understand and reach. For example, our precast-concrete operation can generate a lot of debris and concrete spill. This must be cleaned up every day. It is an undesirable and unfulfilling but necessary task. By assigning an entire crew rather than one cleaning man to clean up around their own work area, the amount of rubbish generated was reduced substantially, which was improvement of productivity by *reducing* waste rather than finding a more efficient way to pick up and remove it. We try to apply this principle in various processes.

### Communication
We review the existing lines and means of communication and encourage more open discussions to create a better understanding of the functions of each department or task group. Sometimes, what one department does or does not do affects the ability of another group to perform its job. For example, the bookkeeper must understand what effort and time are spent on filling out time cards, job reports, materials usage reports, and so on, in order to minimize this task for the production employees and to improve these report processes. If the engineering department can change the location of data on drawings or add additional information, it may save time for the various people who must read and interpret the drawings. To be able to achieve this type of productivity improvement, communication must be open and detailed. Better communication within work crews and between departments is constantly encouraged to promote a better understanding of the functions and parameters of each employee's job. All levels of management must participate in the communication process. In order to encourage maximum involvement of all employees, we must communicate more information than was done under the traditional "need-to-know" policy we have been using in the past.

### Goals and Measurement
Unlike in a manufacturing plant, measurement of productivity in the construction industry is difficult at first review. Measurement

should be made primarily against a standard or specific goal. There are many areas in which we can measure output over input at our plant in what we regard as "standard" terms: (1) the amount of concrete made per hour and per piece of equipment; (2) the number of square feet or cubic yards of product produced per man-hour; and (3) the amount of energy used per cubic yard of concrete. However, our Prestressed Concrete Division is similar to contracting work in that we do not produce standard products for inventory—each product is custom-made for a specific project. Since this type of custom work is difficult to measure against a standard, we have developed several other means of measurement.

1. Measure against the estimated bid item cost. This is a measure against a goal rather than a standard, since the bid item cost for the same type of product will vary from project to project, depending on its complexity.

2. A goal need not necessarily be long-range, and it can be based on yesterday's, last week's, last month's, last quarter's, or last year's outputs. Working with small task groups, it is relatively simple to set a goal to improve on what was performed last week, or in a similar situation, or for a similar product six months ago. Long-term data are desirable but not absolutely necessary to set a goal and measure the output versus input.

3. We do not attempt to set up an elaborate cost-gathering system for each improvement goal and do not avoid attempting an improvement simply because it is too difficult or time-consuming to measure the results within finite two-decimal-point figures. You do not need 100 percent accuracy in numbers to evaluate whether a particular function is being performed with more efficiency, better quality, or fewer people. If the office personnel develop a paperwork procedure that makes fewer copies, uses less filing time and space, and reaches more people quickly, it is not necessary to know the exact number of hours saved in comparison with previous methods.

4. In most cases, the obvious 20 percent to 50 percent improvements have occurred. We want to improve constantly, even if each improvement is only 2 percent to 5 percent. All our employees are capable of this type of improvement and are not apprehensive about attempting such smaller improvements.

5. Once you are successful at small improvements, larger proj-

ects can be attempted with confidence. All of us can work at reachable goals—walk before you run.

## Techniques for Improving Productivity

One of the best methods of improving productivity is to establish and maintain a strong training program for supervisors and their employees. Our training program for our first-line supervisors was a six-session, Saturday morning breakfast meeting that was structured to:

Improve their knowledge of the company, of their position, and of the products they are making.

Improve their attitude toward their position and make them appreciate how their actions and decisions fit into the overall operation.

Improve their skills in planning, organizing, leading, and controlling their work.

Also included was a refresher session, in conjunction with the engineering department, on how to better understand the shop drawings.

Cross-training of personnel—teaching them to handle various jobs or parts of jobs—is a very effective method of improving overall productivity. It is effective in at least two ways. First, when employees are absent or on vacation, the workload can be handled without excessive delay and costs. Second, having several different people handle the same task tends to improve methods and procedures, because it affords an opportunity to approach the task from a different point of view, and eventually the best method for a given task is used by everybody doing that job.

To improve the productivity of materials and energy, we have increased our control of the concrete we produce and use in the precast products, thereby reducing the amount of expensive and scarce cement we use to produce a desired result. Since all our concrete products are heat-cured, either by live steam or by electric radiant heat, every night to achieve high early strengths, we have installed temperature-monitoring equipment and automatic timers to conserve the expensive fuels.

Prevention of waste and scrap is another way to increase net productivity. Product inspection personnel have been added to the quality control department. The inspection procedure was planned and organized to minimize the number of errors that occur during the casting and installing of our products. The individual foremen have close communication with the inspectors. This procedure has greatly reduced repetition of errors and omissions. The percentage of remake costs, compared with sales, has dropped significantly, and a better overall quality awareness has been achieved. These are among the items that good quality control personnel can be assigned to study and implement in order to improve productivity.

The use of time-lapse photography in the construction field has proven to be very helpful in productivity improvement. A relatively inexpensive camera can be set up at a site and run unattended for four to six hours with one 50-foot roll of film. Before the camera is used, discussions are held with *all* employees on why, when, and where the camera will be set up. It is not used as a spy device, and all foremen and squad leaders are shown the final results of the filming. The camera is set up to take pictures at time intervals of two to ten seconds. The film is projected at normal speeds, with stop-action capability. The camera "sees" many things that are not normally apparent to a human observer, and those things become very obvious when viewed on film. Most of the improvements that have come about as a result of the use of the time-lapse camera have been picked up by the actual participants when they viewed the film. Examples of such items are:

The locations of water buckets, distance covered, and time spent going to and from water.

Excessive walking motion in performing certain tasks.

Location and procuring of tools. (Having more tools available saves a lot of time.)

Idle time and placement of equipment.

Concentrations of workers in confined areas trying to do several different tasks and getting in each other's way.

Visible evidence of how planning will ease workers' tasks.

Extending the range of foremen and supervisors. (In order to improve their productivity, they must observe what is going on, and the camera permits them to do this without having to be present.)

### *Motivation*

Productivity doesn't just happen; it must be planned. All employees, from top to bottom, must be involved—and continuously. We follow up on all suggestions—good, bad, or indifferent—and explain the final actions. The employees are involved because improved productivity is also to their benefit and assists in making their jobs more meaningful. You should be prepared to implement some minor and insignificant suggestions and ideas to keep the idea of productivity going.

At the beginning, your brainstorming sessions and follow-up meeting will be gripe sessions, and many alibis, excuses, and reasons will be brought forth as to why something can't be done or why it should not be changed. Continually stress the *positive* nature of improvement.

We attempt to get everyone involved, but this does not mean that no one is responsible for productivity improvement. Some kind of report, oral or written, at regular intervals, should be requested and insisted upon by various levels of management, from chief executive officer down to the line supervisor.

## PRODUCTIVITY IMPROVEMENTS IN THE ADMINISTRATIVE AREAS *

I will discuss some of the measurements and activities in the administrative areas of our company. When we started, we tried to develop some companywide measurements, such as payroll productivity indexes. We quickly realized that there was no one such thing, so we took a number of them. We print the results in monthly reports for the year with comparative information. The figures relate to the company as a whole. We compare such items as number of employees, unionized and nonunionized; total hours of work, including overtime hours; overtime percentage of the hours worked; pay per hour worked; sales per hour worked; operating profit per employee; assets per employee; and payroll percentage to sales. These have become indicative ratios that top management watches month after month. Because we felt that the range covered was rather broad, we are now working on division counterparts of each of these ratios.

Let's look at three of these measurements. In the case of the first one, the overtime percentage, a glance at the past 12 months' figures shows immediately when overtime is getting out of line. You can backtrack and find out where the problem is. The second and

* This section was prepared by Richard F. Martin.

third—sales per hour worked and operating profit per employee—are pretty good indications of what's happening within the company. We are working on some new ratios that will be discussed in the next section.

We don't limit our search for productivity improvement to operating areas. It's been said you can't measure administrative areas, but we think you can, and we've had some success in doing just that. Let's look at our accounting department. The accounting department has about 35 people. There are various small sections within the department: the billing department, the payroll department, a receivables department, and the typical payables department. The people in the billing department, on their own, developed a measurement of delivery tickets processed per employee per month. The range is from a low of 5,990 to a high of about 10,000. We don't have a standard yet, but we're accumulating information on what the average is, and from that we can develop a standard.

This is just one of the areas our accounting department is working on. It is also measuring processing of invoices by invoices-payable-department employees per month, as well as checks received and processed per receivables-department employee per month. Another item measured is manually typed billings per employee per month. Another is fuel cards (used as input for our computerized fuel-measuring system for our equipment) processed per employee per month. These are small items, but as our supervisors and managers measure activities, they begin to look for ways to improve the activity being measured.

Another area in the accounting department (you'll find this in every department, especially administrative departments) is cross-training. It is one of the most important tools we have. As a result of our cross-training program, billing clerks know what a payables clerk does and what every billing clerk in that department does. Cross-training helps you fill in quickly when an emergency arises. We do that consistently throughout all our departments.

Data processing is another one of our major departments, and we mentioned in our definition that the efficient use of information was part of productivity. The form shown in Figure 14-2 was developed by our data processing manager. It becomes a progress report for each project program. The person identified in the upper left-hand corner may be a programmer or systems analyst. It shows the reporting period (usually one month), the goals achieved during that

Figure 14-2. Project progress report—data processing department.

PROJECT STATUS

Name: _____

For: _____ Period Ending: _____

1. SPECIFIC GOALS ACHIEVED DURING REPORTING PERIOD.
2. PROBLEMS ENCOUNTERED THAT HAVE CAUSED OR COULD CAUSE A DELAY IN PROJECT OR SOME SPECIFIC GOAL(S).
3. AREAS IN WHICH THE MANAGER CAN ASSIST.
4. UNRESOLVED DECISIONS.
5. GOALS FOR NEXT REPORTING PERIOD.

reporting period, the problems encountered that might cause a delay in that project, areas about which the manager of the department is concerned, and any unresolved decisions. Goals for the next reporting period are displayed. A month after a report is issued, the data processing department manager reviews it again. This is done for each project within the data processing department.

Data processing is also measuring some rather nitty-gritty things: keystrokes per employee per minute in the keypunch operator department, the report issue date versus the scheduled issue date for each report, and the punches and the verifications per operator per month. It records the problems produced per month per data processing employee (a figure that might be too high). Again, cross-training is a major part of the operation. We mentioned earlier the use of the Data Analyzer, a data-retrieval system introduced to us by a study by Arizona State University's Productivity Institute. This has become a real productivity-enhancement tool for managers, since they normally have to go through a long, detailed process to get a program written and reports produced on a specific item.

Through educational sessions, we can train managers to write a short program in simplified computer language. They can then request directly from the computer, without going through a programmer, the specific report they need. These requests are prioritized and go directly to the computer; the reply comes back the next morning. So managers can receive quick one-shot information on special reports by communicating directly with the computer. This has become a very useful tool for us. It has not only provided a real manager education in data processing but also helped managers improve their own productivity.

We also took measurements in our human resources department. Our personnel services department started counting the masters it processed for the data processing department on employees, terminations, transfers, nonunion time slips, and so on. The first thing we did was count these items to see how many were processed per day. We used that information to compile weekly and monthly figures. Then, as a second step, we started putting down the time it took for each process. An interesting finding was that just by counting we were getting more done from the same people because they were involved and were trying to do better. From these measurements, we hope to set some standards so that we can determine medical claims that should be processed per hour per employee, for example, and identify future measurement and improvement areas.

Another example of productivity improvement occurred when the head of the personnel services department felt she needed another person in the department. She decided the first thing to do was to look at the work flow. So she had the people in her department write up their own work flow. The same group of people analyzed each other's work flow and came up with ideas on how to change the work flow.

The result was that we had almost four new jobs—but the need for an additional person disappeared, because the additional work had been absorbed within this work-flow pattern that the people had created. It was a very interesting and enlightening approach to productivity right down at the clerical level, and it worked. We began cross-training. Through that process, everybody knew what everybody else was doing, because these people had developed their own work flow.

Our purchasing area has a productivity improvement committee that is fairly new. It is beginning to get into the process with cross-training and with reviewing blanket purchase orders. It decided to examine each one carefully. The number of price reductions and corrections that have already taken place just as a result of that one project is amazing.

This gives you some idea of the things that are being pursued in the various administrative areas of The Tanner Companies. They are simple ideas, perhaps, and easy to measure, but they have been starting places. That is probably the first thing we learned in our productivity program: you've got to start somewhere. We started by just counting the pieces of paper we were working on—but it led to complete work-flow change within the department.

## PRODUCTIVITY IMPROVEMENTS IN THE MATERIALS DIVISION *

Within the Materials Division, three recent productivity-related improvement efforts have been particularly successful. The first of these is the development and use of what we call the United Metro Costing System—an operations cost monitoring system designed primarily for operations, not for the accounting function of the company. The second is the use of a data-retrieval system, the Data Analyzer computer software package, which was mentioned previously. The third is the close relationship this division has with our data processing department.

1. The heart of the United Metro Costing System is a group of product reports that have three basic format features: first, a rolling 12-month trend for all data on the report; second, spending levels and unit cost figures; and third, analytical figures. We include a rolling 12-month trend for the data so the superintendent or manager doesn't have to rely on his memory or dig through his files for past months' records. The spending levels and unit cost figures for each product include comparisons of cost with budget or forecast figures. The analytical figures include productivity measurements of direct labor, equipment hours, and total man-hours per ton or cubic yard produced, indicating the reason for changes in spending levels or unit costs. Plant downtime and efficiency percentages are given on some of the reports as well.

This may appear to be too many measurements, but our superintendents helped design these reports to give them needed information. The system has been in operation for some time now, and our superintendents have confidence in the accuracy of the figures and rely on them for evaluating and making decisions concerning their operations. Use of these very detailed measurements has resulted

* This section was prepared by Stephen Jones.

in overall improvements, as indicated by some larger, broader-brush productivity measurements that we monitor, for example, usage of materials (in pounds per cubic yard):

| | 1976 | 1977 | 1978 | 1979 (8 months) |
|---|---|---|---|---|
| Cement | 474 | 454 | 425 | 395 |
| Fly Ash | 44 | 57 | 77 | 110 |

These figures show an improvement in the cement/fly-ash ratio per cubic yard of concrete. As indicated, the pounds of cement per cubic yard of concrete have decreased as we have been able to add greater quantities of fly ash, distributed by a subsidiary of the company. On the average, we are able to use more fly ash—a much cheaper material—per cubic yard of concrete. The fly ash provides the same quality and also helps deal with the cement shortage we have been faced with for many months. Now, let's look at plant production, in tons per man hour:

| | 1976 | 1977 | 1978 | 1979 (8 months) |
|---|---|---|---|---|
| Total Company | 13 | 15 | 16 | 17 |
| Phoenix Plants | 14 | 16 | 19 | 20 |

These figures on plant operations give another indication or productivity improvement. The figures represent a total tonnage for all sand and gravel products produced by our plants. We move on to a transportation productivity analysis for our Phoenix plants only (see Table 14-1).

These transportation figures show improvements that have been achieved in two ways. First, we are running a larger number of ten-yard trucks than eight-yard trucks. Also, because of the volume we are enjoying in the Phoenix area, we are averaging close to a full load in our eight-yard trucks as opposed to a figure that was close to 5½–6 yards per trip per truck for the smaller mixers a few years ago. By having a larger number of larger-capacity trucks and making use of the capacity in all the trucks, improvement in productivity has been achieved.

2. The second area of productivity improvement in our Materials Division is the successful use of a data-retrieval system. It is a computer software system in which the user, after a short training period, writes his own program in a fairly simple computer language and submits this directly to the computer. If the user has

Table 14-1. Transportation productivity analysis for ready mix (Phoenix plants only).

| Productivity Measure | Fiscal Year 1976 | Fiscal Year 1977 | Fiscal Year 1978 | 8 Months, Fiscal Year 1979 |
|---|---|---|---|---|
| (c.y./hr.) | 3.01 | 3.07 | 3.26 | 3.31 |
| Average time per trip (hours) | 2.44 | 2.41 | 2.46 | 2.56 |
| Average size load (c.y.) | 7.33 | 7.41 | 8.02 | 8.47 |
| Cubic yards | 442,265.9 | 517,049.9 | 692,890.8 | 530,870.7 |
| Driver hours | 146,929.7 | 168,539.5 | 212,316.6 | 160,424.7 |
| Trips | 60,316 | 69,810 | 86,445 | 62,688 |

done his homework well, he gets his report the next morning. It has turned out to be a very valuable tool for the Materials Division and for The Tanner Companies in general. It is used to produce one-time reports for the individual manager or to produce reports on a regular basis. We have also found it useful to our programmers in the development of regular programs such as the United Metro Costing System.

As an example of the use we are making of the Data Analyzer, during the month of November, 19 requests a day were submitted, for a monthly total of 411 Data Analyzer requests. It is interesting that we were led to investigate this software package through a project with Arizona State University's Productivity Institute. As a result of the project, we decided to purchase the system and have been very pleased with its results.

3. Finally, the cooperation that our Materials Division has had from our data processing department has been a key element in developing the reporting and measurement systems we use and the confidence our supervisors and managers have in these systems. An important element of this cooperation has been the establishment of a person to act as the interface between operations and data processing in developing and maintaining our systems. Our company is also fortunate to have as manager of data processing a man who is aware of user needs and attempts to meet these needs with the computer services he controls.

## FUTURE OUTLOOK

The following are some of the future objectives and directions for the productivity program in the company. First we have scheduled follow-up meetings with our division and department personnel to generate greater involvement in the process by our hourly employees. Second, we are developing a value-added-per-man-hour measurement, which we feel will be a key productivity measurement. It will monitor those areas, primarily labor and equipment, that we control, and put these labor and equipment costs together with man-hours to measure the value added per man-hour on both a corporate and division level. Third, we will continue the exchange of success stories and techniques among our division and department committees; progress reports from these committees will be given at the monthly meeting of the corporate productivity committee. Finally, we are continuing to stress with all our employees the idea that productivity improvement is a continual process. It doesn't just happen; it must be planned and worked for constantly.

# Part III
# SELECTED ISSUES IN PRODUCTIVITY

CLEMENT F. PREIWISCH

# 15
# GAO Study on Productivity–Sharing Programs

THE GENERAL Accounting Office (GAO) was established by the Budget and Accounting Act of 1921 to assist Congress in its oversight of federal agencies and programs. It primarily conducts three types of audits, reviews, or evaluations:

1. Audits of financial transactions and compliance with federal laws and regulations.
2. Audits of efficiency and economy matters dealing with the operation of federal agencies and programs.
3. Audits of the results or effectiveness of the operation of federal programs and activities.

The GAO is headedby Comptroller General Elmer B. Staats. He was appointed to serve a 15-year term and can be removed only through impeachment proceedings. Operating under his leadership, the office has nine functional operating divisions, a field operations division with 15 regional offices throughout the United States, and an international division with offices in numerous locations around the world.

GAO has a staff of more than 5,000 people, of whom 4,000 are professionals or specialists. These disciplines include accountants, attorneys, economists, engineers, social scientists, actuaries, mathematicians, medical doctors, and computer specialists.

In fiscal year 1979, GAO issued 983 reports, of which 684 went to the Congress, congressional committees, or members of Congress.

GAO's operating expenses in fiscal year 1979 were $181 million, of which $145 million was for personnel costs.

Fiscal savings on the basis of GAO efforts in 1979 amounted to an estimated $2.6 billion. Many important recommendations deal with the way that federal programs are managed and administered and are not quantifiable.

This chapter's discussion of GAO's study of productivity-sharing programs will include the background and scope of the study, findings on the benefits resulting from productivity-sharing plans, factors considered in adopting productivity-sharing plans, difficulties encountered with the plans, the impact of federal policies on the plans, and finally, issues that should be considered by firms in adopting a productivity-sharing program.

## INTRODUCTION

The decline of the nation's productivity is a matter of increasing concern, because productivity growth is an important factor in controlling inflation. From 1948 to 1965, productivity growth in the nonfarm business sector averaged 2.6 percent annually, whereas growth in hourly compensation averaged 4.6 percent. Between 1965 and 1973, the growth rate fell to 2 percent per year, whereas hourly compensation increased to 5.5 percent. Since 1973, the average annual rate of growth in productivity has been less than 1 percent. During the same period, hourly compensation increased at an average annual rate of 9 percent. When wages rise without corresponding growth in output, the costs for businesses increase. In order to maintain profit margins, firms raise prices to cover their higher unit labor costs. The result is more inflation and a reduced standard of living. Many factors are blamed for the productivity slowdown, including:

- The high cost of government regulation and reporting requirements
- A reduction in capital investments to improve productive capacity
- A decline in research and development activities that lead to innovations in technology
- The change in composition of the workforce
- A shift away from manufacturing to service occupations

Researchers, however, have never been able to account for all of the productivity changes, using these variables. Another variable often mentioned is the decreasing motivation or dedication of the workforce to productivity improvement. Management has increasingly recognized that a financial incentive or some method of improving the quality of working life can result in increased productivity. Moreover, businesses have also recognized that workers often know more about their jobs than anyone else and can make valuable suggestions for improvement. As a result, businesses have adopted a wide variety of incentive programs to stimulate performance.

A 1975 study at New York University (supported by the National Science Foundation) investigated worker motivation, productivity, and job satisfaction and found that the principal factor which helped create highly productive and satisfied workers was recognition and reward for effective performance. The study concluded that the reward should be whatever is meaningful to the employee—financial or psychological, or both. Many types of programs exist to motivate employees.

One form of group incentive that has received attention recently is productivity sharing. Productivity-sharing plans are designed to measure the productivity of a plant or firm and to share the benefits of gains in productivity with all participating employees. The three commonly used plans are Scanlon, Rucker, and Improshare.

Productivity-sharing plans differ in the formula used to compute productivity savings and in the implementation method used. Both Scanlon and Rucker plans generally measure the payroll of the plant or firm against total dollar sales, compared with the past average of several years. Improshare measures output against total hours worked. Therefore, Scanlon and Rucker plans use dollars as the measurement unit, and Improshare uses hours. Some plans adjust the formula used for bonus calculations to remove increases or decreases in the selling prices of the product.

All three plans are flexible as to the composition of the group involved in the plan. Direct production workers and management may be included. Engineered standards are not necessary for the functioning of any plan. Scanlon and Rucker plans, however, rely on labor-management productivity committees as the focal points for worker involvement and plan implementation. Improshare plans allow for employee productivity input but are not built around such committees.

## SCOPE OF STUDY

GAO studied productivity-sharing programs as part of a broader congressionally requested review of the Council on Wage and Price Stability's efforts to stimulate productivity. A separate report to the Congress is being issued on this matter. Productivity-sharing programs were selected because the Council was initially unwilling to exempt them from the president's voluntary wage and price standards despite indications that they provide a noninflationary technique for improving productivity. Our goals were to determine how productivity-sharing programs operate and what benefits result; whether long-term increases in productivity can be realized through productivity sharing; and what impact federal policies, particularly those of the Council on Wage and Price Stability, have on productivity-sharing programs at the firm level.

We interviewed officials of 54 firms nationwide to discuss their experiences with productivity sharing and other incentive programs. Although the number of firms involved in productivity-sharing programs is not known, it is thought to be less than 1,000. Through contacts and visits with consultants and productivity organizations, we developed a list of 78 firms believed to have productivity-sharing programs and 18 firms said to have such programs under consideration. We sent letters to these firms, asking them to participate in our study, and followed up with telephone calls to determine their interest.

In order to obtain cooperation, participatng officials were assured that their names and the names of their firms would be kept confidential. Pledges of confidentiality were considered necessary because firms often desire to maintain a low profile about their plans and many of these firms view their programs as giving them a competitive advantage.

From our lists we selected and interviewed 36 firms that had productivity-sharing programs and nine firms that had either rejected adoption of a productivity-sharing program or were still considering implementing one. Firms with productivity-sharing programs were selected to provide a cross section among different types of plans, sizes of firms, and lengths of time in place. Because of the small number of firms identified as considering the adoption of a productivity-sharing program, we interviewed all nine companies that agreed to participate. We found that two of these firms had considered but ultimately rejected a productivity-sharing plan.

The limited number of productivity-sharing plans included in the study suggests a note of caution. The financial and nonfinancial benefits reported by the plans studied should not be construed as being representative of all productivity-sharing plans in existence. Despite this limitation, the benefits reported by the plans studied illustrate the advantages that can be achieved by firms adopting productivity-sharing plans.

In order to broaden the report's focus, we interviewed nine firms that did not have productivity-sharing programs but had other types of incentive programs, such as quality of working life, profit sharing, and incentives based on engineered standards. These were identified through a review of applicable literature and were assured the same degree of confidentiality that was promised the productivity-sharing firms.

We also conducted a roundtable discussion with business and labor leaders, as well as economists and others knowledgeable in the field, to discuss the Council on Wage and Price Stability, inflation, and productivity. Participants were asked to respond to specific questions regarding current Council policies relating to the treatment of productivity sharing and other group productivity programs and on the roles these programs might play in anti-inflation policy.

## TYPES OF INCENTIVE PLANS

Let's look at a profile of the firms we interviewed. Thirty-six of the firms we interviewed had productivity-sharing programs. All but three of the plans were active at the time of our review. The different types of plans investigated in our study were as follows:

| Type of plan | Number of firms |
|---|---|
| Scanlon | 17 |
| Rucker | 8 |
| Improshare | 11 |
| Other | 2 |
| Total | 38 |

The number of plans adds up to 38, because two firms had different plans operating at two or more of its plants.

Twenty-two firms had a productivity-sharing plan in effect for less than five years. The newest plan was eight months old at the time of our review; the oldest was 29 years. Table 15-1 shows the age of the plans.

Table 15-1. Age of productivity-sharing plans in GAO study.

| Age of productivity-sharing plan | Number of firms | Percent |
|---|---|---|
| Less than one year | 2 | 5.6 |
| One year or more, but less than three years | 14 | 38.9 |
| Three years or more, but less than five years | 6 | 16.7 |
| Five years or more, but less than ten years | 6 | 16.7 |
| Ten years or more, but less than twenty years | 3 | 8.3 |
| Twenty years or more | 5 | 13.9 |
| Total | 36 | 100.1 |

Productivity-sharing programs had been considered at nine of the firms we contacted. Seven of these companies had not made a final decision on whether or not to adopt a plan, and the remaining two firms decided against productivity sharing.

The final category of nine firms contacted consisted of those that did not have productivity-sharing programs. The firms interviewed had 13 incentive plans, as follows:

| Type of plan | Number of firms |
|---|---|
| Individual or group incentives based on engineered standards | 5 |
| Profit sharing | 4 |
| Quality of work life | 4 |
| Total | 13 |

### Nature of Businesses

Few service organizations have adopted or considered adopting productivity-sharing programs (see Table 15-2). Most of the firms we contacted were in the manufacturing sector.

Table 15-2. Nature of business of firms in GAO study.

| | Productivity-sharing firms | Firms considering productivity sharing | Other firms | Total |
|---|---|---|---|---|
| *Manufacturing* | | | | |
| Furniture | 4 | — | — | 4 |
| Paper, fiber, and wood products | 1 | 1 | — | 2 |
| Chemicals | 1 | 2 | — | 3 |
| Rubber, plastic products | 2 | — | — | 2 |
| Industrial and farm equipment | 6 | 1 | 1 | 8 |
| Glass, concrete, abrasives | 3 | — | 1 | 4 |
| Metal manufacturing | 3 | — | — | 3 |
| Metal products | 9 | 1 | — | 10 |
| Electronics, appliances | 1 | 2 | 1 | 4 |
| Motor vehicles | 3 | — | 1 | 4 |
| Office equipment | — | — | 2 | 2 |
| Other manufacturing | 2 | 1 | 1 | 4 |
| | 35 | 8 | 7 | 50 |
| *Service* | | | | |
| Hospitals | 1 | — | — | 1 |
| Insurance | — | — | 1 | 1 |
| Banking, savings and loan | — | 1 | 1 | 2 |
| | 1 | 1 | 2 | 4 |
| Total | 36 | 9 | 9 | 54 |

Thirty-five firms were either publicly owned stock corporations or subsidiaries. The remaining 19 firms were private or family owned. Officials at 11 firms described their companies as capital-intensive, 21 said their firms were labor-intensive, and 22 said their firms were both labor- and capital-intensive. Twenty-eight, or 52 percent, of the firms were unionized.

## Size of Firms

The size of the firms contacted ranged from a small manufacturing company with fewer than 100 employees and $1.5 million in sales to a multibillion-dollar corporation with more than 100,000 employees. Table 15-3 reflects the size of firms that employed productivity-sharing plans.

Table 15-3. Size of firms in GAO study.

| Annual sales | Firms | | Number of employees | Firms | |
|---|---|---|---|---|---|
| | Number | Per cent | | Number | Per cent |
| Less than $50 million | 21 | 38.9 | Less than 500 | 17 | 31.5 |
| $50–$99 million | 4 | 7.4 | 500–999 | 7 | 13.0 |
| $100–$499 million | 9 | 16.7 | 1,000–9,999 | 15 | 27.8 |
| $500–$999 million | 7 | 13.0 | 10,000–49,999 | 10 | 18.5 |
| $1 billion and greater | 11 | 20.4 | 50,000 and greater | 4 | 7.4 |
| | 52 $^a$ | | | 53 $^b$ | |

$^a$ Information not available in three cases.
$^b$ Information not available in one case.

## BENEFITS FROM PRODUCTIVITY–SHARING PLANS

Proponents of productivity-sharing programs say such plans can increase a firm's productivity and can provide many benefits to both the firm and its employees, including the following:

Higher wages in the form of bonuses to employees
Increased profitability for the company
A spirit of cooperation among employees and between employees and management
Greater involvement and commitment of employees to their work

We questioned officials at the 36 firms with productivity-sharing plans to determine what monetary and nonmonetary benefits had resulted. Firms were also asked to provide financial information on the savings that had been achieved as a result of their productivity-sharing plan. At 15 firms we interviewed employee or union representatives to obtain their perspectives on the results of the productivity-sharing plan at their company. Employee or union representatives were not interviewed at most of the other firms, because there was no employee representative or they were not readily available. Officials at several firms were unwilling to allow us to interview their employees.

The information we obtained provided ample evidence of the value of productivity sharing. Many firms achieved significant savings from their plans and noted many nonmonetary benefits as well. Also, the majority of firms expressed satisfaction with their productivity-sharing plans. Moreover, most officials we interviewed at firms that had other types of incentive programs believed that these programs resulted in significant savings for their company.

### Monetary Benefits from Productivity–Sharing Plans

Twenty-four firms provided financial information on the results of their productivity-sharing programs. Savings resulting from these plans averaged 16.9 percent of the workforce cost of participating employees, which includes salaries, wages, and fringe benefits (not including productivity-sharing bonuses).

There was little difference in performance between firms on the basis of sales volume. Savings averaged 17.3 percent at the 13 firms that had annual sales of less than $100 million. At the other 11 firms, annual sales were $100 million or greater and savings averaged 18.3 percent.

During our roundtable discussion, several union officials questioned whether productivity-sharing plans could provide long-term benefits. For example, one official stated that productivity-sharing plans can improve productivity in the short term but, as time passes, benefits begin to taper off, causing discontent and finally discontinuance of the program. However, at several of the firms, such criticism was more often directed at incentive systems based on engineered standards than at productivity-sharing plans.

Among the 24 firms providing financial data, those that had productivity-sharing plans in effect the longest showed the best performance. Fifteen of these firms had productivity-sharing plans in operation for less than five years. Savings for these firms averaged 8.5 percent. Nine firms operated plans for five years or more and, of these, seven provided at least five years of financial data. The savings for these seven firms averaged almost 29 percent for the most recent four-year period. Individually, the savings for these seven firms ranged from 13.5 to 77.4 percent.

For example, a large manufacturing company had all 360 employees at one of its plants covered by a productivity-sharing plan. The firm reported savings averaging 77.4 percent of participating workforce cost for the last five years. Savings were attributed to such factors as improved processing techniques, better utilization of equipment, and reduced energy consumption. In the last three years, sales increased by $6 million, and cost of goods sold decreased by $1.2 million.

In another case, a manufacturing firm with approximately 2,000 of its 2,300 domestic employees covered by a productivity-sharing plan saved an average of 24 percent of participating workforce cost in the last five years, and its productivity-sharing plan annual savings ranged from 20 to 35 percent. A company official stated that savings were realized from employee suggestions and because employees were working "smarter and harder." In 1979, the remaining domestic employees were put under the plan.

The majority of firms with productivity-sharing plans did not make periodic assessments of the savings realized to determine their source and nature. Only nine firms indicated that they made such an assessment and, of these, only four told us that these assessments were documented. At a number of firms, officials told us that the source and nature of savings were difficult to measure. One company official said that improvements resulting from employee suggestions made ten years ago still benefited the company. However, the company did not know to what extent these improvements

Table 15-4. Most important factors cited by firms realizing increased savings from productivity-sharing plans.

| Factor mentioned | Number of firms |
|---|---|
| Improved performance of employees | 10 |
| Change in employees' attitudes and job interest | 10 |
| Increased productivity | 8 |
| Reduction in scrap, rework, and waste | 8 |
| Better use of materials, supplies, and equipment | 8 |
| Cost-saving suggestions | 7 |
| Improved processes or procedures | 6 |
| Better product quality | 5 |
| Other | 5 |
| Total | 67 |

contributed to current savings. We asked the 36 firms with productivity-sharing plans what they believed were the most important factors in realizing the increased savings. We received 67 responses, as is shown in Table 15-4.

Since almost all firms providing financial data paid bonuses on a weekly or monthly basis, it was not possible to assess whether the payment cycle influenced performance.

### Nonmonetary Benefits from Productivity–Sharing Programs

We asked the 36 firms whether their productivity-sharing plans have resulted in nonmonetary benefits such as improved labor-management relations, fewer grievances, less absenteeism, and reduced turnover. Figure 15-1 shows the results of our findings.

Other benefits of productivity-sharing plans mentioned by some firms included better teamwork, increased job satisfaction, closer identification with the firm, and less resistance to change.

### Firms' Satisfaction with Productivity–Sharing Plans

Thirty of the firms (or 83 percent) expressed satisfaction with their productivity-sharing plans. At 22 firms, officials said that the benefits originally anticipated when the plan was adopted were

Figure 15-1. Nonmonetary benefits of productivity-sharing plans.

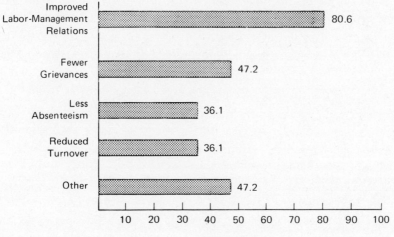

realized. At several firms, we were told that higher bonuses were expected than had actually materialized. Nevertheless, all 30 firms believed that the current benefits to the firm of their productivity-sharing plan warranted its continuation. Twenty-eight firms said they had never considered abandoning their program in favor of another or no program at all. Moreover, 23 firms believed that their productivity-sharing plan gave them a competitive advantage in marketing their products or services.

### Union or Employee Representative Satisfaction with Productivity–Sharing Programs

At most of the 15 firms where we interviewed an employee or union representative, they indicated that the productivity-sharing plan had a positive effect on the workforce. Representatives a 14 firms rated the present climate between labor and management as good or excellent. Of these, 12 told us that this was an improvement over what had existed prior to implementation of the productivity-sharing plan. Representatives at six firms indicated that the improvement in the climate between labor and management was substantial, as can be seen in Table 15-5.

Employee and union representatives most often cited increased wages as reasons for the improved climate between management and the workforce. Other reasons, shown in Table 15-6, include improved labor-management relations, better communication, a greater voice in management of the company, and better acceptance of employees' suggestions by management.

Table 15-5. How satisfied union or employee representatives were with the productivity-sharing programs.

| Number of firms | Present climate between management and the workforce | Present climate compared with climate before introduction of productivity-sharing plan | | | |
|---|---|---|---|---|---|
| | | Substantial improvement | Some improvement | No change | Worse |
| 10 | Excellent | 5 | 4 | 1 | — |
| 4 | Good | 1 | 2 | 1 | — |
| 1 | Poor | — | — | — | 1 |

Table 15-6. What employee satisfaction resulted from.

| Comments | Number of responses |
|---|---|
| Increased wages | 11 |
| Improved labor-management relations | 6 |
| Better communication | 5 |
| Greater voice in management of the company | 1 |
| Better acceptance of employees' suggestions by management | 1 |

## FACTORS AFFECTING THE ADOPTION OF A PRODUCTIVITY–SHARING PLAN

Although productivity-sharing programs have been around for many years, they have not as yet gained widespread acceptance. Nevertheless, there appears to be a growing interest in productivity sharing by many firms. Although the earliest programs were adopted primarily by privately owned companies, many publicly owned corporations have also begun to adopt them.

We asked firms why they were considering or had adopted a productivity-sharing plan, who was covered by the plan, what the bases of bonuses were, and how often they were paid. Firms were also asked whether consultants had any role in the plan's adoption or implementation. In addition, we inquired as to whether employees had any voice in adopting a plan and how they were assured of the fairness and propriety of bonus payments once the plan began functioning.

### Why a Productivity–Sharing Plan Was Adopted

Less than 40 percent of the firms specifically cited improved productivity as a reason for adopting a productivity-sharing program. Other reasons given by firms for adopting a program (see Figure 15-2) included dissatisfaction with existing incentive programs; the desire to establish an incentive program; concern for employees, employee morale, or attitude; price competition; and labor-management problems. Similar reasons were also mentioned by the firms that had considered or were considering adoption of a productivity program.

Figure 15-2. Reasons given for adopting a productivity-sharing plan.

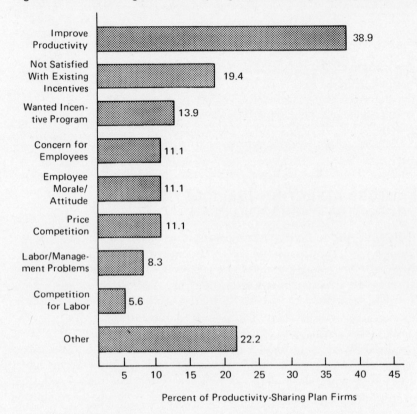

Percent of Productivity-Sharing Plan Firms

Eight of the firms contacted because they operated other types of incentive programs told us they had never considered using productivity sharing.

How these reasons influenced firms can be seen from the following example. An official of one large corporation told us that although the firm was successful, it was believed that productivity could be improved. The company was experiencing high employee turnover, and there seemed to be a general lack of company dedication. Moreover, facilities and equipment were not being used to capacity, and product quality was not completely satisfactory. This official had been interested in productivity-sharing programs for many years and through his efforts convinced others in top management to try the program.

### Employee Coverage by the Productivity–Sharing Plan

In general, the smaller the company, the higher the percentage of employees covered by the productivity-sharing program. Many of the smaller firms had 100 percent participation. The largest corporation contacted, on the other hand, tended to limit coverage to one or two plants, or to a small segment of the workforce.

Usually when a productivity-sharing plan was put into effect, coverage was extended to all categories of employees. Twenty-eight of the firms (or 78 percent) included supervisory, administrative, and/or production support personnel as well as direct production workers. Eight firms reported that their plans covered only production workers. In most cases new employees were covered by the plan after an initial waiting period of from 30 to 90 days. However, at 11 firms new employees participated immediately.

### Relation to Wages, Benefits, and Unionization

Productivity-sharing plans were not used as a substitute for competitive wages and benefits. More than 90 percent of the firms surveyed indicated that employees who earned bonuses also received wages and benefits that were competitive with those of other firms in their geographical areas. This information is shown in Table 15-7.

Table 15-7. Productivity sharing and competitive wages and benefits.

| Salaries, wages, and fringe benefits (not including bonus) | Employees receiving bonuses | | Employees not receiving bonuses | |
|---|---|---|---|---|
| | Number of firms | Percent | Number of firms | Percent |
| Better | 13 | 37.1 | 4 | 11.4 |
| Same | 19 | 54.3 | 11 | 31.4 |
| Worse | 3 | 8.6 | 2 | 5.7 |
| Not applicable | — | — | 18 | 51.4 |
| | $35^b$ | 100.0 | $35^a$ | 99.9 |

$a$ Not applicable because all employees at the facility where productivity sharing was in effect received bonuses.
$b$ Information not readily available from one firm.

It did not appear that productivity-sharing plans were established to avoid unionization. Twenty-one, or almost 60 percent, of the 36 firms with productivity-sharing plans had unions at the locations where a plan was established. Moreover, of the remaining 15 firms, only one indicated that a reason for adopting a plan was a fear of unionization. Among the nine firms that were considering or had considered adoption of a plan, five were unionized.

### Roles of Consultants and Employees

Thirty-two firms used consultants to help design and implement their productivity-sharing programs. Consultants were also used at 6 of these firms after the plan was implemented to monitor progress, attend committee meetings, and help to resolve any problems that arose. The four firms that did not use consultants had productivity-sharing plans that measured output against total hours worked. An official at one of these firms told us that he designed the plan after extensively researching productivity-sharing plans. At another firm, a consultant made a presentation on productivity sharing to company officials. However, the firm ultimately designed and implemented the program itself.

At 18 firms employees voted on the productivity-sharing program prior to adoption. The approval rate ranged from 60 to 96 percent. Seven of these firms polled their employees again after the plan had been operating for a period of time to see if they wanted the plan to continue. In all seven cases, the employees voted to continue the plan and, except in one case, the approval percentage was as high as or higher than the initial vote.

### Bonus Considerations

The bonus formulas used at 18 firms measured the payroll of the plant or firm against gross sales, adjusted for returns and allowances. Twelve firms measured output against total hours worked. Six firms modified their formulas so that they were based on other factors. For example, a manufacturing company had modified its Scanlon Plan so that the formula was based on profit rather than on sales. A bonus was earned in any month to the extent that profit for that month exceeded one-twelfth of 5.25 percent of the company's net worth. Any bonus earned was shared 56–44 between the company and participating employees.

At all 36 firms the savings resulting from the productivity-sharing plan were split between the company and the employees. The firms' share of the savings ranged from a low of 25 percent to a high of 79 percent. In many productivity-sharing plans, a portion of the bonus is set aside to offset deficit periods. At the end of the year, any balance remaining in the reserve is usually distributed to participating employees as a year-end bonus. Twenty firms with productivity-sharing plans reported that a portion of the bonus, ranging from 5 to 33 percent, was retained as a reserve.

A factor that contributes to the success of a productivity-sharing plan is that employees are assured bonus determinations are being made equitably and fairly. Twenty-seven firms said that bonus payments were audited by internal or external auditors, or both. At 17 firms the results of audits were communicated to employees. The remaining 19 firms identified the methods shown in Table 15-8 to assure employees of equitable treatment.

Table 15-8. Methods used to assure employees of the fairness and propriety of bonus payments.

| Response: Method used | Number of firms |
|---|---|
| Financial data available to employees. | 10 |
| Bonus results discussed with screening committees and/or other employee representatives. | 9 |
| Bonus results posted on company bulletin boards. | 7 |
| Bonus results published in company newsletter or paper. | 2 |
| Consultant reviews results and discusses with employees. | 1 |
| Trust exists between management and employees. | 1 |
| Total | 30 |

Having described why the firms in our study adopted productivity-sharing programs and what circumstances were involved, let's look now at the difficulties encountered in establishing and operating these programs.

## DIFFICULTIES ENCOUNTERED WITH PRODUCTIVITY–SHARING PROGRAMS

Despite the numerous benefits claimed for productivity-sharing plans, many pitfalls exist that can affect their success. When a firm attempts to establish a productivity-sharing plan, it may have to overcome resistance by employees and management. Some firms may encounter difficulties trying to develop a workable bonus formula. Once the productivity-sharing plan begins functioning, other problems may develop because the plan was not properly implemented or management was not fully committed to it. Also, if the plan is not closely monitored or if financial reverses occur, expected savings may not materialize. These and other problems can result in the ultimate demise of a firm's productivity-sharing plan.

Eighteen, or 50 percent, of the firms said they had encountered obstacles when they implemented their productivity-sharing programs. These firms most often cited resistance by employees or management as the obstacle. Other problems cited involved market fluctuations, development of an acceptable accounting and reporting system, and the threatened revocation of an organization's tax-exempt status.

Various explanations were mentioned for employee and management resistance. In some cases, employees on piecework feared a loss of income if productivity sharing was adopted. One firm allayed this concern by guaranteeing the wages of its piecework employees for a specified period after productivity sharing was implemented. When another firm implemented a productivity-sharing plan that covered only its production employees, nonparticipating employees resented not being included.

Management resistance at several firms was attributed to the difficult adjustment of some managers to the participative management concept. One firm reported that although employee turnover decreased because of it productivity-sharing plan, turnover among managers had increased.

Three of the seven firms that were considering adoption of productivity sharing indicated that the ability to develop an appropriate bonus formula would be a major influence on whether they ultimately adopted a plan. At one firm a lack of adequate historical records made it difficult to develop a base period. An official at another firm said that determination of an appropriate base period was complicated by the fact that the firm's product mix varied substantially from year to year. The third firm, described by a company official as highly capital-intensive, was trying to develop a bonus formula that accurately reflected productivity gains by the employees and was not affected by price increases.

Other factors being weighed by firms considering adoption of a productivity-sharing plan included fear of rejection by the union, the need for stronger commitment by management, the need to raise current productivity to an acceptable level, and the necessity of improving markets for the company's product and increasing profitability so that a bonus could be paid.

The two firms that elected not to adopt a productivity-sharing plan gave differing reasons for their decision. At one firm, the consultant was too slow in helping the firm implement the plan. This resulted in both management and employees becoming frustrated by the long, drawn-out process. At the other firm, corporate headquarters rejected the plant's request to adopt a plan.

Three firms had discontinued their productivity-sharing plans and three others did not believe that the current benefits from their plans warranted their continuation. Numerous reasons were given for the lack of success at these six firms, including:

Financial difficulties
Lack of commitment or dedication
Inadequate plan design or implementation
Few or no bonus payments
Failure to develop a good communications system between labor
    and management
Insufficient monitoring of performance
Use of a questionable bonus formula

Eight other firms took note of similar problems with their productivity-sharing plans, but of lesser severity. All of these firms believed that the current benefits outweighed any disadvantages.

Most of the problems mentioned in adopting or operating plans were attributed to internal factors. However, there may be conditions beyond the control of a firm that may have an impact on the success of a productivity-sharing plan. One of these factors is business conditions that adversely affect a firm's sales and profitability and force it to lay off employees. Others might be the growth of government regulation and the impact of federal policies.

## FEDERAL POLICIES' EFFECT ON PRODUCTIVITY–SHARING PROGRAMS

The growing cost of government regulation is a major factor in the national decline in productivity. Environmental, health, and safety regulations, for example, have forced businesses to increase their capital expenditures, and reporting and record-keeping requirements have necessitated the expansion of administrative staff. Since businesses do not have unlimited resources, funds needed to comply with federal regulations must come at the expense of monies used to improve output.

Besides increasing costs, government regulations impede managements' freedom to run their businesses. For example, in establishing the pay standards for the first year of the president's voluntary anti-inflation program, the Council on Wage and Price Stability refused to allow exceptions for productivity sharing, as well as most other productivity-incentive programs. The Council's rationale was that these programs do not have any significant value in increasing aggregate productivity, reward all workers regardless of individual performance, and are often measured in dollars rather than units of output. The Council's pay standards, however, allowed a firm to apply for an exception or adjustment in cases of undue hardship or gross inequity.

We asked our study participants whether there were any federal policies that were detrimental to their programs. In particular, we questioned them to determine what effect, if any, the wage and price standards had on their incentive plans. Finally, firms were requested to provide suggestions on what the federal government should do to increase the viability of productivity sharing and other productivity-incentive programs at the firm level. We were really surprised by the responses we got in this area.

The majority of firms interviewed did not believe there were any federal policies that were detrimental to or impaired the operation of their productivity-sharing program. Four firms indicated that overtime requirements of the Fair Labor Standards Act conflicted with their programs. Officials at five firms told us that government regulations and reporting requirements indirectly affected their productivity-sharing plans. Because considerable resources had to be devoted to meeting these requirements, company productivity was less.

At all 36 firms with productivity-sharing plans we were told that the requirements of the Environmental Protection Agency and the Occupational Safety and Health Administration had little or no effect on moving their company closer to adopting a plan.

The lack of an exemption for productivity-sharing programs in the wage and price guidelines had little effect on the firms we surveyed. Although most firms contacted were critical of the Council's wage and price guidelines, none of them indicated that the policy regarding productivity-sharing plans had caused them to reduce or restrict bonus payments. Some firms believed that their plans were exempt because they were in place prior to the wage and price guidelines. Other firms either were not aware of the restriction or, if they were aware, chose to ignore it.

Thirty-five of the 36 firms said that the guidelines did not have any impact on their plans. Officials at the other firm said that the Council's inability to control inflation was hurting its plan because the company paid cost-of-living adjustments from the bonus pool. Higher cost-of-living increases were reducing the amount of bonus paid for productivity improvements and as a result were adversely affecting employees' incentive to perform.

Eight firms criticized the lack of exemption for productivity-sharing plans in the guidelines, but none indicated that this had any effect on their programs.

Among the seven firms that were contemplating the adoption of a productivity-sharing program at the time of our review, only one said that the Council's policy was an important consideration. Two said they would ignore the Council's restriction on productivity sharing. Four firms expressed negative opinions on the need to file with the Council for an exemption for their programs.

We asked firms what positive or negative aspects they saw in the Council's voluntary wage and price guidelines. Forty-six, or 85 percent, of the firms gave negative responses, which are summarized in Table 15-9.

Officials at 24 firms with productivity-sharing plans and at four firms that had considered productivity sharing told us that there were actions that the federal government could take to enhance the viability of productivity-sharing programs at the firm level. Seven firms that had other types of incentive programs mentioned similar actions that could benefit their programs. A summary of their responses is in Table 15-10.

Table 15-9. Negative aspects seen in the Council's wage and price policies.

| Comments | Productivity sharing firms | Firms considering productivity sharing | Other firms | Number of responses |
|---|---|---|---|---|
| Guidelines are inequitable and/or biased in favor of unions | 15 | 2 | 6 | 23 |
| Guidelines are ineffective because they are not being followed | 7 | 2 | — | 9 |
| Guidelines fail to consider productivity, productivity sharing, or other incentive plans | 5 | — | 1 | 6 |
| Guidelines are not controlling inflation | 4 | 1 | — | 5 |
| Guidelines fail to consider all causes of inflation | 4 | — | — | 4 |
| Other | 5 | 1 | 1 | 7 |
| Total | | | | 54 [a] |

[a] Some firms provided more than one response.

## MATTERS OF IMPORTANCE TO FIRMS CONSIDERING A PRODUCTIVITY–SHARING PROGRAM

Finally, let's examine the factors that are important in considering a productivity-sharing program. Productivity-sharing programs are just one of many types of programs to motivate employees. Despite the fact that the programs have received attention in many respected business periodicals, relatively few firms have adopted them. Even more incongruous is that this lack of interest exists at a time when the nation faces a serious decline in national productivity and double-digit inflation. All this affects the competitive position of many firms, as well as the standard of living of every citizen.

The limited scope of the study suggests a note of caution regarding the financial and nonfinancial benefits reported by the firms

Table 15-10. Federal policies favored by firms to enhance productivity sharing.

| Response | Number of responses | Productivity-sharing firms | Firms considering productivity sharing | Other firms |
|---|---|---|---|---|
| Advocacy role, education, and research | 12 | 7 | 3 | 2 |
| Tax incentives for firms | 11 | 7 | 1 | 3 |
| Less government regulation and reporting | 8 | 6 | — | 2 |
| Exempt productivity sharing from the wage and price guidelines | 5 | 5 | — | — |
| Tax incentives for employees | 3 | 2 | — | 1 |
| Other | 3 | 2 | — | 1 |
| Total | 42 $^a$ | | | |

$^a$ Some firms gave more than one response.

studied as being representative of all productivity-sharing plans. However, the performance of the productivity-sharing programs studied suggests that these programs offer a viable method of enhancing productivity at the firm level. These programs warrant serious consideration by firms as a means of stimulating productivity performance, enhancing a firm's competitive advantage, increasing the monetary benefits of a firm's employees, and reducing inflationary pressures.

Although many benefits can accrue from the adoption of a productivity-sharing program, they should not be viewed as a panacea, but should be carefully considered by managements that are willing to devote the time and effort necessary to properly implement them and make them work effectively. A number of suggestions were derived from discussions with firms that have adopted such programs and from other knowledgeable sources.

Both the federal government and the private sector have much to gain from meaningful increases in productivity. At the national level, increases in productivity affect the rate of inflation and the standard of living of every citizen. At the firm level, productivity increases enhance a firm's competitive advantage and result in increased profits for the firm and noninflationary wage increases for the workforce.

Such mutual advantages suggest the basis for the formation of a partnership between the federal establishment and the private sector to work toward the common goal of increasing productivity. Groups such as the American Productivity Center, the Work in America Institute, and other productivity centers around the country should seek to form cooperative linkages within the National Productivity Council and the Council on Wage and Price Stability to promote and encourage the establishment of federal policy that promotes productivity growth in the private sector. GAO hopes that the release of this study will be a catalyst for firms to consider the adoption of these programs when they are compatible with management philosophy and are cost-effective for the firm.

CASS D. ALVIN

# 16
# Managing Productivity Programs:
# A Labor Viewpoint

PRODUCTIVITY may have but one definition in the dictionary, but it has several different meanings and interpretations, depending on who is looking at it. It is a word that defies universal description. Even experts find difficulty in agreeing on what it is and how to measure it accurately. Its multifaceted aspects make it most difficult to arrive at a common denominator.

Over the years, several serious attempts to measure productivity in the steel industry failed, and no consensus exists to this day among economists from industry, labor, or the government on what is an appropriate measurement. All, however, agree that it does exist, if only because we all know it does—a sort of an extension of the *cogito ergo sum* of Descartes's philosophy.

My few limited remarks will shed no new light on this ongoing and complex issue. I aim only to review very briefly some important experiences of the United Steelworkers of America with productivity in the steel industry and to share some personal observations about one or two union-management plans which concern themselves not only with improving this so-called "productivity" but also with how the gains—the fruits of such joint efforts—should be shared among the various elements in a production system.

I will discount any unilaterally imposed schemes that are not derived through joint labor-management participation. I will likewise ignore any practices of mine or factory managements that are described appropriately by the workers themselves as "gyppos," "speedups," and "goose jobs," among a few of the deserving appellations. Such plans are but methods for squeezing out the most effort for the least reward.

Regrettably, such productivity strategies, although often disguised with frilly terminologies, still exist even to this day. Piecework sweatshops in many labor-intensive industries which ignore even the minimal legal standards of pay and working conditions still permeate much of industrial and agricultural America. It is in these deplorable situations where one finds a cult of industrial engineers prostituting their profession with last century's speedups and piecework standards unilaterally imposed on helpless workers. To a degree this also continues in much of the Sun Belt and South, where a few firms still reign over an antebellum slavery-like system.

## PRODUCTIVITY PROGRAMS IN THE STEEL INDUSTRY: A HISTORICAL VIEW

For much of its history, the American steel industry maintained and practiced an assortment of diabolical schemes to nudge the most for the least out of workers. This is square one for me to begin explaining productivity in the steel industry. We've come a long way since then.

Years before the workforce was unionized by the United Steelworkers, the industry became intrigued with peddlers of productivity schemes that considered human workers as machines yet to be invented and creatures that could be easily bought. Persuaded by their charlatanry, company after company installed a variety of productivity schemes. They soon were called "incentives." It suffices to say that these were but brutal extortions to force every ounce of energy out of a human being in exchange for a few pieces of silver and for the privilege of working for those whom God "in His infinite wisdom" has chosen to rule.

From that period to this very date, incentive plans existed. But the drastic refinements and worker earnings protections introduced since then saw these plans evolve far beyond their forerunners. These modern incentives are now the centerpiece of productivity in the steel industry. They provide a substantial yield to as many as 95 percent of the production and maintenance workers in one company and about 80 percent of all workers at other companies. They generate earnings ranging from 35 percent to as high as 250 percent of the worker's hourly wage. The percentages for so-called "indirect" groups are somewhat lower, perhaps from 12 to 20 percent in addition to the standard hourly rate.

This is the one single, major system practiced in the steel industry to encourage a greater production output. Whether it in fact does so is not easily measured. But cut it, and down goes production. "Sweeten" it, and up goes production, with more and more steel produced by the same crew. But all attempts to replace these plans with other types of productivity schemes—however exotic or enticing—failed, and no new approaches are anywhere in sight.

A few years ago, a new idea was tried by Kaiser Steel Corporation at its mill in California, where in 1963 a long-range sharing plan was mutually developed by the union and the company, with assistance from three professionally neutral public members. Among its several goals, the plan envisioned the elimination of traditional incentives in favor of a broader concept of sharing gains on the basis of total performance of the entire workforce. Productivity gains were measured monthly by comparing standard labor and materials costs during a month in an average year (agreed to in advance) with the costs in a current month and then sharing the savings between the workers and the company on a ratio of 32.5 percent for labor and 67.5 percent for the company. (Incidentally, this ratio is about the same as the one used to this day in the industry. It's a ratio of labor costs to material and supply costs in steelmaking, which hasn't changed significantly since the late nineteenth century.)

While the much-heralded plan of sharing was in full operation at Kaiser (and also in a modified version at Alan Wood Steel in Pennsylvania), some very valuable lessons were learned about how and how not to launch or manage any productivity-sharing plan in the steel industry. Although the plan still exists, it no longer has its former sparkle. It is dimming out as inflation costs run four and five times higher than productivity gains. It was doomed to die, perhaps because it was imposed alongside the existing direct incentive plan, and it quickly was submerged in a morass of interest conflicts, attitudinal as well as political, which the parties could not deal with successfully.

The experiment at Kaiser came out of the long 116-day strike of 1959 in the steel industry—the last such strike that the nation witnessed. At the heart of the impasse was the issue of work practices, which the industry was claiming stifled its ability to increase its productivity and its chance of competing successfully with newer and more efficient foreign mills. Labor, on the other hand, fearing all sorts of adverse changes in long-established work practices as well as other rights protected by what is known as a *past practices clause* in the labor agreements, resisted giving up such rights to management, because it was afraid that management might unilaterally change work rules and take away hard-fought gains without mutual consent.

The industry certainly watched the Kaiser experiment with considerable interest. But, seemingly because it held a grudge against Kaiser's break-away settlement with the union while the others stood fast in their demand, the industry, company by company, chose instead to stay with the old way but to extend existing incentive plans to a greater percentage of the workforce and provide minimum guarantees in the bonus rewards—all this in agreement with the union's collective bargaining proposals. But the issues of productivity and foreign competition still linger. Discussions between the union and the major companies about productivity continue to this day, but not about any plans to replace the incentive system to which both parties now seem wedded.

The steel union, from its very inception, did not display eagerness for any form of productivity or incentive plans. Its leadership came from a coal miners' union background, where incentives (tonnage plans) were the very antithesis of unionism. One leader called incentives "a form of industrial cannibalism." The fledgling union tolerated incentives but hoped that, as collective bargaining raised wages, incentives would somehow go away, as they did in coal mining.

During World War II, a most unusual experience in an Ohio independent steel company led to the creation of a productivity plan that was later refined and formalized by a research employee of the then young union. It still is performing satisfactorily in several companies within and outside the steel industry. The Scanlon Plan (bearing the name of its author, Joseph Scanlon) put into rational form a practice of an aging steel employer who rewarded his workers through a system based on production values and on the employee contributions to it. It apparently also lacked appeal to the rest of the industry, and the union made no all-out effort to press for it with other employers. More recently in the steel productivity anthology, two developments which were initiated in collective bargaining are worthy of mention.

The first came in 1971 when the union and the major companies included a clause calling for the establishment of a joint advisory committee on productivity in every basic steel local union and at every plant site. The intent was to have such committees work cooperatively as union and management teams to devise ways to improve productivity and promote use of domestic steel. This concept was extended to several smaller steel mills in addition to the nine major steel companies. In all, several hundred were formed, and all were supposed to be looking for ways to promote productivity without either side giving up any of its rights or prerogatives.

They were free to discuss such matters as making more efficient use of production time; reducing equipment breakdowns and delays; improving quality; eliminating waste and negligent use of materials, supplies, and equipment; reducing excessive overtime; boosting employee morale; improving safety experiences; and generally focusing employee awareness on the productivity problems and "the real threat of foreign competition." But none of this was to have any effect on employees' rights under the labor contract. A special top-level national committee of union and management was established to develop guidelines and oversee the entire operation. Few, if any, such committees are still noticeably functioning.

While the parties do not discount some of the notable successes reported, these committees received far less than an enthusiastic acceptance from local management and labor union members. An industrywide recession brought about by a sagging, stagflation-ridden economy made it difficult to talk about productivity at a time when workers were being furloughed from jobs and production dipped to low levels of capacity.

The other development worthy of mention is that in the 1977 agreement a provision was added that establishes a new-member orientation program to be conducted by the union to explain to new job entrants how the union works on the job and also, again, to promote understanding of the need for improved productivity and to explain the threat of foreign steel competition. Similar clauses were added to agreements with companies outside the Big Nine (steel firms) and to contracts in the aluminum industry and the metal container industry, but without any reference to productivity or foreign competition. Such orientation programs are expected to be in full operation in the months ahead.

That concludes my thumbnail round-up of past and present programs in the steel industry, which in most cases are operated mutually by the union and management. The one arrangement for increasing output, or productivity, that survives is the group incentive that links rewards directly to performance. These plans are worked out on the shop level between the affected group and plant management, following certain guidelines in the master labor agreement.

## KEY ELEMENTS OF SETTING UP A PRODUCTIVITY PLAN

Permit me to share some thoughts I have about installing and operating any productivity plan. I mention these opinions and views in the hope that I can add something worthwhile from my experience, especially with the Kaiser sharing plan.

First and foremost, for a plan to be successful, there must exist a climate of mutual respect. Success or failure of any plan hinges on cooperation. It cannot survive tensions between labor and management; nor can it be carried out when a backlog of unresolved grievances clogs the procedural channels or when neither side respects the rights of the other.

Without constructive attitudes and a mature relationship that takes into account all the human factors involved, no cooperation is possible. Among the human factors to be considered are:

The need of workers for security, both of job and of income.

Workers' legitimate expectations for a rising standard of living and for upward mobility.

Protection against cost-of-living income erosion.

Safe and healthy working conditions as well as normal work schedules.

Assurance that participation in a productivity plan will *not* negate reasonable long-standing work practices.

Guarantee that gains achieved through greater efficiency of labor or through technological changes will not result in loss of job or earnings.

Decisions related to achieving a company's objective to maximize its return are outside the traditional sphere of labor prerogatives. Such matters as sales, purchasing, research, management salaries and other compensations, expansion, and capital investment are beyond the control of labor. Yet each of these can have a great bearing on productivity, on the need for growth, and even on workers' morale. On the other hand, usage of materials and supplies, yield improvement, fuller utilization of technology, and the like are indeed affected tremendously by the cooperation and performance of employees and these and only these factors should be used in determining the productivity performance of labor.

Any plan must be practical and must be easily understood by all who will participate. It should avoid complicated calculation formulas, computer simulations and projections, and cumbersome methods of determining the yield. Above all, it should be free of engineering gobbledygook or esoteric terminology. It should also be based on the performance of the smallest possible unit rather than on total plant performance.

All rewards for improved yield should be made as soon as possible after the actual performance so that the individual worker or the group can promptly relate performance to the reward and make adjustments as needed. Rewards should be based on a percentage of the classified wage rate and not be a flat and equal sum to all. In that way, the pay structure is not distorted or compressed.

Special creativity and inventiveness rewards should be a part of any plan, and judging should be done by workers in the unit. But gamelike competitiveness along other lines should be avoided to minimize the friction that such contests create.

*At every stage, from planning to administration, worker input is essential.*

Free exchange of information through a two-way communications system is also vital to any program. There should be no secrets about any planned changes, expansion of facilities, new processes or products, and contemplated schedules. Only through openness can rumors, gossip, and the formation of cliques be minimized and false reports, suspicions, and political pressures avoided.

Any plan must apply equally to workers and supervisors. The same rules and standards should apply to both, and a balance should be maintained. Implementation of the plan should be supervised by a joint committee selected by the workers and management. No changes, alterations, adjustments, or amendments should be made without at least a two-thirds voting consent. Finally, do not attempt to install a productivity plan of any kind or a worker incentive program during a period of unemployment or at a time when it is obvious that what is needed is not productivity of labor but an infusion of capital to modernize and otherwise improve the operation. You just cannot save a poorly managed, obsolete enterprise with any wage cuts or productivity schemes.

Now all this time I assumed, of course, that productivity programs should have a payoff that workers who contribute can see in their paychecks. If such is not the case, I cannot in my wildest imagination see cooperative participation from workers in an industry such as steel. If the only reward is a promise, to be fulfilled sometime between now and eternity, forget it! Enhancing a company's financial well-being so that it can remain competitive or reduce its prices because of lowered production costs are very noble goals, but they're not going to impress the worker unless they bring with them some tangible benefits.

CASS D. ALVIN

# 17
# In Defense of American Worker Productivity

IN THE PREVIOUS chapter I dealt with programs that existed in the steel industry for stimulating worker output. I included the group incentive plans, which constitute the centerpiece of productivity in the steel industry as well as our union's experience with such programs as the Scanlon Plan, the Kaiser long-range sharing plan, and the productivity committees established contractually by the United Steelworkers of America and the major steel companies. This most limited and narrow appraisal was a micro view of productivity, focused on but one industry and the workplace level. In this chapter I will attempt to widen the scope and offer a broader, long-range view of the problem of our shrinking productivity.

About a generation ago, the American railroad industry, sensing its demise, fashioned an assault on what it considered to be a principal cause of its rapidly approaching derailment. Unable or unwilling to face the stigma of its own failures, it resorted to the use of an old and proven propaganda technique of shifting the blame for its shortcomings to someone else. Those of you who have researched the history of railroads or talked to your elders who still remember may have come across the word "featherbedding." It was applied by the managers of the railroad hierarchy to a practice they originally agreed to establish but which they later condemned as villainous work habits of the workers. The charge was that the railroads were forced to accept fixed crew sizes and makeups, mandatory safety personnel, relief periods, "dead-heading," and other arrangements which in their judgment could no longer be supported in a new and modern railroad technology.

The effect of this widespread propaganda was to shift the blame for the railroad industry's loss of profitability to the workers and their unions, when in reality the problem was not featherbedding at all but a series of management blunders, prolonged and compounded by a government that listened to industry and paid little or no attention to the data before it, which clearly showed that a change was needed in the corporate behavior of the railroad giants and which led to the creation of the highway trust fund. Most of the regulatory agencies sanctioned indefensible industry practices and showed little or no concern for the public will.

## WORKERS AND GOVERNMENT ARE NOT THE CULPRITS

Today, some 30 years later, American industry is again trying to shift the blame for its dilemma from itself to what it considers to be the culprits.

If I read correctly, what much of American industry is saying these days through its spokesmen is that it cannot fulfill its obligation as a viable segment of the economy because of the many impediments placed in its way by unions, foreign producers, and especially the government. Today's equivalent of "featherbedding" is "overregulation." It shackles freedom. It thwarts growth and productivity. Productivity problems are also blamed on a number of structural, social, and moral changes in our society. These, along with overregulation, then, are said to prevent the needed rate of productivity—a word that defies accurate definition but generally is understood to refer to the generation of greater output of goods and/or services with the same or lesser input.

Whenever productivity is mentioned, the culprit is immediately fingered, directly or indirectly: it is the American worker. To the minds of too many, productivity is something that only the worker and his attitude can do anything about. Somehow, whether productivity is not being enhanced or is being reduced depends on the workers' attitude. Hardly ever are the other more important factors mentioned, such as poor management, lack of imagination in product design, unwise research and development strategies, need for infusion of capital, and the fiscal and monetary policies of government. Hardly anybody discusses the destructive practices of monopolies, oligopolies, conglomerates, and multinational corporations that thwart the very creativity needed to expand our system of enterprise and keep it within the boundaries of our nation.

Let me give you an example of how the government can help. The most modern steel facility in the North American continent is being completed within eyesight of the United States by Steelco, Inc.—in Canada! The entire facility is being amortized rapidly under the tax policy of Canada in less than three years. A similar facility in this country requires a 15- to 20-year write-off. Why our government cannot adopt a policy to encourage modernization and building of industrial plants that can meet the challenge from off-shore competitors whose governments are in a virtual partnership with industry is difficult to understand.

Also, in certain situations it is a distinct technological advantage to build facilities with joint capital outlay from several competing firms. We may need to examine such arrangements, presently outlawed by antitrust laws, in light of modern realities, taking into account both the need for more efficient technology and cost-benefit considerations.

With decisions being made by these corporate giants on a global basis, it hardly is worth our time to think about how we can improve our productivity by focusing on some kind of behavior schemes or work arrangements that will eke out of workers degrees of higher performance. Engineering of human beings has very definite limits, but sound, creative engineering by human beings provides a never ending opportunity for greater productivity.

Let me make one thing perfectly clear: American labor unions are in full support of improving productivity. The record shows it. Productivity is a way of making the pie bigger, and it is the very essence of the American system of enterprise. It is one of the major elements in the collective bargaining criteria of unions. And we in labor are ready to match our performance against that of any group of workers in any other nation or under any system in the world.

We in labor think we know something about work, its sweat and blisters. We challenge anybody to show proof that American trade unionists want a free lunch or that their productivity efforts lag behind those of their counterparts in any nation. We are sick and tired of being made the culprits by people who are entrusted by our system of enterprise to manage production, but who do not.

The current charge of our corporate leaders is an indictment of our efforts to make America first again—number one in the world. If there is a failure, let's honestly place the blame where it belongs and not on American workers or their unions.

The other contributors to this book address themselves to ways of making the workplace more conducive to higher productivity. This is good and should be applauded. The rise of organized labor in our society came about largely because many felt that industrial democracy would have a positive impact on productivity. Unions won support in America because productivity schemes unilaterally imposed by management had failed to meet the challenge posed by growth and concentration of power in corporate industry. I can recall no example of labor refusing to cooperate as a member of a team in order to make the pie bigger, provided the workers were promised a fair share in return.

## SOME MYTHS ABOUT PRODUCTIVITY

We all are too often victims of myths. Rather than face reality, we choose the comfort of escape. We all tend to believe in simplistic "do-it-quick" formulas to end all our problems, and we adhere to values or dogmas that give comfort to the stereotypes we shelter from the past—values which now dictate our decisions and our very lives.

Among the many myths we revere are a few that apply to productivity. Instead of showing you some magic scheme to get a scant overall percentage increase in the output per worker, I choose instead to debunk the myths which are being promulgated, but which have little or no relevance to the problem of productivity slippage experienced in the past few years.

*Myth #1: The work ethic is disappearing. People no longer believe in the virtue of hard work and care nothing about personal pride of accomplishment or making a better product more efficiently.* So we are told. The fact is that if the work ethic is dead, it has been destroyed not by the workers but by a system that feels that profits could be made bigger and bigger by using less human effort and more energy in production.

The skill and craftsmanship of the individual worker have long been ignored in favor of building quality and speed into the machine. The craftsman with pride in his work was turned into a lonely, numerically controlled machine tender, because industry wanted to take the control of quality from his hands and put it in some capital-intensive mechanical device. Therefore, the blame must be put not on "the man with the hoe" but on the decisions of profit-oriented enterprise.

*Myth #2: Organized labor's resistance to change in work practices cuts productivity.* This is but another technique of shifting the blame from where it properly belongs to a convenient scapegoat. Admittedly, a few archaic practices do exist in industry today which no longer are realistic, but work rules are being altered each and every day with full consent of unions and management. When pressed on the issue, a high official of Kaiser Steel told our union that if his company had the unilateral right to do as it pleased about work practices, it would not change the productivity by more than 5 percent—and he wasn't sure which way.

*Myth #3: The increasing number of women in the workforce reduces productivity.* Employment of women has absolutely nothing to do with our declining productivity. In fact, women are probably *more* productive than men as a gender and in the workplace. They can outproduce most of their critics, and for anyone to put the blame for the drop in productivity in our system on the increasing number of women in our workforce exposes a disgraceful ignorance of facts and displays the lowest form of male chauvinism. Many, if not most, entrance jobs structured by management engineers in our industrial society today can be performed equally by males and females (and, in all too many cases, by chimpanzees). So, let's put that indictment of womanhood to rest once and for all.

*Myth #4: Overregulation by government is stifling productivity.* There may well be more supporters of this thesis if we included in the definition of overregulation *all* elements—labor, corporations, consumers, banks, youths, stockholders, and so on. What I understand this overregulation argument to be about is that government intrusion is OK if it serves the need of a particular business or business in general, but that it is definitely undesirable if it provides any controls that business objects to—such as occupational safety and health; mine safety and health; protection of the environment, air, and water; land use; pure food; federal trade; and so on. All these are intrusions on the free market. But such controls as the right of corporations to have priority and protection even over people; bankruptcy laws that protect the mistakes of business; depletion allowances for the extraction industries; loans and land grants to railroads, industries, to Lockheed and Chrysler; subsidies to agriculture and others—these are perfectly consistent with the so-called free enterprise system.

There is a duplicity here that is not very hard to detect: those who have it want to keep it; those who don't have it want to have a chance to get some of the action. How does the system work? Who knows? But to blame the government for protecting the citizens from blatant abuses is sheer lunacy. The air we breathe, the water we use, the land that sustains us *need* protection and cannot be left in the hands of those who are by their own credo interested only in maximizing profit.

More important to our discussion here is that none of this has anything to do with higher productivity. In fact, it can be proven that investments in abatement of air, water, and land pollution have contributed more to an increase in productivity than to its decline.

*Myth #5: Because of the declining productivity of American workers, we have become a service economy rather than a producing industrial society.* The fact is that one out of every four automobiles is made off-shore because Detroit, among its other failings, ignored the realities of energy and public preference. The same holds for such industries as shoes, flat glass, electronics, TVs, radios, cameras, musical instruments, toys, apparel, and tools. Most of these products are being made overseas. Steel, rubber, and plastics are next on the list. We have defaulted and given up on the American industrial system and on the shrewdness of the Yankee trader and have become literally panders for the multinationals and those who defend the exportation of American capital, technology, and scientific know-how to countries outside the United States. All this results in bringing boatloads of unemployment back to America—and we pay about $15 billion to $20 billion for every percentage point of unemployment in welfare costs, crime increase, and so on.

Industry claims that we cannot outproduce the Japanese, the Europeans, and the Hong Kong and Taiwan industries because Americans are soft, lazy, unproductive, booze- and dope-addicted, and so on. All that is nonsense. The only element of truth in this myth is that we are indeed becoming a service nation—and we cannot survive as such for long.

Think of it! In less than a generation, we have written off American enterprise, and nobody in this nation even had a chance to cast a vote on it. The culprits are not the working people or their trade unions. Clearly, the blame must be placed on those who today feel they are being held captives by the government, by Ralph Nader, and by anybody who dares to question their economic primacy. It is their wealth and influence, not the will of the people, that controls political thought in Washington.

*Myth #6: If we would only let the marketplace be freed of government-imposed impediments, everybody would be better off.* Indeed so. The free market has been manipulated. The free enterprise system has been altered. Its "founder," Adam Smith, would not recognize it today. But on whom should the blame be placed? Who intruded on the ideals of the free marketplace? Perhaps all of us. But certainly General Motors as one of the Fortune 500 corporations claiming to be enslaved, or the others who also would not be in the economic primer of Mr. Smith as examples of free enterprise. Surely they, along with trade unions, which were formed to challenge the corporate abuses, as well as an ever adjusting and accommodating government, are guilty of manipulating the free-market concept.

So who is kidding whom? The economic theory of freedom being advanced by Milton Friedman has no model anywhere in the world and, as many social economists state, could exist only by dogma. As always in the past, those who speak for absolute freedom need a totalitarian regime to implement that concept.

We, of course, all know that the concept of a free market has been twisted and distorted in its meaning, even totally uprooted by a system of misleading advertising. Although what's left of our free market still constitutes a viable mechanism that influences some decisions in the private sector, it is no match for the Fortune 500, for Big Business, foreign multinationals, the OPEC cartel, or others who know how frail freedom of any kind is and how it can be manipulated.

## THE WORK ETHIC IN AMERICA IS NOT DEAD

Allow me to return for a moment to just one of these myths—the claim that the work ethic has disappeared in America. Historians among you will recall that the work ethic is a European Christian concept, which, some say, was devised to assist the acceptance of the Church as a center of social and economic authority. The harder one works, the greater the reward will be for him in heaven. The Orientals hold to no such ethic. It is often referred to as the Protestant ethic, because work for a heavenly reward was central to some major Protestant reform movements and to the rise of capitalism.

Today we are told that this ethic is gone—that the Protestants lost it, but the Japanese now have it. It is still practiced in Europe, we're made to believe, but our permissive welfare society has destroyed the urge to work. How plausible it all sounds, but how wrong it is.

Let us examine two cases: first, the Volkswagen factory in Pennsylvania, compared with the one in Germany; second, the Honda motorcycle plant in Ohio, compared with its counterpart in Japan. This should be a real contest—a battle of the work ethic. Which team will you bet on? What are the facts, as discovered by the studies of the United Automobile Workers and the companies at both plants?

In the case of Volkswagen, the Pennsylvania plant is far more productive than the one in Germany—as much as 10 percent better, while putting out a product of at least the same quality as the plant in Germany.

The difference between Volkswagen and American automobile manufacturers is that the managers of Volkswagen insist on quality built into every part, subassembly, and system. The company gets full cooperation from the union and from the workers. Nothing leaves the plant that is not thoroughly inspected at every stage of production. The Detroit philosophy has been for more than 20 years now to do away with or minimize most of the inspection or repair of the product before it leaves the plant. The policy is to save on quality control and let the customer be the inspector. That is the reason for the huge number of recalls of cars. One or more of *Fortune*'s captive 500 are guilty of this anticonsumer practice. No wonder they hate Ralph Nader!

The Honda case is an even brighter story of American worker productivity and pride of workmanship. The Japanese-owned American Honda is an example of what can be done if there is a commitment to precision, quality, and efficiency. Workers want this kind of management and are willing to be partners in such a production system. The work ethic may no longer hold that there is a reward in heaven for hard work. The new ethic may be that workers are more than machines not yet invented and, given a chance, will put themselves out to show that they are special.

## CONCLUSION

I believe it is important that we establish a proper climate—a humanized environment in the workplace, one that will lessen the boredom, filth, monotony, frustrations, anguish, and the dangers to the body from toxic substances; a workplace that will provide safety and health, physical and mental, for the working person. As important, there must be an emphasis on democracy in the workplace and on the relevance of the individual human being. Humanizing the workplace should be a top priority in a nation where polls continue to show that up to 70 percent of workers are dissatisfied with their jobs.

The productivity we are measuring by today's formula is an output scaled in dollar and cent values. But let's look at other factors, at other values. America indeed needs greater productivity. That, I suppose, is the name of the game in any industrial society. It's the way to achieve a higher standard of living for everybody. And it is the way America has grown and prospered. But let's remember that the required 4 to 5 percent annual rate of productivity cannot possibly be met by a more efficient system of human engineering. Productivity depends on the latest and best of tools and machines, on equipment, on availability of energy and raw materials, on research and development, on capital, on investment policy of the private and public sectors, on imaginative and creative incentives, on a government that is a partner in this productivity effort, on industry that accepts its responsibility to invest and to produce for social and overall economic good and not just on its immediate profit goals.

Let us honestly look at ourselves and determine what our current sickness is and how it came about, and then let us plan with boldness and imagination to once again be the greatest of all the greats—to be the America that must continue to be the model for the world to imitate.

MURRAY L. WEIDENBAUM

# 18
# "Free the Fortune 500"— An Economist's Response to Big Business Day

VARIOUS PRIVATE GROUPS and individuals (such as Ralph Nader) designated April 17, 1980, as Big Business Day. If those corporate activists had had their way, that would have been the day all business executives tore their garments, donned sackcloth and ashes, and recited from the Book of Lamentations. But mine is not a plea for business to engage in acts of contrition. Rather, I would like to turn the tables and show how the actions of the corporate activists have, wittingly or not, done so much harm to the American economy and ultimately to the consumer.

To begin, we must acknowledge the obvious: the American business system is under assault. If you have any doubt about that, just turn on the evening news or pick up any daily newspaper. You will see allegations of companies "polluting" the environment while forcing their employees to work under "cancer-inducing" conditions to produce "unsafe" products, "constantly" raising their prices, and earning "windfall" profits to boot. Sometimes, it seems that the media coverage of business presents little else. We should acknowledge that presenting the positive side of business accomplishments is not dramatic and perhaps not even newsworthy. The positive side rarely lends itself to photographic or visual "opportunities," to use the media jargon. Nevertheless, the steady drumbeat of criticism of business performance is used to justify an ever increasing expansion of government intervention in business.

Do not mistake my intent. As one who has worked in both business and government, I am keenly aware of the shortcomings of corporate practices and the need for public-sector intervention. But in my current role of academic observer of business-government relations, it is apparent to me that we are already in the midst of an unprecedented expansion of government involvement in private enterprise, far more rapid than the celebrated New Deal period of the 1930s. And we must note that this expansion was motivated in large part by prior actions of the sponsors of Big Business Day.

## ADVERSE EFFECTS OF GOVERNMENT REGULATION

It should be clear by now to any observer that the adverse effects of government regulation touch every part of the economy. And it is the citizen-taxpayer-consumer who pays the costs of overregulation.

We are witnessing several highly visible reforms. Congress has deregulated the airlines and has cut back on trucking controls. The Occupational Safety and Health Administration (OSHA) has eliminated what it calls "Mickey Mouse" regulations—those silly rules concerning the difference between a hole and an opening, when a roof is a floor, and how often spittoons are to be cleaned. But that overlooks the vast amount of new regulation that already is in the pipeline. I am referring to the many laws passed by the Congress in recent years for which the agencies are just beginning to issue the regulations. Let us just hit the highlights. To opera buffs, *Tosca* is a melodrama ending in tragedy; for the specialists in federal alphabet soup, however, TOSCA is the Toxic Substances Control Act of 1976. The government is still inventorying the situation before promulgating the stiff regulations that are contemplated. But this is only the beginning. The Clean Air and Clean Water statutes of 1977 are just becoming effective; when they do, it will be extremely difficult to build any major new facility in most parts of this country. And then there is the Resource Conservation and Recovery Act. Under that law, the Environmental Protection Agency (EPA) will be setting up cradle-to-grave controls over all substances designated as hazardous. And we should not overlook OSHA's General

Carcinogenic Standard. That one new and far-reaching ruling is likely to generate far greater compliance costs than all of the existing OSHA standards put together; preliminary estimates are in the tens of billions of dollars a year.

Frankly, it is difficult to overestimate the rapid expansion and the great variety of government involvement in private enterprise now occurring in the United States. The very concept of a regulated industry—such as the railroads—has become out of date. We already live in an economy in which every business in this country feels the rising encroachment of government in all major aspects of its day-to-day operations. The regulators must be consulted on practically every aspect of business activity—where to set up a business, who can be hired, how to operate the business, what to sell, to whom to sell it, and, of course, how much of the proceeds to keep. No business, large or small, can operate without obeying a myriad of government rules and restrictions.

Virtually every major department of the typical corporation in the United States has one or more counterparts in a government agency that controls or strongly influences its internal decision making. There is almost a shadow organization chart of public officials matching the organization structure of each private company. The scientists in corporate research laboratories now do much of their work to ensure that the products they develop are not rejected by lawyers in regulatory agencies. The engineers in manufacturing departments must make sure the equipment they specify meets the standards developed by engineers in the Labor Department. Marketing staffs must follow procedures established by product safety agencies. The location of business facilities must conform to a variety of environmental statutes. The activities of personnel staffs are increasingly geared to meeting the standards of the many agencies concerned with employment conditions. And finance departments bear the brunt of the rising paperwork burden imposed by government agencies.

In short, there are few aspects of business activities that escape some type of government review or influence. In turn, important adjustments are taking place in the structure and operation of the typical corporation. These changes tend to be in one direction—to increase the overhead costs of doing business and to deflect management and employee attention from the conventional tasks of designing, producing, and distributing new and better or cheaper goods and services.

Some of the most fundamental impacts are discernible in the research and development area, with a resulting slowdown in product innovation. Here is a striking example in the pharmaceutical area. Cardiovascular disease (heart attack and stroke) has been the main cause of death in the United States for many years. What does the government do to help? The Food and Drug Administration (FDA) continues to block the availability of new and improved drugs. In the case of one drug alone—the beta-blocker practolol, which could be used to prevent heart attacks and coronary death—the FDA is still studying it, even though it is in general use in England. According to Professor William Wardell of the University of Rochester Medical School, if this drug were approved for use in this country, it would save at least 10,000 lives a year. Remember that fact the next time a corporate activist tells you that economists and business executives are just "green eyeshade" types who do not care about people.

Government imposition on business of socially desirable requirements may seem to be an inexpensive way of achieving national objectives. However, the public does not get a free or even low-cost lunch when government imposes burdens on private industry. In large measure, the costs of government regulation show up in higher prices of goods and services that consumers buy. These higher prices represent the hidden tax imposed on the public by government regulation. And, to many people in politics, the best tax is a hidden tax. Those corporate activists who view regulation as a good way to "sock it to business" ignore that business is the middleman, acting, in effect, as a tax collector for government. The ultimate burden of regulation, as with traditional sales taxes, is borne by consumers.

The regulatory tax hits the consumer especially hard through automobile regulation. The newly produced automobile in the United States carries a load of equipment from catalytic converters to heavier bumpers that the federal government has mandated must be installed. All in all, there was approximately $666 in government-mandated safety and environmental control equipment in the typical 1978 passenger car. But these direct costs are only the initial or first-order effects of government regulation.

## SECOND- AND THIRD-ORDER EFFECTS OF REGULATION

It is the indirect or second-order effects that are truly huge—the various changes in a company's way of doing business in order to comply with government directives. One indirect cost of regulation is the growing paperwork: the expensive and time-consuming process of submitting reports, making applications, filling out questionnaires, and replying to orders and directives. Ultimately, every consumer feels those effects in the form of higher prices. According to my estimates, the total cost of federal regulation came to approximately $121 billion in 1979. That is approximately $500 for each man, woman, and child in the United States—a hidden tax from regulation of close to $2,000 for a typical family of four. We should not, of course, ignore the benefits that government regulation can generate. But that does not lessen the impact of the costs; neither does it obviate the need to ensure that regulations are made more cost-effective than they are now.

The most fundamental impacts of government intervention are what we can call the third-order or induced effects on the corporation. These are the actions that the firm takes to respond to the direct and indirect effects of regulation. These responses include such negative actions as cutting back on research and development and on new capital formation because of the diversion of funds to meet government-mandated social requirements. The basic functioning of the business system is adversely affected, notably in the reduced pace of innovation, the lessened ability to finance growth, and, ultimately, the weakening of the capability of the firm to perform its central role of producing goods and services for the consumer. These difficult-to-measure induced impacts in the long run far outweigh the more measurable direct costs of regulation.

Government adversely affects capital formation by introducing uncertainty about the future of regulations. It is becoming increasingly difficult for American companies to move ahead with building any new energy facilities. A cogent example is furnished in the report by a task force of the president's Energy Resources Council dealing with the development of a new synthetic fuel industry. The task force stated that a major uncertainty was the length of time that a project would be delayed pending the issuance of an environmental impact statement that would stand up in court. It noted that the cost of such delays—additional interim financing and further cost increases in labor and equipment—is an obvious potential hazard for any new project. The report concluded, "In summary, some of these regulatory requirements could easily hold up or permanently postpone any attempt to build and operate a synthetic fuels plant."

Where the impact of government is less dramatic it is no less profound. A significant but subtle bureaucratization occurs in the corporate activity that is undertaken. The pension reform law (the Employee Retirement Income Security Act of 1974, or ERISA) shifted much of the attention of the management of pension funds from maximizing the return on the contributions to following a more cautious approach of minimizing the likelihood that the fund managers will be criticized for their investment decisions. It thus becomes safer, although not necessarily more desirable to the employees covered, for the pension managers to keep more detailed records of their deliberations, to hire more outside experts (so that the responsibility can be diluted), and to avoid innovative investments. The federal rules also tend to make the pension fund manager unwilling to invest in other than blue-chip stocks, thus depriving newer and smaller enterprises of an important source of venture capital.

From such regulatory experiences, it is apparent the nation is paying yet another price for the expansion of government power—the weakening of the risk-bearing and entrepreneurial characteristics of the private enterprise system. But my main concern is the effect of the expansion of government power on the individual.

The matter of the ban by the Consumer Product Safety Commission on spray adhesives is a fascinating case. In August 1973, the Commission banned aerosol spray adhesives as an imminent hazard. Those are not Band-Aids, but a form of art supply. The Commission's decision was based on the preliminary findings of one academic researcher who claimed that if pregnant women used the sprays, they might produce children with brain defects. Then the Commission did something unusual and commendable: it did a full-scale study of the spray adhesives. That more careful research failed to corroborate the initial report, and the Commission lifted the ban in March 1974. Why do I mention this case? After all, depriving consumers of spray adhesives for artwork for less than seven months does not seem to be too harsh in view of the desire to avoid serious threats to people's health.

The Commission's admission of error and lifting of the ban were commendable. But unfortunately, there is an O. Henry twist to the story. Nine pregnant women who had used the sprays reacted to the news of the Commission's initial decision by undergoing abortions. They decided not to carry through their pregnancies for fear of producing babies with birth defects. But they could not reverse their actions when the regulators changed their minds. The sadness of this case is hardly reduced by the fact that everyone involved was trying to promote the public health and safety, but they all underestimated the awesome power of government over our daily lives.

## SOME RECOMMENDATIONS

What are we to do? Fundamentally, we should not focus our attention on technical measurements and administrative procedures or on extensions of government power over the private sector. Rather, we need to take a different view of the regulatory mechanism. Instead of relying on regulation to control in detail every facet of private behavior, the regulatory device should be seen as a powerful tool to be used reluctantly and with great care and discretion. Basically, attitudes need to be changed.

Experience with the job safety program provides an example. Although the government's safety rules have resulted in billions of dollars in public and private outlays, the goal of a safer work environment has not been achieved. A more satisfying answer requires a major change in the approach to regulation. If, for example, the objective is to reduce accidents, then public policy should focus directly on the reduction of accidents. Excessively detailed regulations are often merely a substitute—the normal bureaucratic substitute—for hard policy decisions.

Rather than placing emphasis on issuing citations to employers who fail to fill out forms correctly or who do not post the required notices, emphasis should be on the regulation of those employers with high and rising accident rates. Perhaps stiff fines should be levied on the basis of accidents that actually occur in a given factory or office. As the accident rates decline, the fines would be reduced or eliminated. That would strengthen the usual business incentives to reduce these disruptions of the workplace. But the government should not be much concerned with the way a specific organization achieves a safer working environment. Some companies may find it more efficient to change work rules, others to buy new equipment, and still others to retrain workers. The making of this choice is precisely the kind of operational business decision making that government should avoid, but that now dominates many regulatory programs.

In the traditional one-industry type of government regulation (as of airlines, trucking, and railroads), a greater role should be given to competition. Unlike the newer forms of regulation, the older regulations mainly protect existing firms from competition.

In the consumer protection area, an information strategy can provide a sensible alternative to compulsory standards. For the many visible hazards to which consumers voluntarily subject themselves, the most important consideration of public policy is to improve the individual's knowledge of the risks involved rather than to limit personal discretion. In their daily lives, citizens rarely opt for zero-risk alternatives but trade off, for example, between speed and safety.

Any realistic appraisal of government regulation, however, must acknowledge that important benefits have resulted—less pollution, fewer product hazards, reduced job discrimination, and so on. But that does not justify government's attempting to regulate every facet of private behavior. A reasonable approach requires great care in sorting out the serious hazards that should be regulated from the lesser hazards that can best be dealt with by the prudence of consumers, workers, and business firms.

We must recognize that the pressure for more regulations continues. Here it is important to be aware of the source of that pressure—the self-appointed, self-styled public interest groups. The public, the media, and government decision makers all need to realize that these public interest groups do not represent the total public interest. Yet, large sements of the media, as well as many legislators, view them automatically as the underdog. This attitude portrays the people who disagree with them as the "heavies." Just because I may disagree with Ralph Nader or Jane Fonda should not inevitably be taken as my representing some special interest opposed to the public welfare. It just may happen that, on occasion, Ralph (or Jane) may be wrong. They may not be aware of the full burdens that their proposals would place on the consumer.

Many, but not all, representatives of public interest groups confuse their personal prejudices with the national well-being. As one who was intimately involved in government policymaking, I know that making good policy is far more difficult than merely choosing between "public" or "consumer" interests, which are presumably good and to be endorsed, and "special" or "business" interests, which are presumably evil and to be opposed. Sensible policymaking consists not of dramatic confrontation but of carefully balancing and reconciling a variety of legitimate interests—such as clean air, low inflation, safe products, high employment, healthy working conditions, and rising productivity.

It is intriguing that these public interest groups often view the corporation as simultaneously venal and omnipotent. Many critics of the American business system automatically accept the positive accomplishments produced by corporations, but they cavalierly reject the role of material incentives in obtaining the desired material benefits. They seem to think that the corporation could continue to produce all the material abundance, at least as effectively as now, while simultaneously turning its efforts to a host of social concerns.

The one thing these groups lack is a sense of humor. For example, they attacked OSHA for stopping the distribution of one of its pamphlets. OSHA has issued a pamphlet on farm safety that treats farmers as dummies. One of the newspapers in the Farm Belt answered with the following editorial in the form of a Dick and Jane book, the kind a child reads in the first grade.

### DICK AND JANE VISIT THE FARM

See the book.
See the little book.
See the little OSHA book.
What is OSHA?
OSHA is your government.
OSHA is the Occupational Safety
  and Health Administration.
OSHA helps people.
OSHA helps people to be safe.
OSHA made the little book for
  farmers.
What does the little book say?
This is what it says:

"Be careful around the farm . . . Hazards are one of the main causes of accidents. A hazard is anything that is dangerous."

"Be careful when you are handling animals. Tired or hungry or frightened cattle can bolt and trample you. Be patient, talk softly around the cows. Don't talk fast or be loud around them. If they are upset, don't go into the pen with them."

"DON'T FALL."

"Be careful that you do not fall into the manure pits. Put up signs and fences to keep people away. These pits are very dangerous."

See the farmer.
See the farmer go to the mail box.
See the farmer get the little book.
The farmer can read.
The farmer can read big words.
The farmer can read long sentences.
The farmer knows about fences.
The farmer knows about manure pits.
Now the farmer knows about OSHA.
See the farmer kick the mail box.
Hear the farmer say bad words.
See the farmer throw the little book.
See the farmer throw the little book
  into the manure pit.
See OSHA.
See OSHA write.
See OSHA throw money into the manure
  pit.
Say bad words about OSHA.

Business is surely responsible for its share of goofs, and the standard reaction to criticism—launching another public relations campaign—is clearly inadequate, if not counterproductive. The most fundamental response to the widespread public dissatisfaction with the business system is to do a better job of "minding the store." The basic way for business truly to satisfy the American people on a long-term, sustainable basis is to produce higher employment, a lower rate of inflation, and a rising standard of living for the average family—with one key provision, to do all that in an environment of maximum freedom for the individual. The essence of improving the business image rests not in trying to conjure up a good story when performance fails but in improving performance so that there will, in fact, be a good story to tell.

It is far too easy for business to ask the rest of society to support those sensible actions that will strengthen the market economy—less regulation, elimination of union featherbedding practices, and so on—so long as the burden of those sensible actions is placed elsewhere than on business. Those of us who advocate the deregulation of energy, for example, are motivated to do so because the good that will result in the form of higher production and more effective use of domestic energy supplies will far outweigh the added costs. But, of course, it is the consumer who will bear those added costs in the form of higher gasoline prices. Although deregulation makes excellent economic sense, it is easy to see why business firms, rather than consumer groups, endorse it so enthusiastically.

To be truly creditable, business also needs to advocate those actions that are difficult or even distasteful to business. This does not include such counterproductive moves as reducing profits and dividends as a way of "punishing" business for whatever shortcomings it may possess. That would be akin to attempting to cure an illness by starving the patient. What would be useful is a course of action which, although painful to individual business executives, would not harm but might strengthen the overall business system. That would be analogous to urging a flabby person to undertake a regimen of vigorous exercise.

One specific question which, like tough exercise, would be as unpopular as it would be helpful is to curtail what is the Imperial Presidency in the private sector. Members of top management of corporations often have acquired perquisites ("perks") that smack more of the prerogatives of royalty than of the needs of competitive, profit-maximizing management.

Those "perks" range from using the company plane for taking the children of executives to college to entertaining friends at the company's hunting lodge, or requiring employees to wash and wax the personal vehicles of senior management as part of their work for the company. None of these items in themselves is large in comparison to the sales or earnings of the companies, but they send a powerful message—a negative one—to the public.

What is needed within business is conscious self-restraint in the use of perquisites. Surely, a great many corporations conduct themselves in a circumspect and prudent manner, but not all do. One company spent $6,000 for a dinner to entertain the members of its board of directors and various friends and advisors. The executive of another company used the firm's private jet to fly his pedigreed bull terriers to and from dog shows across the United States and Canada. The fundamental question here is not whether such expenditures are legal. Rather, the overriding concern is the harm such actions do in reducing public support for the business system. The prospects for the future of private enterprise in the United States surely would be enhanced by raising the prevailing mores.

Finally, we need to remind the public of something so obvious that we all overlook it. Spin the globe and identify the various nations of the world that provide their citizens a substantial degree of personal freedom. Then spin the globe again and identify those countries that have a large and strong private business sector. There is a striking overlap of the two groups. We find that the capitalistic nations are also the free nations. Correspondence between those countries with economic freedom and those with personal freedom is not mere coincidence. Those societies that have a large and independent profit-making private sector have avoided the concentration of power that results in a totalitarian state. Capitalism has its share of faults. We should be frank to admit them and eager to correct them where we can. But we also should remind our fellow citizens of the superiority of our system over any existing alternatives. Thus we ever need to stress the importance of maintaining a society containing diverse, independent, voluntary institutions—in both economic and noneconomic spheres of activity.

Thus, the concern with the future of the American economic system really reflects our more basic desire to maintain and strengthen the free and voluntary society of which the economy is a vital but only a constituent part. Boiled down to its essence, economic freedom is inseparable from political freedom. We foster one as we pursue the other. Thus, I say, with all seriousness, that the proper response to Big Business Day is, "Free the Fortune 500."

# Part IV
# MANAGING PRODUCTIVITY IMPROVEMENT PROGRAMS

Y. KRISHNA SHETTY and
VERNON M. BUEHLER

# 19
# Managing Productivity Improvement: Guidelines for Action

PRODUCTIVITY IMPROVEMENT has tremendous appeal to businessmen, judging by the number of firms that have instituted or are in the process of instituting such programs. The concept involves designing and implementing programs and practices that supplement management's continuing efforts to enhance productivity.

The purpose of this section is to synthesize the current state of knowledge on the basis of the experience of selected companies so as to provide guidelines for promoting productivity improvements.

## CRITICAL PROGRAM ELEMENTS

Company practices show that a wide variety of techniques and programs have the potential to enhance productivity. An analysis of company programs also suggests that companies differ in their program organization and content. Despite these differences, certain elements are similar from company to company. These elements are

Top-management support.
Organizational arrangement.
Company climate.
Measurement of productivity.
Productivity improvement plans.
Implementation and monitoring.

*Top-management support.* Management is ultimately responsible for providing direction for productivity improvement. If a productivity improvement plan is to succeed there must be top-management support. Unless managers and employees are convinced that a productivity improvement program has the support and commitment of top management, as demonstrated through visible and tangible evidence, they will probably not take the program seriously.

Top-management support can be expressed in many ways. The top-management support at Beatrice Foods includes, among other things, top-management emphasis in all major speeches, a letter from the chairman of the board encouraging productivity improvement as a top priority for the company, encouragement of divisional meetings on productivity, and the publication of a Beatrice productivity philosophy booklet. Top management supports the program by providing corporate staff services through its operating services department, establishing productivity goals and objectives, allocating corporate capital resources for productivity improvement projects, and monitoring their results.

At Kaiser Aluminum & Chemical Corporation, the annual productivity improvement plan has been part of operating philosophy for more than a decade. Management support is expressed through a corporate productivity coordinator and productivity committee. The CEO of the company shows his support by involving himself in key activities, including a review of each plant's annual productivity improvement goals and monthly monitoring of results.

Effective top-management support can be expressed in company goals and policies, and through executive speeches, publications, annual reports, and so on. Top management must make a definitive policy commitment to the company efforts, establish an appropriate organizational mechanism to implement such efforts, and require the operating units to develop goals and means of implementation. Allocating sufficient resources and monitoring the overall program also are essential elements of management support and ongoing commitment. Such commitments help members of an organization at all levels to think and act on productivity.

*Organization structure.* Once a company has visibly demonstrated top-management support, it must develop a suitable organizational unit to do the job. Organizational arrangements also take many forms.

Tanner Companies' organization structure for its productivity program involves the corporate productivity committee, a productivity coordinator, and divisional productivity committees for each division of the company. The corporate productivity committee members are selected from different parts of the company to get the program under way. The divisional committees consist of management representatives and, in some cases, union leaders, as well as office, sales, and production people. Division productivity committees formulate plans of action, set goals, discuss techniques, and follow up on the progress of productivity improvement efforts.

At Beatrice Foods, the operating services department, representing financial services, materials management, and industrial engineering, is responsible for productivity improvement efforts. This department provides project assistance to the operating units at their request and conducts corporate-level productivity improvement projects. At the Detroit Edison Company, a top-level productivity committee is responsible for surveying operations of the company's 65 departments, establishing productivity-training programs for managers and supervisors, and assisting departments in establishing measurement systems and action programs.

The type of organizational unit depends upon the size of the company, the nature of its business, and its unique operating structure. Organizational units can take the form of a special committee (as at Detroit Edison), an expansion of responsibility of an existing department (as at Beatrice Foods), or the combination of a committee and a special coordinator (as at Tanner Companies). Or the program may be carried on through existing line management alone.

Regardless of the organizational arrangements, all companies feel that no single employee has the sole job of productivity improvement. That is a part of a total management process and the responsibility of all managers and employees. However, the productivity committee, with the help of the productivity coordinator, provides a number of useful services. It helps to develop a favorable climate for continuing productivity improvement; coordinates the program; and helps functional or divisional managers to implement programs. The committee also conducts studies in specialized areas, recommends company policy and strategy in the productivity area, and advises top management on major technical, environmental, and human developments affecting company productivity.

Although organizational mechanisms may not guarantee productivity improvement, they provide the kind of top-management support and organizational assistance that are prerequisites for substantive and positive company action.

*Company climate.* Companies in the forefront of productivity improvement programs believe that a conducive company climate is another essential ingredient of effective productivity improvement. According to a number of companies (such as Kaiser, Detroit Edison, Hughes Aircraft), an important element of this climate is productivity awareness. In order to develop a company climate conducive to promoting productivity, organization members—managers, supervisors, and employees—must be aware of the productivity problem. They must be aware of what productivity is, what it means to their jobs and companies, and how it can be measured and improved.

Awareness. The awareness level of employees can be raised through top-management support, organization structure, and systematic training and educational programs.

The productivity awareness plans at Beatrice Foods include emphasis on the theme of productivity in all major corporate and divisional meetings, publication of a booklet on productivity, and discussion of the issue in the management newsletter. Beatrice also conducts seminars and workshops. The agenda for one of the seminars included the following: why productivity is important to Beatrice Foods; improving managerial skills to achieve productivity results; the productivity process; effective tools to improve manufacturing productivity; and case studies featuring selected divisions of the company.

In addition to an educational program, other effective techniques for developing awareness are a statement of company policy, the measurement of productivity, and the establishment of productivity goals. A number of companies also use meetings, memoranda, company papers, and bulletin boards—all aimed at raising employee awareness of productivity. Education and training programs and other methods, systematically used, can greatly enhance employee understanding and awareness. They can stimulate employee interest in improving productivity and encourage employees to actively recognize opportunities for improvement. The experience of many companies shows that the education of employees on the job by their supervisors and managers may be the best method of stimulating such interest.

Communication. Effective communication throughout the organization is an essential component of a climate conducive to productivity improvement. A full understanding at all levels of the organization of the purpose and objectives of the program is essential. Open communication between departments and between labor and management can foster productivity improvements by disseminating ideas and creating a cooperative atmosphere within the organization. Employees at all levels should have full knowledge of all facts relating to their jobs and the company.

Productivity is often mistaken as a code word for cost reduction, layoffs, and speed-ups. It is often misunderstood as getting employees to work harder for the same wages. The climate conducive to productivity improvement involves an environment in which employees work smarter and creatively instead of harder. This achieves more output with a relatively smaller increase in input or with the same or less input. There should be no secrets about any planned changes, expansion of facilities, new processes or products, and contemplated schedules. Productivity programs should be planned and implemented within the framework of the collective bargaining agreement.

The Tanner Companies constantly reviews the existing lines and means of communication and encourages more detailed and open communication between department and task groups. Open communication at the Nucor Corporation takes into account the legitimate concerns of employees, such as job security and income, when productivity programs are implemented. Most companies believe that open communication between labor and management creates better understanding of the functions of productivity improvement programs, the barriers to such programs, and the potential benefits of such programs for both the employee and the company. Effective communication emphasizes the role of the company's employees and convinces them that every effort will be made to improve productivity without impairing job security.

Employee involvement. Another aspect of the company climate is employee involvement in the development and implementation of productivity programs. According to a number of companies (such as Beatrice Foods, Continental Group, General Foods, and Kaiser

Aluminum & Chemicals), employees must be involved in such programs from top to bottom and in between, and continuously. Personnel at all levels need to be involved through meetings at the plant, departmental, or divisional levels. These may be work groups aimed at employee involvement, informal discussions, and joint labor-management committee sessions. Whenever appropriate, labor-management joint involvement is an essential aspect of a successful program.

Employees can help in planning training programs, in the measurement of productivity, and in the development of programs for improving productivity. Employee involvement promotes teamwork in that the workers have information of value to share with management, and management in turn has information that will be shared with workers. This sharing of information provides the worker with the desire and means to collaborate. Furthermore, the greatest potential exists with employees who face the day-to day operating problems. They can more effectively recognize opportunities for change, and their involvement provides motivation.

Sharing benefits. Sharing the benefits of productivity improvement is another essential element. Not only should the employees be involved but their contributions should be recognized through appropriate rewards. This is somewhat of a controversial area as to just how monetary rewards should be worked into the plan. Different programs could involve differing reward systems. The Scanlon Plan kinds of productivity programs provide bonuses for improved productivity. As their measures show reduced costs per unit, or increased profit, a bonus is periodically paid to workers. In other cases, individual workers are paid bonuses for particular cost-saving suggestions. The Nucor Corporation uses a group incentive system for improving productivity. The foreman and maintenance crew are part of the group in its incentive system. The company pays bonuses promptly so that employees can directly relate the added effort to increased rewards. Beatrice Foods uses employee recognition methods such as employee or supervisor of the month, attendance recognition, monetary awards for employee suggestions, cost reduction contests among employees, and nonmonetary rewards.

*Productivity measurement.* Productivity information is essential for any kind of productivity improvement. At the company level, productivity can be calculated by using labor units, such as employees or man-hours—partial productivity measure—or using all inputs, such as capital, labor, material, and energy—total productivity measure.

Most companies prefer the total productivity index, since it relates all factors of production to final output rather than focusing on any single factor of production. However, the calculation of total productivity measure poses complex technical and conceptual problems about which consensus is not available. As a result, most companies with productivity improvement programs use partial productivity measures. For example, Kaiser Aluminum & Chemical measures labor productivity, material productivity, and energy productivity in a combined index by plant. It does not include capital or white-collar costs on the input side. Corning Glass Works and Crompton Company also use partial productivity indexes. Next year, Corning Glass is planning to install a productivity measurement system that will measure the total factor productivity of each plant. This will tell the company how labor, capital, energy, and materials are used. Beatrice Foods' experience suggests that the following productivity measures are most useful:

*Employee productivity*, measured as output per employee or per man-hour.

*Equipment productivity*, measured as output per machine-hour.

*Assets productivity*, measured as output per asset dollar.

*Energy productivity*, measured as product output per energy input.

The experience of companies with productivity measurement programs suggests a number of problems. In most companies, productivity information is not easily available, and specific plans must be developed to get productivity information routinely. Also, the perfect measures of productivity are difficult to obtain, but useful productivity measures can be developed and used. The measurement task will require direction and technical help from company coordinators of the program or from an outside expert. Some immediate improvement in performance can be achieved by measurement, because it makes employees more aware of the meaning of and opportunity for productivity improvement. Finally, there is an increasing effort to promote the use of total productivity measure.

Appraising the productivity information and setting realistic goals are part of this step. The productivity information must be appraised to learn whether the company or the department concerned is doing well by historical or competitive comparison, or both, and where problems might exist in the company. Once the company knows its productivity position, it is time to develop productivity improvement plans with specific goals and programs. Immediate and visible goals can be set, such as increasing efficiency and quality, reducing turnover, reducing scrap, saving energy, increasing output, increasing safety, and reducing tardiness and rework. To be meaningful, productivity goals should be realistic. Goals that are either too high or too low can have a detrimental effect on performance. At Beatrice Foods and Tanner Companies, divisional and departmental managers are responsible for identifying productivity goals for their respective subunits; these managers are closer to the operations and hence are in a much better position to set quantitative goals.

*Productivity improvement plan.* The process of productivity improvement planning involves the application of available tools and development of a plan of action. The experience of Beatrice Foods suggests that improvement can be achieved through such techniques as work simplification, short-interval scheduling, value analysis, automation, and methods analysis. The Detroit Edison Company uses time study, work sampling, and management by objectives. Crompton Company uses a three-day, 12-hour work schedule along with incentive wages. Burger King uses time and motion studies and simulation models to enhance productivity. Still others use Scanlon-like group incentive plans, job enrichment, goal setting, zero-base budgeting, autonomous work groups, and so on.

The experience of the companies suggests that there is no single technique such as a work simplification system, a cost reduction plan, or an MBO program that can be applied universally to generate productivity improvements. Companies have used these and other techniques with varying degrees of success. Each technique has its own strengths and weaknesses and each has to be evaluated for its ease of understanding and implementation and for its cost and benefits. Each company is unique, and the suitability of a particular technique to a company situation has to be evaluated. Factors such as the size of the company, age of the company, kind of facility, technology used, labor content of the manufacturing process, nature of the raw materials being processed, employee attitudes and capability, management attitude and capability, type of employees, and labor relations climate in the company all have a bearing on the technique and the approach used in a particular company, or in a particular division or plant of a company, or at any given time.

*Implementation, monitoring, and evaluation.* The success of the productivity improvement program depends on effective implementation. Company experiences suggest that managers must devise a schedule for implementing the effort and committing resources. Managers must also be aware that there will be problems in implementation. Schedules will slip; some middle managers and employees may not take the effort seriously; and some phases of the process may unleash criticism of the managers. There is no quick, one-shot solution to the productivity problem; it requires commitment from all levels to make it work. To be effective, there must be patience, slow but steady progress, and constant monitoring of the progress. When a company attempts to implement a plan of action, it may have to overcome many difficulties. Once productivity improvement programs begin functioning, other problems may develop because the plan was not properly implemented. If the program is not closely monitored, expected benefits may not materialize. Other problems involve accurate measurement of output and development of an acceptable reporting system.

Most companies believe that monitoring, evaluation, and feedback should be essential components of the implementation process. At Detroit Edison, periodic reviews of the program include reports that compare actual performance of departments or groups with their productivity objectives and identify groups that fall below standard performance. After this evaluation, decisions are reached between supervisors and their superiors as to remedial measures to be taken. Kaiser has a similar program. Quantitative and qualitative assessment of divisional progress is made at regular meetings of corporate officers and divisional managers. Without monitoring, evaluation, and feedback, the effectiveness of such programs could not be determined. Feedback should be timely and meaningful; learning and improvement may be directly proportional to the timeliness and detail of feedback. The primary purpose of the evaluation is to note the benchmarks achieved and to analyze difficulties that have been experienced to date. Obviously, unforeseen circumstances will arise to force altering of plans. The evaluations will help to facilitate the corrective action necessary for the removal of roadblocks, to employ other techniques, and, when the circumstances dictate, to redefine productivity goals consistent with more realistic appraisals.

## GUIDES TO MANAGERIAL ACTION

From management's point of view, there is a clear need for an organizational response through which concern for productivity can be recognized and formed into company policy, structure, and action. Without top-management commitment, organizational mechanism, some measurable productivity objective, and specific action plans aimed at achieving these objectives, neither the organization nor the individual has a sense of direction in productivity improvement.

What generalizations or principles might one derive from the experiences of these companies? The following list combines those of the participant companies about productivity improvement efforts.

1. For productivity improvement to succeed, top management must be wholly committed to the program. When top management's support is lacking and no resources are specifically committed to productivity programs, no amount of good intentions will succeed. It requires clear policy commitment and tangible budgetary and staff support.

2. There must be an effective organizational arrangement, regardless of its specific form, with someone who is responsible to top management for the program.

3. A full understanding must exist at all levels about the objectives of the productivity improvement program: education of managers, supervisors, and employees covering the concept of productivity, its role, how to measure it, and how to improve it.

4. Communication throughout the organization—between labor and management and between departments—can foster productivity improvement by disseminating ideas and creating trust and a cooperative atmosphere within the firm.

5. Recognition of the key role of the company employees in productivity improvement is crucial. The employee must be involved in improvement efforts. If productivity improvement is to be successful, employees must also share financially in programs that increase productivity. There is convincing evidence that labor will

cooperate with management in productivity improvement if it is promised a fair share in return. Job enrichment, flexible hours, and increased participation in organizational decision making are not by themselves enough to guarantee improved productivity. Productivity improvement should be achieved to the extent possible without impairing job security.

6. Productivity improvement should be linked with measurement. Measurement of productivity makes it possible to set goals, understand the problem, and evaluate results.

7. It must be recognized that a variety of productivity improvement techniques are available—technological, behavioral, and managerial. The choice of technique or techniques has to fit the company situation, needs, resources, and implementation capabilities. No one single technique is a cure for all productivity ills.

8. Monitoring, evaluation, and feedback should be built into the program. A periodic review, evaluation, and analysis of the program, the results, the benefits, and barriers faced should be conducted. Such an evaluation may warrant a change in the existing program or the introduction of a new one.

In short, productivity improvement in an organization does not automatically happen; it requires commitment from all levels to make it work. It has to be planned, directed, and monitored.

## CONCLUSION

Productivity enhancement is essential to our way of life. It is the best tool we have to fight inflation, create employment opportunities, increase our competitive position at home and abroad, provide for increasing capital investment, improve corporate profits, and improve the quality of life in general. Most companies agree that productivity is the key to our economic survival. However, most of them do not have an explicit, goal-oriented, ongoing program. In order to derive tangible results, the function of productivity improvement should assume an integral place in company activities. It has to be planned, monitored, and directed for results. Reversing the trend in productivity is a major task of corporate managers in the coming years.

# Appendix: Productivity and Stagflation

An economic recession is probably upon us, and the outlook for inflation is grim. There is no reason to believe that the recession will cure our short-run inflation problem, and in the long run it is likely to make it worse.

Moreover, the disproportionate burden of a recession falls on blacks, Hispanics, and other minority groups. And the disincentives to investment spending caused by idled machines and plants are something our economy can ill afford. Not only would a shut-off of capital spending severely limit our future growth potential; it would virtually guarantee yet another sharp increase in prices once the economy turns up.

In brief, the solution to our long-run stagflation problem does not lie in short-run policy initiatives designed to maintain aggregate spending far below our nation's productive potential. Rather, the solution lies in the adoption of longer-run policies aimed at expanding the supply side of the economy; that is, at expanding our nation's productive potential in a manner that raises dramatically the growth of American productivity. Although we have discussed different aspects of the productivity problem in previous reports, it is so fundamental and so pervasive that it merits the careful review which follows. Only by understanding our productivity problems will we be able to develop solutions to the stagflation that dominates the economic outlook in the foreseeable future.

*The Recent Performance of Productivity*

In the past few years, economists and public officials have reached a consensus that an important cause of our stagflation and poor growth record is our dismal productivity performance.

Currently, official productivity measures refer only to labor productivity—output per hour of labor input. Other single-factor productivity indicators would also be useful in analyzing economic growth:

*Source: Midyear Review of the Economy: The Outlook for 1979—Report of the Joint Economic Committee, Congress of the United States, Washington, D.C.: U.S. Printing Office, 1979, Chapter II, pp. 28–44.

capital productivity (output per unit of capital input); energy productivity (output per unit of energy input); and materials productivity (output per unit of materials input). Additionally, a broader measure of multiple-factor productivity, obtained by combining inputs, would be valuable. But labor productivity would still be of paramount importance—it is the measure most directly tied to individual economic welfare.

Since World War II, the United States has experienced three distinct periods of productivity growth, as shown in Table A-1. From the late 1940s until the mid- or late 1960s, private-sector productivity increased at an annual rate of slightly more than 3 percent; from the mid- or late 1960s to the early 1970s, it rose at an annual rate of slightly more than 2 percent; and from the early 1970s to the late 1970s, it increased at a rate of slightly more than 1 percent. For the first half of 1979, output per hour in the private business sector actually decreased at an annual rate of 3.3 percent.

Table A-1. Growth of labor productivity (average annual rates of change).

| Sector | 1947– 1965 | 1965– 1973 | 1973– 1978 | 1978 (4th Quarter)– 1979 (4th Quarter) |
|---|---|---|---|---|
| Private business | 3.2 | 2.3 | 1.1 | – 3.3 |
| Nonfarm business | 2.6 | 2.0 | 1.0 | – 4.3 |
| Manufacturing | 3.2 | 2.4 | 1.6 | 0.6 |
| Nonfinancial corporations | 3.7 [a] | 1.9 | 1.1 | – 1.8 [b] |

[a] 1958–65; data not available for years prior to 1958.
[b] 1978 (fourth quarter) to 1979 (first quarter)
Source:   Bureau of Labor Statistics.

### International Comparisons

When we compare our growth in productivity with that of other major industrialized countries, our record is the least enviable. Our growth in productivity since World War II has lagged behind the rates posted by every one of our major trading partners. The Joint Economic Committee, in its 1979 annual report to Congress, examined international productivity rates and found that productivity in Japan grew four times faster than in the United States from 1950 to 1977. In France, Italy, and Germany, it grew 2½ times faster. From 1967 to 1977, the British economy scored productivity gains two or three times our own.

Although our working men and women still outproduce foreign workers, the gap is closing quickly: if present trends continue, German and French workers will be outproducing us within six years; Japanese and Canadian workers will follow soon thereafter. Major gains in our standard of living could have been obtained if our productivity performance had been better.

What accounts for our poor relative showing on the productivity growth front? In our view, an important part of the explanation can be found in the savings and investment rates of the United States and the other major industrialized countries. According to statistics compiled by the Organization for Economic Cooperation and Development (OECD), U.S. nonresidential fixed investment since 1965 has commanded a smaller percentage of Gross National Product (GNP) than in all other major industrialized countries. Thus, for the years 1966–1978, Japan devoted, on average, 18 percent of its GNP to nonresidential fixed investment, West Germany devoted 13 percent, while the United States devoted only 10 percent. Additionally, the U.S. savings rate (personal savings as a percentage of disposable income) has consistently been well below the rates experienced by these same countries. For the years from 1966 to 1978, the U.S. savings rate averaged only 6.6 percent, while for Japan and West Germany the corresponding rates were 18.7 and 13.4 percent respectively.

## Causes of the Productivity Slowdown

Two of the leading analysts of productivity growth are Edward Denison and John Kendrick. In Table A-2 we have presented Kendrick's latest estimates of the sources of productivity growth for the business economy and his projections for 1980–1990. Some of these estimates are based on previous work by Denison. Kendrick has also divided the post-World War II years into three parts, but the rates of growth differ slightly from those in Table 14-2 because the periods chosen and the measure of productivity differ slightly from those in Table 14-2. The conclusion is nonetheless the same—a drop of somewhat more than 2 percentage points in the annual growth rate between the first two postwar decades and the last five years.

We have grouped these eight sources of growth into three categories: five major causes of the slowdown, one minor cause, and one offsetting factor. (The eighth factor, "Actual/Potential Efficiency and Not Elsewhere Classified," the residual after the impacts of other factors have been estimated, had the same impact in 1948 to 1966 and 1973 to 1978.)

The five major causes of the slowdown are:

1. *Slower growth of the capital-labor ratio.* Due to indadequate capital formation (relative to the rapidly growing labor force), the contribution to labor productivity growth of the capital-labor ratio (weighted by capital's share of national income) declined steadily over the period. This fact, and possible policies to deal with it, were discussed in more detail in the committee's *Joint Economic Report 1979.* For the next decade, Kendrick foresees some improvement, back toward the 1966–1973 level.

2. *A reduction in the contribution from advances of knowledge.* This is primarily due to the lessened contribution of formal research and development and to a slower rate of diffusion of existing knowledge. The

Table A-2. Estimated sources of growth of labor productivity (average annual growth rate).

| | 1948– 1966 | 1966– 1973 | 1973– 1978 | 1973– 1978 Minus 1948– 1966 | Pro- jected 1980– 1990 |
|---|---|---|---|---|---|
| Real Product per Unit of Labor | 3.5 | 2.1 | 1.1 | – 2.4 | 2.1 |
| *Sources of Growth* | | | | | |
| Growth of Capital- Labor Ratio | 0.7 | 0.5 | 0.3 | – 0.4 | 0.5 |
| Advances of Knowledge: | 1.4 | 1.1 | 0.8 | – 0.6 | 0.9 |
| R&D Stock | 0.85 | 0.75 | 0.6 | – 0.25 | 0.6 |
| Informal Innovation | 0.3 | 0.25 | 0.2 | – 0.1 | 0.2 |
| Rate of Diffusion | 0.25 | 0.1 | 0.0 | – 0.25 | 0.1 |
| Changes in Labor Quality: | 0.6 | 0.4 | 0.7 | 0.1 | 1.0 |
| Education and Training | 0.6 | 0.7 | 0.8 | 0.2 | 0.8 |
| Health | 0.1 | 0.1 | 0.1 | 0.0 | 0.1 |
| Age/Sex Composition | – 0.1 | – 0.4 | – 0.2 | – 0.1 | 0.1 |
| Changes in Quality of Natural Resources | 0.0 | – 0.1 | – 0.2 | – 0.2 | – 0.3 |
| Resource Reallocation: | 0.8 | 0.7 | 0.3 | – 0.5 | 0.3 |
| Labor | 0.4 | 0.2 | 0.1 | – 0.3 | 0.1 |
| Capital | 0.4 | 0.5 | 0.2 | – 0.2 | 0.2 |
| Volume Changes: | 0.4 | 0.2 | – 0.1 | – 0.5 | 0.4 |
| Economies of Scale | 0.4 | 0.3 | 0.2 | – 0.2 | 0.3 |
| Intensity of Demand (Cyclical) | 0.0 | – 0.1 | – 0.3 | – 0.3 | 0.1 |
| Net Government Impact: | 0.0 | – 0.1 | – 0.3 | – 0.3 | – 0.2 |
| Services to Business | 0.1 | 0.1 | 0.1 | 0.0 | 0.0 |
| Regulations | – 0.1 | – 0.2 | – 0.4 | – 0.3 | – 0.2 |
| Actual/Potential Efficiency and Not Elsewhere Classified | – 0.4 | – 0.6 | – 0.4 | – 0.0 | – 0.5 |

*Source:* John W. Kendrick, *Contemporary Economic Problems—1979*, edited by William Fellner, American Enterprise Institute, forthcoming.

latter is measured by the average age of the capital stock, because the latest technological advances are embodied in new capital. Between 1948 and 1966, this average declined by about three years, but there was virtually no change between 1973 and 1978.

3. *Reduced gains from resource reallocation.* These reflect both a slower rate of movement of labor out of lower-productivity agriculture and a slower rate of capital reallocation out of low-productivity industries and geographic areas.

4. *A change from a net gain to a slight net loss from volume changes.* The drop arising from this factor is approximately evenly divided between lessened economies of scale and the impact of intensity of demand, Kendrick's term for the cyclical productivity pattern discussed below.

5. *Effects of government regulation.* Government services continued to contribute slightly to growth from 1973 to 1978, at the rate of 0.1 percent per year. But regulations multiplied, changing from a slight negative factor to a significant deterrent of productivity growth. Of course, these regulations yield some benefits, many of which are not included in the current measures of GNP and productivity.

The one minor cause of the productivity slowdown was a reduction in the quality of natural resources used in production. This mainly showed up in mining (primarily coal) but also in agriculture. A further deterioration is projected, particularly if we become more dependent on domestic energy sources.

The only factor which contributed more to productivity growth for 1973 to 1978 than for 1948 to 1966 was the overall quality of labor, reflecting primarily greater average levels of education and training. The latter is projected to have the same impact on productivity over the next decade as it did for 1973 to 1978.

Kendrick's estimate of the effect of the changing demographic composition of the labor force differs somewhat from those of others. In his view, the reduced average experience level arising from the influx of women and baby-boom teenagers had its most severe impact (0.4 percent per year) during the 1966–1973 period. For 1973 to 1978, this reduced the rate of labor productivity growth by only 0.2 percent per year, versus 0.1 percent over the 1948–1966 period. This factor should become a net source of productivity growth as women and teenagers gain experience.

These data on the sources of productivity growth are not precise, but they are useful "order of magnitude" estimates. They do give us some guidance with regard to the policy areas which must be addressed to reverse our productivity slide over the long run.

### The Relationship Between Inflation and Productivity Growth

The relationship between productivity and inflation is double-edged. A slowed rate of productivity growth causes inflation to accelerate, and escalating prices depress productivity. As we detail below, even a marginal increase in the rate of productivity advance could bring about a significant slowdown in the rate of increase of prices.

The most obvious way in which reduced productivity growth increases inflation arises from the fact that in the long run, unit labor costs and the price level move virtually in tandem. Employee compensation accounts for more than 75 percent of national income, thus for the economy as a whole unit labor cost (labor cost per unit of output) is the most important component of total unit cost and average price.. By definition, the percentage change in unit labor cost in any period is equal to the difference between the percentage change in average hourly compensation and the percentage change in output per hour. For any given rate of increase in average hourly compensation, each increase of one percentage point in productivity growth reduces by one percentage point the rates of increase in unit cost and inflation, barring major changes in profit margins or other costs. That is, productivity growth is the only way we can achieve growth in real compensation.

However, this mathematical identity understates the benefits from productivity growth, because it ignores the dynamic feedback effects of today's inflation on tomorrow's wage settlements. Taking these into account, the impact on inflation of a sustained improvement of one percentage point in the rate of productivity growth may be substantially greater than 1 percent.

This conclusion is extremely important, for we are all aware of how difficult it will be to reverse the decline in productivity growth. If a 1 percent increase in productivity led to only a 1 percent reduction in our nation's ultimate inflation rate, policies designed to raise productivity would look less attractive than they actually are. For example, suppose that each increase of one percentage point in this year's inflation is reflected in an increase of 0.6 percent in next year's average hourly compensation. Then if an increase of one percentage point in productivity is maintained in each year of the 1980s, inflation will be reduced by:

- 1 percent in 1980—the direct impact on prices of the 1980 productivity gain.
- 1.6 percent in 1981—the direct impact of the 1 percent gain in 1981, plus the indirect feedback on 1981 wage settlements of 0.6 percent from the reduced inflation rate of 1980.
- 1.96 percent in 1982—the direct impact of the 1 percent gain in 1982, plus the indirect feedback on wage settlements of .96 percent (0.6 × 1.6) from the 1981 inflation reduction.

By 1985, the total reduction in the annual rate of inflation would be 2.38 percent; the long-run equilibrium reduction would amount to 2.5 percent. This example is hypothetical, but everyday observation and the structures of several econometric models confirm the existence of these feedback effects of productivity gains. Unfortunately, this cumulative effect on inflation cuts in both directions: a reduction of one percentage point in the rate of productivity growth may lead to an increase in the rate of inflation of several percentage points. However, the example assumes that workers do not adjust to inflationary expectations.

As discussed above, in the long run, increases in real hourly compensation can arise only from, and will closely parallel, increases in productivity. But this may not occur in the next few quarters. As shown in Table A-3, in the first quarter of 1979, productivity in the nonfinancial corporate sector decreased at an annual rate of 1.8 percent, but real hourly compensation nearly held even, decreasing at an annual rate of only 0.3 percent. This occurred because the gain in nominal hourly compensation of 11.3 percent combined with the productivity decrease to raise unit labor costs by 13.4 percent. But because unit nonlabor costs increased by only 6.8 percent, total unit cost rose by 11.7 percent; this combined with a decrease in unit profits of 22.1 percent to increase average prices by 7.6 percent (as measured by the GNP deflator—the Consumer Price Index rose by 11.0 percent).

These relationships may be reversed over the next few quarters. Due to the increase in energy prices, increases in unit nonlabor costs may outstrip the increases in unit labor costs, and unit profits may increase, or at least not continue to decline at the first quarter's rate. Thus a gain in productivity of at least 1 percent may be necessary simply to keep real hourly compensation from falling.

The other side of this double-edged relation is the impact of inflation on productivity. We focus our attention on the effects of inflation in general and the effects of escalating energy prices in particular.

With respect to inflation in general, inflation and the existing tax rules have combined to depress the rate of capital formation. Firms are allowed to depreciate their plant and equipment on a "historic cost" basis only, even though inflation raises their replacement costs. Also, at least some portion of inventory profits, if measured as the difference between the original and the replacement cost value of inventories, is illusory. For these two reasons, inflation automatically raises the effective tex rate on corporate income. One estimate is that understatement of depreciation allowances and inventory replacement costs raised the tax burden on the income of nonfinancial corporations by more than $30 billion in 1977, the most recent year for which detailed data are available. This represents a 50 percent increase in the total tax paid.

Personal savings is a major source of funds for investment and productivity increases. Unfortunately, inflation reduces the incentive to save. Small savers in particular have difficulty finding safe investments with

Table A-3. Compensation, costs, and productivity (average annual rates of increase for the nonfinancial corporate sector).

| | 1958–1968 | 1968–1973 | 1973–1978 | 1978:4–1979:1 |
|---|---|---|---|---|
| (1) Nominal Hourly Compensation | 4.1 | 6.5 | 8.9 | 11.3 |
| (2) Productivity | 3.3 | 1.9 | 1.5 | −1.8 |
| (3) Unit Labor Cost | 0.8 | 4.5 | 7.3 | 13.4 |
| (4) Unit Nonlabor Cost | 0.7 | 5.8 | 7.0 | 6.8 |
| (5) Total Unit Cost | 0.8 | 4.9 | 7.2 | 11.7 |
| (6) Unit Profits | 2.8 | −2.2 | 11.8 | −22.1 |
| (7) Implicit Price Deflator | 1.1 | 4.0 | 7.6 | 7.6 |
| (8) Consumer Price Index | 1.7 | 4.9 | 7.7 | 11.0 |
| (9) Real Hourly Compensation | 2.3 | 1.6 | 1.2 | 0.3 |

*Notes:*    (3) = (1) − (2)
        (5) = weighted average of (3) and (4), with weights based on the relative shares of labor cost and nonlabor cost in total cost
        (7) = weighted average of (5) and (6), with weights based on the relative shares of total cost and profit in total price
        (8) and (7) are both measures of inflation, but are, as indicated, the specific values of these two measures over any period
        (9) = (1) − (8)
*Source:*  Bureau of Labor Statistics, based on trend lines. (Relations may not hold exactly. Nonfinancial corporations account for approximately two-thirds of the private business sector.)

rates of return high enough to compensate for inflation. When interest rates are lower than the inflation rate, the interest is insufficient to offset the loss in purchasing power of the principal. The saver has a negative real rate of return to start with and then must pay taxes on the interest. This problem is made worse as inflation forces taxpayers into higher tax brackets.

With respect to the effects of higher energy prices, the fourfold increase in petroleum prices during 1973–1974 may have been a contributor to our most recent productivity slowdown. If this past experience serves as a guide to the future, the rapid escalation of energy prices this year, in cmmbination with further prospective rapid increases in the future, may imply continued sluggish productivity growth.

Economists have traditionally stressed the importance of the capital-labor ratio as a determinant of labor productivity. Higher energy prices influence that ratio. On the one hand, higher energy prices encourage capital spending on more fuel-efficient equipment. On the other hand, higher energy prices reduce the effective capital stock by making the most energy-inefficient equipment obsolete. Some recent analyses suggest that in the short run the latter effect predominates, although the magnitude of the effect is unclear. Productivity growth began slowing down before the energy crisis occurred.

*The Short-Term Outlook for Productivity and Unit Labor Costs*

The short-term outlook for productivity growth is unfavorable for two reasons: the recent low trend of productivity growth and the cyclical performance of productivity. In the early stages of an economic slowdown, management is hesitant to make major cutbacks in labor, and labor overhead is spread over fewer units of production; thus the rate of increase in productivity falls, or the level may actually decrease. This offsets partially or even fully any slowdown in the rate of increase in hourly compensation that occurs during a recession. This offset has been especially significant in the past two recessions. If this pattern should hold today, the effects of a recession on inflation would be minimal.

There is no quick fix for our productivity problem. That is something we need to keep uppermost in our minds as we wrestle with the economic problems confronting our country. Testifying before our committee during the midyear hearings, Barry Bosworth, Director of the Council on Wage and Price Stability, said:

> In the long run, the control of inflation requires that the vulnerability of the economy to extraneous shocks be reduced. This could be brought about, in part by a resurgence of productivity growth. Thus, as we grapple with the immediate problem of preventing the food and fuel price increases from spreading throughout the remainder of the economy, we should not lose track of a fundamental long-term malady—slow productivity growth. We must redouble our efforts to revive the growth in productivity.

# Biographical Notes

CASS D. ALVIN is Director of Public Relations and Education of District 38, United Steelworkers of America, AFL-CIO, in the Western Region. Among his responsibilities, he is entrusted with arranging union leadership training programs for members and officers, and serves as a union-management consultant on apprenticeships and training. He was a member of the subcommittee of the USWA–Kaiser Steel Corporation Long-Range Sharing Plan Committee, which developed a plan that allows employees to share in cost reduction resulting from productivity and material savings, while protecting the workers against job losses because of automation.

ARNOLD J. BENES joined Detroit Edison in 1941 and progressed through several positions to become General Auditor in 1968. He is Chairman of the Productivity and the Foreign Corrupt Practices Act committees. Mr. Benes is a member of the Edison Electric Institute's Internal Auditing Committee and served as its chairman in 1972.

VERNON M. BUEHLER is Professor of Business Administration and Assistant Dean of the College of Business of Utah State University. He holds an MBA degree from the Harvard University Graduate School of Business Administration, and a Ph.D. in economics from George Washington University in Washington, D.C. He has been active in the field of government-business relationships and has taught at the Industrial College of the Armed Forces, Ft. McNair, Washington, D.C. His articles have been published in the *Academy of Management Journal*, *Management Review*, and other journals.

DONALD J. DONAHUE has been Vice Chairman of the Board of Directors and chief financial and administrative officer since joining Continental Group, Inc., in 1975. He has been the president and a director of AMAX Inc., and is currently serving as a director of other major corporations, banks, and educational institutions.

TED J. GUTT is Assistant Vice President for Research, Development, and Quality Control for the Prestressed Concrete Division of The Tanner

Companies, a Phoenix-based organization providing heavy-construction services and rock and concrete products in Arizona and Southern California. He has been with Tanner since 1971 and currently serves as Chairman of the Corporate Productivity Committee.

F. CECIL HILL has been affiliated with Hughes Aircraft Company in various technical management capacities for the last 17 years. He has served in his present capacity as Corporate Manager of the company's Motivation and Cost Reduction programs for the last four years. He is involved with developing and implementing productivity improvement programs at Hughes.

CARL C. JACOBSON is currently Vice Chairman of the Board and Assistant to the President of The Tanner Companies. In this capacity, he has been responsible for developing and implementing the company's productivity program. He has been with Tanner for over 35 years, holding a number of executive management positions, including that of President in the early 1970s.

JERRY JENSEN directs the operating services' industrial engineering staff in project activities at Beatrice Foods Company's operating units. Before joining Beatrice in 1976 as a management systems specialist, he had advanced through various industrial engineering and production scheduling positions to Production Control Manager during 5½ years with General Foods. He became a project manager with Beatrice in 1977 and Manager of Industrial Engineering in 1980.

DR. STEPHEN JONES is Corporate Productivity Coordinator for The Tanner Companies. In this position he is responsible for implementing and coordinating the firm's productivity program throughout the three operating divisions (Contracting, Materials, Prestress) as well as the accounting, data processing, and administrative functions of the organization.

DR. JOHN W. KENDRICK is a Professor of Economics at George Washington University and is a member of the Board of Directors of the American Productivity Center in Houston, Texas. He has been chief economist for the U.S. Department of Commerce and, in 1972–1973, was Vice President for Economic Research at The Conference Board. He is currently on the research staffs of The Conference Board and the National Bureau of Economic Research. Dr. Kendrick has written several books, including *Productivity Trends in the United States*.

MACK R. LARSON is Vice President for Equipment and Maintenance of The Tanner Companies. He has been with Tanner since 1956 and has been responsible for the introduction of maintenance programs and reporting procedures which have been the subject of numerous articles in national maintenance publications.

DAVID E. LEIBSON has been Vice President of Corning Glass Works and director of its Manufacturing and Engineering Division since 1969. He joined Corning in 1949 and has served in numerous positions there.

WILLIAM G. LORD II was with Burlington Industries from 1947 until 1961, when he joined Crompton Company, Inc. He returned to Burlington from 1963–1972 and rejoined Crompton in 1972 as Executive Vice President. He was elected President in 1976 and CEO in December 1977. He is Chairman of the Export Committee of the American Textile Manufacturers Institute.

WILBURN G. MANUEL is the General Manager of Nucor Corporation's new $60 million steel mill in Plymouth, Utah. Charged with first building and then operating the plant, he brings 15 years of steel mill management experience to the area. As a metallurgical engineer, Mr. Manuel was active in the manufacture and development of numerous aerospace and high-temperature alloys.

RICHARD F. MARTIN is Senior Vice President for Human Resources and Administration of The Tanner Companies. He has been with Tanner since 1972 and has been instrumental in assisting Carl Jacobson with the implementation of the company's productivity program.

JAMES W. MASON, JR., is Director of Industrial Engineering for Kaiser Aluminum & Chemical Corporation. Mr. Mason has had extensive manufacturing experience in metals fabrication, machining, molding, casting, assembly, finishing, chemicals processing, and maintenance. He was a management consultant for five years with H.B. Maynard and Co., and was a plant manager and division general manager for Rockwell International.

ANTHONY W. OLKEWICZ is an internal OD consultant with General Foods Corporation. His experience includes work in manufacturing management, process engineering, personnel administration, and joint union-management participation problem solving. His current assignment is in the manufacturing function in General Foods, and the range of his activities includes job design, group problem solving, team building, and the development of management skills required to manage participative work systems.

TED OLSON directs Beatrice Foods Company's operating services staff, which provides internal consulting assistance to operating units in financial systems, materials management, and industrial engineering. He also coordinates outside consulting services. Before joining Beatrice in 1972, he had extensive operating experience at several companies, including Baxter Travenol and Horner-Waldorf.

CLEMENT F. PREIWISCH is a supervisory auditor with the U.S. General Accounting Office's Chicago Regional Office. He was the team leader in GAO's review of the value of productivity-sharing plans in the private sector. He has been with GAO since 1954 and has served on a variety of financial, compliance, economy and efficiency, and program results reviews, including reviews concerned with the productivity issue.

FRANK J. RUCK, JR., is Vice President of Chicago Title and Trust Company. As chairman of the standing committee on productivity for the Lincoln National Corporation, Mr. Ruck has invested 18 months of study and planning to introduce management strategies for enhancing productivity with the Lincoln family of companies. He is head of five of Chicago Title's subsidiary companies.

Y. KRISHNA SHETTY, Professor of Management at the College of Business of Utah State University, is currently engaged in research on problems of productivity at the firm level. His articles have been published in *California Management Review, Advanced Management Journal, Management Review, Business Horizons*, and other journals. He is co-author of *An Introduction to Multinational Management*.

WILLIAM W. SWART joined the Burger King Corporation in 1979 as Manager of Operations Research and is now the Director of Industrial Engineering and Operations Research. He is responsible for development and analysis of systems to optimize productivity through the proper blending of human, physical, and space resources. Dr. Swart was Professor of Management and Associate Dean of the School of Business at California State University. His industrial experience includes positions with Du Pont and the International Paper Co.

MURRAY L. WEIDENBAUM is Chairman of President Reagan's Council of Economic Advisers. He is also Edward Mallinkrodt Distinguished Professor of Economics and the Director of the Center for the Study of American Business at Washington University in St. Louis. In 1979–1980, he was resident scholar at the American Enterprise Institute in Washington, D.C. He served as Assistant Secretary of the Treasury for Economic Policy and has held a variety of other positions, including economist of the U.S. Bureau of the Budget and corporate economist at the Boeing Company. A member of the board of economists of *Time*, he is the author of several books, including *The Future of Business Regulation*, published by AMACOM.

# Selected Bibliography

Adkins, L. "Getting a Grip on White-Collar Productivity." *Dun's Review*, December 1979.

Bakewell, K.G.B. *How to Find Out: Management and Productivity.* New York: Pergamon Press, 1970.

Balt, William L., Jr., and Wernberg, Edgar. "Labor-Management Cooperation Today." *Harvard Business Review*, January–February 1978.

Barks, Joseph V. "Getting a Big Payback from Those You Pay." *Iron Age*, January 28, 1980.

Baxter, J.D. "Productivity Bombs Out: What's Gone Wrong?" *Iron Age*, July 4, 1977.

Baytos, C.M. "Nine Strategies for Productivity Improvement." *Personnel Journal*, July 1979.

Beer, M., and Ruh, R.A. "Employee Growth through Performance Management." *Harvard Business Review*, July 1976.

Bergeron, P.G. "Why Government Managers Aren't More Productive." *CA Magazine*, June 1978.

Bloom, G.F. "Productivity: Weak Link in Our Economy." *Harvard Business Review*, January–February 1971.

Bobela, H.U., and Buchanan, P.J. "Building a More Productive Environment." *Management World*, January 1979.

Bohlander, George W. "Implementing Quality-of-Work Programs." MSU *Business Topics*, Spring 1979.

Boner, Barbara, and Neef, Arthur. "Productivity and Unit Labor Costs in 12 Industrial Countries." *Monthly Labor Review*, July 1977.

Brennan, D.P. "Management—Assessing its Role in Improvement of Productivity." *Paper Trade Journal*, December 15, 1978.

Buehler, Vernon, and Shetty, Y.K. *Managing Productivity Enhancement: Company Experiences.* Logan, Utah: College of Business, Utah State University. 1979.

Burch, E. Earl. "Productivity: Its Meaning and Measurement." *Atlanta Economic Review*, May–June 1974.

Burham, D.C. *Productivity Improvement.* New York: Columbia University Press, 1973.

Butterworth, N. *Productivity Now.* New York: Pergamon Press, 1969.

"Campaign to Improve Productivity Seen as Economic Growth Tool." *Commerce Today*, September 3, 1973.

Capdevieue, P., and Neef, A. "Productivity and Unit Labor Costs in the U.S. and Abroad." *Monthly Labor Review*, July 1975.

Cooper, M.R., Morgan, B.S., Foley, P.M., and Kaplan, L.B. "Changing Employee Values: Deepening Discontent?" *Harvard Business Review*, January–February 1979.

Craig, C.E., and Harris, R.C. "Total Productivity Measurement at the Firm Level." *Sloan Management Review*, Spring 1973.

Cummings, L.L. "Strategies for Improving Human Productivity." *The Personnel Administrator*, June 1975.

Davis, Hiram S. *Productivity Accounting*. Philadelphia: University of Pennsylvania Press, 1979.

————. "The Meaning and Measurement of Productivity." In *Industrial Productivity*. Madison, Wisc.: Industrial Relations Research Association, 1951.

Davis, L.E., and Taylor, James C., eds. *Design of Jobs*. Santa Monica, Cal.: Goodyear Publishing Company, 1979.

Dearden, J. "How to Make Incentive Plans Work." *Harvard Business Review*, July–August 1972.

Denison, Edward. "Effects of Selected Changes in the Institutional and Human Environment upon Output per Unit of Input." *Survey of Current Business*, January 1978.

Devlin, James. "Improving Productivity: One Company's Wage Incentive Program." *Supervisory Management*, March 1976.

Dewitt, Frank. "A Technique for Measuring Management Productivity." *Management Review*, June 1970.

Dowling, W. "At GM: System 4 Builds Performance and Profits." *Organizational Dynamics*, Winter 1975.

Dreyfack, Raymond. *How to Boost Company Productivity and Profits: Step-by-Step Guide to Corporate Growth*. Chicago: Dartnell Corporation, 1976.

Driscoll, J.W. "Working Creatively with a Union: Lessons from the Scanlon Plan." *Organizational Dynamics*, Summer 1979.

Dunlop, John T., and Diatchenko, Vasilli P. *Labor Productivity*. New York: McGraw-Hill Book Company, 1964.

Eilon, S., Gold, B., and Soesan, J. *Applied Productivity Analysis for Industry*. New York: Pergamon Press, 1976.

Eisenberg, William M. "Measuring the Productivity of Nonfinancial Corporations." *Monthly Labor Review*, November 1974.

Fabricant, Solomon. *A Primer on Productivity*. New York: Random House, 1971.

Farris, George F. "Chickens, Eggs and Productivity in Organizations." *Organizational Dynamics*, Spring 1975.

Fein, Mitchell. "Improving Productivity by Improved Productivity Sharing." *The Conference Board Record*, July 1976.

Frease, M., and Zawachi, R.A. "Job-Sharing: An Answer to Productivity Problems?" *Personnel Administrator*, October 1979.

Fly, R.D. "Why Rotating Shifts Sharply Reduce Productivity." *Supervisory Management*, January 1980.

Ford, R.N. "Job Enrichment Lessons from AT&T." *Harvard Business Review*, January–February 1973.

————. "The Art of Reshaping Jobs." *Bell Telephone Magazine*, September–October 1968.

Gale, Bradley T. "Can More Capital Buy Higher Productivity?" *Harvard Business Review*, July–August 1980.

Gehring, Don. "Productivity Means Working Smarter at Tanner." *Concrete Products*, January 1979.

Gellerman, S.W. *Motivation and Productivity.* New York: American Management Association, 1963.

Geohegan, E.H. "How to Attack Inflation by Increased Productivity." *Public Utilities Fortnightly*, April 26, 1979.

Gerstenberg, Richard D. "Productivity: Its Meaning for America." *Michigan Business Review*, July 1972.

Gibson, Charles H. "Volvo Increases Productivity through Job Enrichment." *California Management Review*, Summer 1973.

Gilroy, Edwin B. "A Primer on Productivity." *Supervisory Management*, March 1975.

Glaser, E.M. "Productivity Gain through Worklife Improvement." *Personnel*, January–February 1980.

Gold, Bela. *Productivity, Technology and Capital: Economic Analysis, Managerial Strategies and Government Policies.* Lexington, Mass.: Lexington Books, 1979.

Grayson, C.J., Jr. "An Expanded Concept of Productivity and its Implications for Economic Policy Makers." *Sloan Management Review*, Spring 1974.

————. "How to Make Productivity Grow Faster." *Business Week*, July 14, 1973.

————. "Eight Ways to Raise Productivity—and Profits." *Nation's Business*, November 1972.

————. "Productivity Slide." *Dun's Review*, September 1976.

Greenberg, Leon. *A Practical Guide to Productivity Measurement.* Washington, D.C.: The Bureau of National Affairs, Inc., 1973.

Groff, G.K. "Worker Productivity: An Integrated View." *Business Horizons*, April 1971.

Guest, Robert H. "Quality of Work Life—Learning from Tarrytown." *Harvard Business Review*, July–August 1979.

Gutenberg, A.W. *A Primer For Productivity Management.* Pasadena, Cal.:

California Institute of Technology, Industrial Relations Center (Circular No. 39), February 1976.

Gyllenhammar, Pehr G. *People at Work*. Reading, Mass.: Addison-Wesley Publishing Company, 1977.

Hackman, J.R., and Suttle, J.L. *Improving Life at Work: Behavioral Science Approaches to Organizational Change*, Santa Monica, Cal.: Goodyear Publishing Company, 1976.

Hamlin, Jerry. "Productivity Improvement: An Organized Effort." *AIIE 1978 Spring Annual Conference Proceedings*.

Harrison, Jared F. *Improving Performance and Productivity (Why Won't They Do What I Want them to Do?)*. Reading, Mass.: Addison-Wesley Publishing Company, 1978.

Hershfield, David C. "Barriers to Increased Labor Productivity." *The Conference Board Record*, July 1976.

Hickey, James J. *Employee Productivity: How to Improve and Measure Your Company's Performance*. Stratford, Conn.: Institute for the Advancement of Scientific Management and Control, 1974.

Hinricas, John R. *The Motivation Crisis*. New York: AMACOM, 1974.

Hodge, M.H., Jr. "Rate Your Company's Research Productivity." *Harvard Business Review*, November–December 1963.

Hollander, S. *The Source of Increased Efficiency*. Boston: M.I.T. Press, 1965.

"How to Promote Productivity." *Business Week*, July 24, 1978.

Howe, R.J. "Building Teams for Increased Productivity." *Personnel Journal*, January 1977.

Howell, W.J. "A New Look at Profit Sharing, Pensions, and Productivity Plans." *Business Management*, December 1967.

"Is Productivity Lag a New Problem?" *Industry Week*, January 1, 1973.

Jacobs, Herman S., and Jillson, Katherine. *Executive Productivity*. New York: AMACOM, 1974.

Judson, A.S. "New Strategies to Improve Productivity." *Technology Review*, July–August 1976.

Katzell, M.E. *Productivity: The Measure and the Myth*. New York: AMACOM, 1975.

Katzell, R.A., et al. *A Guide to Worker Productivity Experiments in the United States, 1971–1975*. New York: New York University Press, 1977.

_____. *Work, Productivity, and Job Satisfaction: An Evaluation of Policy-Related Research*. Report to the National Science Foundation. New York: Psychological Corporation, 1975.

Katzen, R. "Measuring the Productivity of Engineers." *Chemical Engineering Progress*, April 1975.

Kellogg, M. *Closing the Performance Gap*. New York: American Management Association, 1967.

Kendrick, John W. *Postwar Productivity Trends in the United States*

*1948–1969* (prepared for the National Bureau of Economic Research). New York: Columbia University Press, 1973.

————. *Productivity Trends in the United States.* Princeton, N.J.: Princeton University Press, 1961.

————. *The Formation and Stocks of Total Capital.* New York: National Bureau of Economic Research, 1976.

————. *Understanding Productivity.* Baltimore: Johns Hopkins University Press, 1977.

Kendrick, John W., and Creamer, D. *Measuring Company Productivity* (handbook with Case Studies, Studies in Business Economics No. 89). New York: The Conference Board, 1965.

Kendrick, John W., and Grossman, E.S. *Productivity in the United States.* Baltimore: Johns Hopkins University Press, 1980.

Kendrick, John W., and Vaccara, Beatrice N. *New Developments in Productivity Measurements and Analysis.* Chicago: University of Chicago Press, 1980.

Kolmin, F.W., and Cerullo, Michael J. "Measuring Productivity and Efficiency." *Management Accounting,* November 1973.

Kraft, W.R., Jr., and Williams, K.L. "Job Design Improves Productivity." *Personnel Journal,* July 1975.

Kravis, Irving B. "A Survey of International Comparisons of Productivity," *Economic Journal,* March 1976.

Kreitner, R. "Identifying and Managing the Basics of Individual Productivity." *Arizona Business,* May 1976.

Lakein, Alan. *How to Get Control of Your Time and Your Life.* New York: P.H. Wyden, 1973.

Lawler, Edward E., and Ozley, Lee. "Winning Union-Management Cooperation on Quality of Worklife Projects." *Management Review,* March 1979.

Lehman, Edward J. *Productivity, A Bibliography with Abstract.* Springfield, Va.: National Technical Information Service, U.S. Department of Commerce, October 1974.

Lesier, F.G., and Puckett, E.S. "The Scanlon Plan Has Proved Itself." *Harvard Business Review,* September–October 1969.

Louviere, Vernon. "Raising Productivity with Flexible Work Hours." *Nation's Business,* November 1976.

Lovelock, Christopher H., and Young, Robert F. "Look at Consumers to Increase Productivity." *Harvard Business Review,* May–June 1979.

Maccoby, Michael. *Alternatives in the World of Work.* Washington, D.C.: Committee on Alternative Work Patterns and the National Center for Productivity and the Quality of Working Life, Winter 1976.

Maclean, David. "Productivity: Everyone Says You Need It; How Do You Get It?" *Nation's Business,* September 1972.

Macy, Barry A., and Mirvis, Philip H. "A Methodology for Assessment of

Quality of Work Life and Organizational Effectiveness in Behavioral. Economic Terms." *Administrative Science Quarterly*, June 1976.

Maher, J., ed. *New Perspectives in Job Enrichment*. New York: Van Nostrand Reinhold, 1971.

Mali, Paul. *Improving Total Productivity*. New York: John Wiley & Sons, 1978.

Malkiel, Burton G. "Productivity—The Problem Behind Headlines." *Harvard Business Review*, May–June 1979.

Margolis, J. "Productivity, Performance and Professionalism." *Training and Development Journal*, October 1979.

Mark, Jerome A. "Progress in Measuring Productivity in Government." *Monthly Labor Review*, December 1972.

Masterson, T.R., and Mara, T.G. *Motivating the Underperformer*. New York: American Management Association, 1969.

McBeath, Gordon. *Productivity through People: A Practical Guide to Improvement*. New York: Halsted Press (Wiley), 1974.

McConnell, Campbell R. "Why Is U.S. Productivity Slowing Down?" *Harvard Business Review*, March–April 1979.

Meadows, Edward. "A Close-Up Look at the Productivity Lag." *Fortune*, December 4, 1978.

Meyer, Herbert H. "The Pay-for-Performance Dilemma." *Organizational Dynamics*, Winter 1975.

Miller, Donald B. "How to Improve the Performance and Productivity of the Knowledge Workers," *Organizational Dynamics*, Winter 1977.

Mills, Ted. "Europe's Industrial Democracy: An American Response." *Harvard Business Review*, November–December 1978.

Miner, J.B. *The Management of Ineffective Performance*. New York: McGraw-Hill Book Co., 1973.

Montana, J. "Managing an Effective Suggestion System." *Administrative Management*, October 1966.

Moore, Brian, and Ross, Timothy L. *The Scanlon Way to Improved Productivity: A Practical Guide*. New York: John Wiley & Sons, 1978.

Nadiri, M. Ishaq. "Some Approaches to the Theory and Measurement of Total Factor Productivity." *Journal of Economic Literature*, December 1970.

Nance, H.W., and Nolan, R.E. *Office Work Measurement*. New York: McGraw-Hill Book Co., 1971.

Nassr, M.A. "Productivity Growth through Work Measurement." *Defense Management Journal*, April 1977.

National Center for Productivity and Quality of Working Life. *A Plant-Wide Productivity Plan in Action: Three Years of Experience with the Scanlon Plan*. Washington, D.C.: U.S. Government Printing Office (U.S.G.P.O.), 1975.

————. *Annual Report to the President and Congress of the National Center for Productivity and Quality of Working Life*. U.S.G.P.O., 1976.

————. *Annual Report to the President and Congress of the National Center for Productivity and Quality of Working Life.* U.S.G.P.O., 1977.

————. *Directory of Productivity and Quality of Working Life Centers.* U.S.G.P.O., Fall 1978.

————. *First Annual Report of the National Commission on Productivity.* U.S.G.P.O., 1972.

————. *Second Annual Report of the National Commission on Productivity.* U.S.G.P.O. 1973.

————. *Third Annual Report of the National Commission on Productivity.* Washington, D.C.: National Technical Information Service, U.S. Department of Commerce, 1974.

————. *Fourth Annual Report of the National Commission on Productivity and Work Quality,* U.S.G.P.O., 1975.

————. *Improving Productivity through Industry and Company Measurement.* U.S.G.P.O., October 1976.

————. *Productivity in the Changing World of the 1980s: The Final Report of the National Center for Productivity and Quality of Working Life.* U.S.G.P.O., 1978.

————. *Total Performance Management: Some Pointers for Action.* U.S.G.P.O., 1978.

National Commission on Productivity and Work Quality. *A National Policy for Productivity Improvement.* U.S.G.P.O., 1975.

National Research Council. *Measurement and Interpretation of Productivity.* Washington, D.C.: National Academy of Science, 1979.

Nekvasil, Charles A. "Taking the Hocus-Pocus Out of Productivity." *Industry Week,* January 5, 1976.

————. "Turning Employees on Boosts Productivity, Too." *Industry Week,* January 26, 1976.

"New Tool: 'Reinforcement' for Good Work." *Business Week,* December 18, 1971.

Newburn, R.M. "Measuring Productivity in Organizations with Unquantifiable End-Products." *Personnel Journal,* September 1972.

Nollen, S.D. "Does Flexitime Improve Productivity?" *Harvard Business Review,* August–September 1979.

Nunn, H.L. *Partners in Production: A New Role for Management and Labor.* Englewood Cliffs, N.J.: Prentice-Hall, 1961.

Patton, A. "Why Incentive Plans Fail." *Harvard Business Review,* May–June 1972.

Peloquin, J.J. "Training: the Key to Productivity." *Training and Development Journal,* February 1980.

"Productivity: Our Biggest Underdeveloped Resource." *Business Week,* September 9, 1972.

"Productivity: The End of the Drought." *Fortune,* May 1975.

"Productivity: The Federal Government's Role." *Industrial Engineering,* February 1973.

Quick, J.H. "Measuring Office Productivity." *The Office*, December 1972.

Rockart, John F. "An Approach to Productivity in Two Knowledge-Based Industries." *Sloan Management Review*, Fall 1973.

Rosow, Jerome J. "Solving the Human Equation in the Productivity Puzzle." *Management Review*, August 1977.

Ross, Joel E. *Managing Productivity*, Reston, Va.: Reston Publishing Company, 1977.

Ross, Joel E., and Kami, Michael T. *Corporate Management in Crisis: Why the Mighty Fall*. Englewood Cliffs, N.J.: Prentice-Hall, 1973.

Ruch, William A., and Hershauer, J.C. *Factors Affecting Worker Productivity*. Tempe, Ariz.: Bureau of Business and Economic Research, Arizona State University, 1974.

————. "Worker Productivity Model and Its Use at Lincoln Electric." *Interfaces*, May 1978.

Rudge, F. *The Key to Increased Productivity: A Manual for Line Executives*. Washington, D.C.: Bureau of National Affairs, 1977.

Runcie, John F. "By Days I Make the Cars." *Harvard Business Review*, May–June 1980.

Rush, H.M.F. *Job Design for Motivation: Experiments in Job Enlargement and Job Enrichment*. New York: National Industrial Conference Board, 1971.

Salmans, S. "Total Productivity Bonus Increases Involvement." *International Management*, May 1978.

Schulhof, R.J. "Five Years with a Scanlon Plan." *Personnel Administrator*, June 1979.

Scott, Walter B. "Productivity: A Program for Improvement." *Industrial Engineering*, October 1973.

Shallman, William S., and Beasley, William E. "Productivity Measurement in the Federal Government." *Atlanta Economic Review*, May–June 1974.

Sherman, George. "The Scanlon Concept: Its Capabilities for Productivity Improvement." *The Personnel Administrator*, July 1976.

Sibson, Robert E. *Increasing Employee Productivity*. New York: AMACOM, 1976.

Siegel, Irving H. *Company Productivity: Measurement for Improvement*, Kalamazoo, Mich.: The W.E. Upjohn Institute for Employment Research, 1980.

Simpson, D.H. "Increasing Productivity of Engineers and Designers." *Chemical Engineering Progress*, July 1975.

Smith, I.G. *The Measure of Productivity*, Brooklyn, N.Y.: Beekman, 1973.

Staats, E.B. "Measuring and Enhancing Federal Productivity." *Sloan Management Review*, Fall 1973.

Staley, J.O., and Bellof, I.A. *Improving Individual Productivity.* New York: American Management Association, 1963.

Stansbury, W.M. "Reducing Clerical Turnover." *Personnel Journal,* January 1973.

Starr, Martin K. "Productivity Is the USA's Problem." *California Management Review,* Winter 1973.

Stein, H., and Mark, J.A. *Meaning and Measurement of Productivity.* Washington, D.C.: National Commission on Productivity (U.S. Department of Labor, Bureau of Labor Statistics), September 1971.

Stein, J.M. "Using Group Process Techniques to Develop Productivity Measures." *Public Personnel Management,* March 1979.

Strong, E.P. *Increasing Office Productivity: A Seven-Step Program.* New York: McGraw-Hill Book Co., 1962.

Stutermeister, Robert A. *People and Productivity.* New York: McGraw-Hill Book Co., 1976.

Tagliaferri, L.E. "The Productivity Crisis and What You Can Do About It." *Training and Development Journal,* August 1973.

Terleckyj, Nestor. *Effects of R&D on the Productivity Growth of Industries: An Exploratory Study.* Washington, D.C.: National Planning Association, 1974.

Thackray, J. "America's Output Problem." *Management Today,* June 1978.

Tubbs, S.L., and Widgerg, R.N. "When Productivity Lags, Check at the Top: Are the Managers Really Communicating?" *Management Review,* November 1978.

U.S. Department of Health, Education, and Welfare. *Work in America:* Report of a Special Task Force to the Secretary of Health, Education, and Welfare (prepared under the auspices of the W.E. Upjohn Institute for Employment Research). Cambridge, Mass.: M.I.T. Press, 1973.

U.S. Department of Labor, Bureau of Labor Statistics. *Improving Productivity: Labor and Management Approaches.* September 1971.

——————*Productivity: A Selected Annonated Bibliography, 1976–1978.* Bulletin 2051. Washington, D.C., April 1980. [Previous Publications by Bureau of Labor Statistics on Productivity include Bulletin 1776 (1971), and Bulletin 1933 (1977).]

Vough, Clair F. *Tapping the Human Resources: A Strategy for Productivity.* New York: AMACOM, 1974.

Vough, Clair F., and Asbel, Bernard. *Productivity: A Practical Program for Improving Efficiency.* New York: AMACOM, 1979.

Walters, Roy W. & Associates, Inc. *Job Enrichment for Results: Strategies for Successful Implementation.* Reading, Mass.: Addison-Wesley Publishing Company, 1975.

Walton, R.E. "Improving the Quality of Work Life." *Harvard Business Review,* May–June 1974.

———— "Quality of Working Life: What Is It?" *Sloan Management Review*, Fall 1973.

Ward, D.L. *How to Motivate the Ineffective Employee.* Evanston, Ill.: Ward, 1973.

Weber, A.F. "Productivity: The Road to Improvement Leads Back to Basics." *Dun's Review*, July 1, 1977.

Wegger, John J. *Motivating Supervisors.* New York: American Management Association, 1971.

Weinburg, E. "Labor-Management Cooperation: A Report on Recent Initiatives." *Monthly Labor Review*, April 1976.

Weiner, G.A. "Working Productivity into a Four-Day Week." *Iron Age*, June 4, 1979.

Wooton, L.M., and Tarter, Jim L. "The Productivity Audit: A Key Tool for Executives." *MSU Business Topics*, Spring 1976.

Wunnenberg, C.A., Jr. "Productivity in the Warehouse: Who Needs to Automate?" *Management Review*, October 1977.

Zenger, John. "Increasing Productivity: How Behavioral Scientists Can Help." *Personnel Journal*, October 1976.

# Index